THE UNITY PRINCIPLE

The Shaping of Jewish History

Ellis Rivkin

With a Foreword by Robert M. Seltzer
Edited by Seymour Rossel

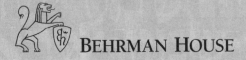

BEHRMAN HOUSE

The quotations from the Bible on pages 5-6, 9, 26-28 are from The Holy Scriptures *(Philadelphia, 1970). The quotations from Ecclesiasticus on pages 50, 51-53 are from the* Revised Standard Version *and the quotations from Josephus on pages 62, 63-64, 65 are from* Josephus: Against Apion, *The Loeb Classical Library, translated by H.St.J. Thackeray, Harvard University Press; the quotation on pages 63 is from* Josephus: The Jewish Wars *Loeb Classical Library, translated by H. StJ. Thackeray, Harvard University Press, and that on pages 71-72 is from* Josephus: Jewish Antiquities, *Loeb Classical Library, translated by H. StJ. Thackeray, Harvard University Press. In all instances the italics are mine.*

Cover design by Red Rooster Group
Book design by Seymour Rossel

Published by Behrman House, Inc.
Springfield, NJ 07081
www.behrmanhouse.com

Library of Congress Cataloging-in-Publication Data

Rivkin, Ellis, 1918-
   [Shaping of Jewish history]
   The unity principle: the shaping of Jewish history / [Ellis Rivkin].
      p. cm.
   Includes index.
   ISBN 0-87441-174-2
    1. Jews--History--Philosophy. I. Title.
DS115.5 .R585 2003
909'.04924'0072--dc21

2002034268

Manufactured in the United States of America

To **Zelda**
for her steadfast love and for the fruits thereof —
our children: **Rosalyn** and **Sharon**;
and our grandchildren: **Talia, Elana, Tashi,** and **Sofia**.

Editor's Note

ɞ Since the publication of the first version of *The Unity Principle* (called *The Shaping of Jewish History*) in 1971, language usage has steadily moved in the direction of inclusion. Among our goals in preparing this newly revised and expanded edition was the goal of achieving gender neutral language. Within the narrative, this posed little problem. History itself, however, and particularly primary historical documents, including the Bible, cannot always be amended and rendered in gender neutral language, lest the intention of writers of particular periods be entirely lost to us. A good example of this is the use of the terms "patriarch" and "Patriarchal Period." Such terms are employed not to diminish the importance of the matriarchs to the development of Judaism and the Jewish people, but because they make clear the intention of thinkers and writers at the time of their composition. For this reason, no changes were made to biblical and other texts quoted directly or to terminology that was clearly intended by earlier writers. At the same time, significant changes to the language of the narrative were made throughout the book to reflect the importance of gender neutral usage in our time. — SR

Foreword

Robert M. Seltzer

ä⚫ For those of us who had the good fortune to study with Ellis Rivkin, the appearance of *The Unity Principle*, a new edition of *The Shaping of Jewish History*, is splendid news. This remarkable book captures much of the scope, passion, originality, and incisiveness of an inimitable teacher and cherished mentor who opened new vistas for our understanding of Jewish history—indeed of history itself. Over and over as I reread the book I had the "aha" experience of "now I recall where I got that insight." Rivkin conveyed to his classes (and conveys in this book) a fresh approach to history on every level: how to deal with primary sources, how to think through historical problems, how to formulate generalizations that hold their own across varied periods and distinct situations—above all, how to situate each slice of history against its proper background. For Rivkin, the larger background of Jewish history was the diverse string of civilizations in which the Jews participated, constituting almost all of world history.

In the course of his teaching and writing, Rivkin explicated in his own way concepts that have become shibboleths of recent historical and literary scholarship: among them, *method, perspective, synergy, context,* and *structure.* Thus, he reiterated that adequate solutions to controversial issues in historical reconstruction could be obtained only if the historian clearly lays out his or her methodology and takes into account the perspective that colors every document and report. He called our attention to the synergy of interacting factors, each of which by itself had only a limited impact. He taught the need to contextualize each historical item in its proper setting. Above all, he insisted that we had to look for the social and political structure in which events took place and world views were expressed — the underlying structures that made it possible to grasp the deeper meaning of historical occurrences, personages, and developments.

For Rivkin, each period had its dominant coercive systems that underpinned the appropriation and distribution of wealth. He repeatedly pointed out the malleability of ideology, in contrast to the definiteness of power structures. As the reader will see, in this book he applies this approach to several intractable issues in Jewish historical interpretation: for example, the process by which the finished Pentateuch came into being. Rivkin proposes that this question can best be approached not by concentrating on hypothetical pre-Pentateuchal documents, each with its own literary style, but by reconstructing the history of leadership forms which conveyed supreme authority. He postulates a sequence of leadership in ancient Israel from early patriarchs and prophets of the monarchy to Aaronide priests (especially High Priests) during Persian domination of the Middle East. Although one authority system is dominant at any time, in a continuous tradition successive elites must deal with the previous structures so as to legitimize their own rule and override the authority asserted by their predecessors. Hence the Torah preserves the earlier patterns while at the same time canceling their efficacy by overlaying it with the new shape of authority. This focus on who has (or claims to have) supremacy to determine what is correct practice or belief provides him with the key to interpreting various historical controversies that appear, on the surface at least, to be abstract or trivial by modern standards. The recorded disputes between the Pharisees and the Sadducees, for example, or between the followers of Hillel and the followers of Shammai, like the controversies between the Orthodox patriarchs and the Pope in the early Middle Ages or between the Trotskyites and the Stalinists in the 1930s, ultimately revolve around who has the coercive power to demand obedience and therefore the right to define the dominant ideology. Hence matters which seem recondite to us may have been powerfully important to the historical actors at the time.

In his youth, Rivkin was an Orthodox Jew and a budding historian but also a perspicacious reader of Karl Marx. His critical take on Marxism proved to be immensely insightful to his students because he showed what is useful in Marxian analysis while exposing what was deceptive. Some features of his analysis show up in the last chapters of the present book: that an understanding of religious ideology illuminates Marxist movements and regimes as well as vice versa, and that Marxist ideology hardly prevented the elite espousing it from becoming a highly privileged class despite a theoretical egalitarianism. One of the central motifs of Rivkin's insistence is a striking reversal of the conventional Marxist interpretation of capitalism as exploitative. Up to a point, the historical Marx could even view capitalism as furthering progress through a dynamic, open-ended process of remaking the social world by creating new forms of wealth through innovative entrepreneurship. Despite his crediting capitalism with subverting the hierarchy of feudal privileges and the *ancien régime*, however, Marx demonized the bourgeoisie as a parasitic class that socialism must overthrow to establish true equality. Positing capitalism as the enemy par excellence, Rivkin pointed out to his students, flows from the Marxists' aspirations to power (adding an ominous meaning to Marx's well-known "thesis on Feuerbach" that "the philosophers have only interpreted the world differently; what matters is to change it"). On the contrary, for Rivkin, capitalism has been the primary motor for the spectacular increase in wealth and improvement in living conditions in modern times, as long as it did not run into obstacles that dammed up its dynamic and thereby exacerbated human destructiveness.

The reader will discover that, in Rivkin's analysis, the crucial political form furthering capitalism yet creating obstacles for its advance is the nation-state, which brings Rivkin to consider the development of Judaism and its vulnerability in the modern world. Each stage of capitalism opened opportunities for Jews, some of which they were remarkably well situated to play. When the nation-state system faced economic stagnation and political reaction Jews paid a terrible price. It is a historical principle of Rivkinian analysis that as expansive economies —premodern and modern—are conducive to social peace, Jewish distinctiveness is not a liability, whereas contracting economies exacerbate social tension and facilitate the scapegoating of Jews. This systolic and diastolic rhythm of economic expansion and contraction is a subset of a more general historiographical principle: that to be rendered understandable Jewish history itself must be envisioned against its general historical background.

The reader will find that *The Unity Principle*, while arranged chronologically, is not a narrative history but an effort to understand the deeper dynamics of the past, à la the Hegelians in the nineteenth century and Toynbee in the twentieth. Rivkin looks for the crucial evolutionary leaps in Judaism's adaptation to the challenges of successive historical periods. He employs biological metaphors in his analysis ("replication," "adaptation," and "mutation" of communal and other structures), but I would not categorize him simply as a Darwinian, like the distinguished historian of Eastern European Jewry, Simon Dubnow. Dubnow's multi-volume *World History of the Jewish People* served Rivkin as a model for periodizing distinctive diaspora cultures and calling attention to the positive role of the diaspora as an indispensable stimulant for the creative survival of the Jews. Perhaps a closer parallel to Rivkin would be Heinrich Graetz, the preeminent nineteenth-century historian of the whole of the Jewish past, because of Graetz's concern for the unfolding of the implications of monotheism.

For idealist Jewish thinkers of Graetz's generation, Jewish religious history was the working out of the implications of the original biblical belief in one God. Rivkin's "Unity Principle" seems its functional equivalent. If I understand Rivkin correctly, Judaism was irrevocably committed to a principle of oneness in the sense that chaotic features of experienced reality must be rendered coherent by being subsumed under a dynamic, ever more inclusive rationality which connects with a transcendent universal Oneness. As the Jewish people was forced to cope with one social and intellectual setting after another, its conception of this ultimate higher unity attained greater comprehensiveness by subsuming diverse new modes of experience and organization, rather like a personality learning to cope with more and more challenges as it matures, or as nature bringing forth greater levels of stable complexity as cosmic eons unfold. One hopes that Rivkin will explain his Unity Principle more fully in his future writings, and explicate how his approach relates to thinkers from Spinoza in the seventeenth century to twentieth-century process philosophers such as Whitehead.

This Foreword is not intended to be a summary of *The Unity Principle* but to highlight some of its salient features. A summary would be inappropriate; the reader has the book in hand and should react to its contents without an intermediary. You will probably encounter ideas with which you will disagree, sometimes vehemently. No problem. Rivkin himself would be delighted if this book forces the reader to reconsider the way he or she views some of the most significant aspects of Jewish history. Some have criticized Rivkin on the grounds that his view of Jewish history is excessively rational and oversimplified, but without the search for causes no cause would never be isolated, and one can say that every original thinker (Freud, for example) latches on to certain notions which make the irrational meaningful. As his friends know, for many years he has had some remarkable intuitions concerning the undercurrents of contemporary world power politics — intuitions that have turned out to be more insightful than the conventional wisdom of the time. Behind even his most extravagant passages are suggestive and stimulating ideas which prompt a reconsideration of long-held assumptions and the impetus to look at Jewish history afresh.

To be sure, there are places where passionate rhetoric overtakes dispassionate analysis. Rivkin's oeuvre of essays, reviews, and monographs on almost every phase of Jewish history will supply the concrete details and critique of primary sources that a survey must omit. Chapter III summarizes his classic *A Hidden Revolution: The Pharisees' Search for the Kingdom Within*. Chapter VI is drawn from his archival work and published essays and reviews on the Marranos and the Mendes family. There is hardly a period in Jewish history where Rivkin has not suggested a fresh start based on critical research. His students can testify that many ideas that he tossed out in his classes or broached in his essays anticipated conclusions reached later by specialists in almost every era of Jewish history.

Primarily a historian in the grand manner, Rivkin's work also has theological implications. As his students and colleagues know very well, he made much use of the term *globalism* long before it became fashionable to do so. *The Unity Principle* examines the Jewish past, especially the recent Jewish past, against the background of global history. A global perspective has enabled Rivkin to look for hopeful signs of a future age of universal peace and well being but not from a position of historical or theological determinism. He admits that we do not know if an eventual age world-wide prosperity and security will emerge necessarily from the competitiveness, conflicts, and agonies of the present. If this does occur, however, historians of the future will be able to discern how it came about and to note the exemplary role of Judaism in this process. In the "Postlude," it is evident that Rivkin's is a new version of what has been called "prophetic Judaism," the Judaism of Amos, Isaiah, and the other classical prophets of ancient times, refined in light of twenty-five or so subsequent centuries of intellectual growth.

In *The Unity Principle: The Shaping of Jewish History* the reader will encounter the distilled thought of someone deeply informed about the Jewish religious tradition, expertly trained in the modern scientific study of the Jewish past, an experienced practitioner of the historical profession, a man at home in the advanced intellectual world of our day and committed to the adventure of ideas, and a beloved teacher who seeks to bring these constituents together into a daring vision of what Jewish history can mean to future generations and what Judaism can mean to ours.

ð Robert M. Seltzer is Professor of Jewish History at Hunter College. He is the author of *Jewish People, Jewish Thought: The Jewish Experience in History.*

THE UNITY PRINCIPLE

The Shaping of Jewish History

Introduction

৯৯ This is a new kind of book on Jewish history. It is not a storehouse of information, facts, or dates; nor is it a catalogue of battles, books, and heroic personalities. It is a far more audacious effort. By deliberately setting for myself the goal of redesigning Jewish—and, as a consequence, world—history, I have been compelled to rearrange, reallocate, and restructure the data already known. I have, in a word, attempted to make intelligible the entire range and sweep of Jewish history, and to expose all of its remarkable complexity as the working through of a concept of the unity of all reality, which I call the Unity Principle. I try to demonstrate that Jewish history reveals itself to have been a process of elaboration of this simple, fragile, tenuous concept, espoused by a group of semi-nomadic sojourners in the Ancient Near East. As historical circumstances raised novel and unanticipated problems of survival, the original concept became more sophisticated and complex to underwrite the development of new forms of Jewish life, each connected with the others, together forming the entire sweep of Jewish history.

I was encouraged in this undertaking by what appeared to me to be the paradoxical nature of the great conceptual breakthroughs in scientific thought. The crowning accomplishment always seems to have been to arrange under a simple, single principle or formula the rich variety of the phenomena themselves. If variety and differentiation are explained by some simple principle in the world of atoms and in the world of biological beings, why should one not look for an equivalently simple source of the variety and differentiation and unique happenings in the history of man; why should the discovery of a simple principle preclude complexity and variation in history any more than it does in the natural sciences? The paradox of a simple principle explaining phenomenal complexity is so rooted in the remarkable accomplishments of science that it ought to encourage us to look for such a principle in human history without the fear that the diversity of historical phenomena will dissolve as a consequence. It is this paradox that I have sought to transfer to the realm of the historical processes.

Jewish historical experience lends itself to such an enterprise. It is unique, not in any supernatural sense, but in a phenomenal sense; i.e., there is no other historical experience quite analogous to it. It is not simply the history of a religion or of a people or a nation. It is, rather, interlocked with the emergence and development of Western civilization—a minority interlocking in reciprocal interaction with large, complex, and enveloping cultures, societies, and civilizations. For though each phase of Jewish history bears the stamp of the enveloping society, it is, nonetheless, highly differentiated from it. Its individuality is the outcome of successive interactions with the encompassing culture, society, or civilization. Unlike any other entity, it cannot be treated, even temporarily, in isolation. Ancient Near Eastern motifs, patterns, and modes of dealing with reality cannot be separated from Israel's without distorting our picture of ancient Israel. Yet Israel's distinctiveness keeps it separate from Egypt, Assyria, Babylonia, or Persia. Likewise, though one can write a history of England without simultaneously writing a history of Russia, one cannot write a history of the Jews without regard to English, or

Russian, or French, or German, or American, or Ottoman, or Christian, or Islamic, or Roman, or Hellenistic, or Ancient Near Eastern history.

This, I submit, has no historical analogue. Though it is true there have been, from time to time, minorities interlocked with phases of Western civilization, there is no continuous entity that has been so interlocked — from the dawn of civilization in the Ancient Near East to the postindustrial era of our day. Jews have been interlinked with every phase, and without a single disruption of their individuality. Furthermore, though always a minority, Israel was neither passive nor inconsequential. It not only fashioned the notion of a single omnipotent deity out of the stuff of Near Eastern experience, but it spun off two world-girdling religions: Christianity and Islam. And it did not lose its generative powers after procreating two independent religious systems. In virtually every territory of medieval Christendom and Islam, Jews fashioned forms and structures of bewildering variety as individualistic responses to changing historical circumstances. Indeed, this quality of creative adaptation was so efficacious that not only do Jews throughout the world today sustain at least three basic denominational divisions, but they also sustain a wide variety of national and secular identities as well. And most significant is the fact that the State of Israel, created by westernized Jews in the twentieth century, is alive and vibrant and developing and grappling with the complex problems of the contemporary Middle East. An analogous phenomenon just does not exist.

The larger world thus can no more be extricated from the Jew than the Jew can extricate himself from the larger world. To reconstruct the history of the Jews in the Ancient Near East, the historian is compelled to grapple with the interrelationships within that region, with the patterns, motifs, and events of its civilizational complex; to reconstruct the history of the Jews in the Hellenistic and Roman worlds, one must pay almost as much attention to the Greco-Roman framework as to what is distinctively Jewish. Similarly, one distorts the Jewish experience if one neglects either the Church or the Mosque, or the institutions of the caliphate and feudalism, or the basic developments in Christian and Muslim thought, or the evolution and development of capitalism and the modern system of nation-states.

This book represents an effort to lay bare these interconnections. I seek in these pages to share with the reader a novel way of looking at *all* of Jewish history. And because Jewish history is a history of such interconnections, this new angle of vision necessarily involves refocusing certain crucial aspects of historical development.

The Unity Principle

ஃ The operative principle of this book is utterly simple: The problems of Jewish history can be understood by means of the Unity Principle. For most of Jewish history, this concept was the affirmation that God was one and omnipotent. But though this God was believed to be one and omnipotent, the concept of God changed, as changing historical circumstances confronted Jews with new problems. Each successive form of Jewish history represents a solution to problems posed to the idea of unity by changing historical circumstances. The Unity Principle became the source and justification for variation and even radical transmutation of Jewish life. Commitment to unity did not breed repetitive conformity, but creative diversity, for the idea of God's omnipotence was drawn upon to multiply and diversify God's powers and attributes. Indeed the Unity Principle proved to be so resilient that it was successfully elaborated and extended to embrace ever more complex systems on earth as well as in heaven.

Jewish history is thus the history of the evolution, development, and elaboration of the Unity Principle through a sequence of historically interrelated and interdependent forms, none of which is identical with any other. The Unity Principle became the organizer, systematizer, and processor of diversity, rather than its negation. The commitment to unity did not end with unity — it ended with diversity.

This can be illustrated by the fact that millions of Jews today publicly proclaim adherence to the Unity Principle, though they differ radically as to what they mean, and in no single instance is the concept identical — not even for the most orthodox Jews who believe that God gave the Pentateuch to Moses — with the Unity Principle that flourished in biblical Israel. Yet every one of today's differing concepts is the outcome of a sequence of interconnections that ultimately reaches back to the Unity Principle associated with the semi-nomadic patriarchs. Similarly there are hundreds of Christian variations of the Unity Principle, each of which, though reducible to prior Christian concepts, must trace its origins back to the birth of Christianity, and *then* must connect with pre-Christian Judaism through a historical sequence of interconnected forms, all adhering to the Unity Principle back to the Book of Genesis.

This book then is, I believe, unique. It is neither an apologia nor a panegyric. At no time do I claim that the Unity Principle is a guarantee of the religious, moral, or ethical quality of Jews or Judaism. I have been a student of history for too many years to have any illusions that people, Jews or otherwise, are more than human. I know the embarrassing biblical texts as well as the elevating ones. I am firmly convinced that Jews are neither better nor worse than other folk. But it is nonetheless true that they have had a different history. Whether their religion, or ethics, or morals, or ideas, or concepts were or were not at any given moment higher than those held by others is

irrelevant. What is relevant is that, higher, lower, or in between, they were fashioned under the aegis of the concept of
unity; and that we can learn something about historical process from examining how this concept worked in history. Po-
lygamy was, at one time, as compatible with it as monogamy
is in our own day. The total eradication of the Amalekites
was, at one time, as pleasing to it as was unbounded compassion at another. The simple revelation of God to Moses in a
wilderness Tent of Meeting was neither more nor less a commitment to it than was the medieval philosophical belief that
God was the Unmoved Mover.

It should also be stressed that the Unity Principle is in no
way committed to the perpetuation of any of the content attached to it by any of the forms, or, for that matter, to the perpetuation of the forms themselves. Jewish history reveals that
no law, idea, custom, or dictum has been preserved intact
from the beginning. It further reveals that, far from sustaining
any single form of the Unity Principle, Jewish history is the interconnected sequence of *changing* forms. Yet all content and
all forms, however diverse, fit under the Unity Principle,
which is simply the notion that reality, be it simple, complex,
or changing, is amenable to a unifying idea.

The one stubborn empirical datum of Jewish history, which
is difficult to challenge, is that the Jews, and only the Jews,
have actively participated in *every* phase of the development of
Western civilization. If this can be shown to be causally related to the Jews' adherence to the concept of unity, then it is
only appropriate to raise the question whether this concept affords greater survival value than a concept that attaches some
kind of independent power to every diversity in nature, man,
and historical experience. I doubt whether any scientist, for
example, operates in the belief that reality is a congeries of un-
related, unconnected, and independent items, however much
the scientist may vociferously insist that metaphysics has been

transcended. I also wonder whether the survival of humanity in our own day might not be dependent on whether we can conceptualize reality as a "unity of diversity" — with individual, national, racial, intellectual, and other differences as necessary and legitimate consequences of unity. I raise these questions of larger meaning since Jewish history gives evidence, not of the triumph of a single form, belief, or set of practices, but of the proliferation of many forms, ideas, beliefs, and practices — as many as survival necessitated. Jewish history testifies that the Unity Principle generated diversity, rather than stifled it.

The Unity Principle is the *essential* differentiating feature of Jewish history and it is the *constant* in every situation in which the Jews were required to solve problems through the millennia. But it is not in and of itself a sufficient explanation of Jewish history. It was used to solve problems, but because the Jews lived within larger societies the problems themselves were generally set by extrinsic forces. Thus the threat of Assyrian and Babylonian imperialism posed the question of how omnipotent Yahweh really was. The answer given by Amos, Isaiah, and Jeremiah was that God was so omnipotent that God used the great imperial powers as the rods of God's anger. The problem was raised by imperialism; its resolution was sought by expanding the scope of the Unity Principle.

A Developing Principle

૨ૐ The Unity Principle thus developed dialectically: the idea spawned new possibilities through interaction with the external world, and the new possibilities themselves brought about new interactions. The idea constantly responded to economic, social, and political forces. Indeed, the evolution and development of the Unity Principle was the outcome of that very "Challenge and Response" that Arnold Toynbee set as his essential criterion of a civilization and of its power to sur-

vive. How ironic that the Jews, the one civilization which reveals this principle as empirically verifiable, are considered
by Toynbee to be a fossil civilization. Toynbee, oddly, sees
fossilization setting in at the very moment when the Jews
were fashioning a form of Judaism — Pharisaism — that was to
give rise to Christianity, endowing it with the Jews' own techniques of responding to historical challenge.

The most difficult problems confronting the Unity Principle were usually those created by economic situations. The
semi-nomadic life of the patriarchal period was a way of
wresting survival from nature. The conquest of Canaan was
an effective use of coercion to achieve economic and political
goals that were obstructed by those in possession of the land.
The settling down of the semi-nomads to till the soil, build
towns, and establish a monarchy was an economic, social, and
political process. The loss of the land of Israel and of the Temple were the consequences of foreign imperial expansion
motivated by economic, social, and political goals. The penetration of Hellenistic civilization into the Near East on the
heels of the conquests of Alexander the Great was an economic, political, and social intrusion as well as an intrusion of
ideas. An economic movement — the rise and spread of capitalism in Europe since the sixteenth century — was, as I shall
endeavor to show, the fundamental generator of emancipation for the Jews. The spread of imperialism at the end of the
nineteenth century, during the heyday of British, French, German, and Russian rivalry for choice segments of the Ottoman
Empire, initiated a complex process that gave life to the Jewish nationalist idea. The decline of imperialism after World
War II opened up the opportunity for the creation of the State
of Israel. The stagnation of nation-state capitalism between
the two world wars was, I shall contend, the necessary prerequisite for the rise of Nazism. The economic, social, and political problem of dealing with surplus labor and surplus

production makes intelligible the Nazi plan for exterminating Jews and thirty million or so Slavs long before Stalingrad. The existence of the State of Israel and the freedom Jews enjoy throughout the West can both be attributed to the rise and spread since 1945 of a new form of social revolutionary capitalism. The chronic anti-Semitism that was prevalent in the Soviet Union and in some of its satellites — along with the hostility to Israel — was, I would maintain, the consequence of the failure of Marxist systems, when in power, to solve the problem of agricultural productivity; i.e., anti-Semitism there can be directly correlated with the failure of the food supply.

The reconstruction that I am advocating is thus no artful idealistic ploy. It is hard-boiled and radical, making no pretense that the history of the Jewish individual or the individual Jew is elevated above the crude, the sordid, the cheap, and the tawdry. Power and its arrogance are as much the *leitmotif* of the book as is soaring spirit. Indeed, this book is a study of the interplay of an idea with history — not an idea vaulting over history, but an idea confronting it.

This interplay will become evident virtually from the first page. In applying the Unity Principle to Israel's beginnings, I take a tack different from contemporary biblical scholars. I do not approach the Pentateuch as primarily a literary work, but as the record of successive stages of problem solving spanning a thousand or more years of Israel's history. Unlike Wellhausen, Albright, Noth, Kaufman, and others, I do not take as my starting point J, E, D, or P — the various sources that are considered to underlie the Pentateuch. I do not assume redactors. I do not take for granted that the Pentateuch is primarily a record of traditions, religious themes, or stories. These are assumptions for which there are good and persuasive grounds, but they are assumptions nevertheless. No one really knows — no matter how vast his erudition and how agile his mind — how the Pentateuch evolved. There is overwhelming evidence that it is a composite, but even the most superficial reading of the most learned scholars will reveal that what one considers early, the other considers late; what for one is "obvious" for the other is "absurd." No one really knows, simply because there are no records that tell us how this composite became the Pentateuch, which even today is believed by millions to be God's revelation to Moses.

I therefore see no cogent argument against approaching the Pentateuch from a very different angle of vision. Whatever else it may be, it is a work that deals in the most concrete ways with problems of power. Indeed, the most explicit and unambiguous verses in the entire Pentateuch are those that spell out the penalty for any unauthorized individual who approached the altar. In the entire Pentateuch no single episode is treated in such detail as the challenge by Korah and his fellow Levites to the supremacy of the priestly caste, the Aaronides; no other single act of disobedience, not even the making of the Golden Calf, was punished in so decisive and dramatic a manner: burial alive, fire, and devastating plague. Nor was any other act followed with so detailed a spelling out of lines of authority.

With such texts clamoring for recognition, I see no reason why the Pentateuch should not be studied as a record of the evolution and development of power and authority in Israel from semi-nomadic times till the fifth century B.C.E. The culmination was the fashioning of the Pentateuch, not by editors or by redactors of traditions or stories and narrative, but by a class of priests who sought to solve the problems confronting the community after its return from exile in Babylon by having Yahweh and Moses assign absolute power to Aaron and his sons. They did not compile the Pentateuch, but created it; i.e., they so designed the work that a class that had never exercised power previously was now to enjoy it as a God-given monopoly. The promulgation of the Pentateuch was thus a revolutionary act launching a form of Judaism that had never previously existed.

The promulgation of the Pentateuch, ushering in a new ruling class and a new form of Judaism, was by no means the only revolutionary act based on the Unity Principle. The Pharisaic revolution was even more thoroughgoing, even more discontinuous with what had gone before. Not only did it bring to power a scholar class that had no sanction in the Pentateuch, but it proclaimed that God had given Moses on Sinai not one Law but two: one written, the Pentateuch, and the other oral. The Oral Law was known only to the scholar class, and it was on it that the scholar class based its new power and authority. Armed with the twofold Law, the Pharisees transmuted Judaism radically — into a system of salvation for the individual. Thereby they prepared the stage for the emergence of Christianity. To my knowledge this concept of the Pharisaic revolution has never been advocated by any other scholar. The idea is at odds with the prevailing scholarly consensus. Yet the sources give firm evidence of its validity.

Likewise, I have broken new ground in my theory of Christian origins and especially in my treatment of Paul. I attribute his remarkable transfiguration and stunning critique of the Law solely to his struggle with the twofold Law. There is no other primal source, be it Hellenism, the mystery cults, or philosophy. Paul's unique visualization of Christ was compounded out of inner turmoil, not out of books or academic contemplation.

I stress the fact that Christianity, even after its break with Judaism, preserved the Unity Principle and developed it along independent lines. Indeed, the expansive and flexible quality of this concept enabled societies to draw upon it for all the kaleidoscopic variations of Judaism and Christianity — and Islam too — throughout the Middle Ages.

How Societal Change
Impacts Religious Thought

ε❧ In seeking to make intelligible the diversities spawned by the Unity Principle and their interaction throughout the Middle Ages, I focus on the fact that the Jews were not treated in a consistent way by either Christians or Muslims. Highly positive treatment was followed by negative; negative, in turn, was replaced by positive. Even more impressive is the fact that Jews expelled from one part of Christendom were welcomed by other parts; Jews under a cloud in one part of Islam would find clear skies elsewhere in Islam.

I suggest that the explanation of this phenomenon is to be found in the patterns of economic growth and economic decline, a pattern decisive not in one or another instance, but in every single instance. The implications of this hypothesis are wide-ranging: *Ideological differences alone, no matter how mutually antagonistic they become, are not enough to sustain negative patterns of conduct. However, when some breakdown, crisis, or structural stress — e.g., economic, social, or political disintegration — occurs, such differences become vital.* Diversity in thought, ideas, beliefs about God, etc., had little killing power when they were not attached to economic, social, and political conflicts; but, when they were conjoined with them, such diversity was lethal. Discriminatory treatment, ghettoization, expulsion, and pogroms were visited on the Jews, not primarily because they were believed to have killed Christ, but because the feudal system and the Church experienced several hundred years of economic, social, and political disintegration.

The recognition of this peculiar interplay between the economic, social, and political — what I shall call concrete structural — systems and the realm of ideas is another factor that distinguishes this view of Jewish history from others. Although I am thoroughly aware that every historical phenomenon arises from a number of causes, I do not believe that every cause is as weighty as every other. Of all the causal factors, stated above, for me the most elemental is the economic, simply because the rise and fall of available wealth compels human response. Below a certain level, the failure to produce food *necessitates* a reduction of nurture, and, when severe enough, starvation and death. The disintegration and collapse of modes of production and distribution have direct effects on human life and hence provoke the most profound response. This also holds true for the operation of the political system: its malfunctioning is quickly translated into a matter of life and death.

The vital role of the economic factor has been depreciated largely because it has seemed to reduce us merely to economic creatures—as if all spiritual and intellectual concerns are stripped of their value once it is pointed out that they are interconnected in some way with economics. But poverty must be reckoned with by the mind and heart as well as by the body. This fact, in and of itself, tells us very little about the way in which poverty will be handled. Poverty may bring any number of responses in the mind and in the heart. It may lead to apathy or to aggressiveness. It may generate callousness or compassion. It may even be spiritualized, as the history of Christianity makes evident. Economic change may raise the problem but it does not determine the response, which may be a mystery cult, a redeeming Christ, esoteric cabalism, unrestrained hedonism, or self-imposed asceticism. The economic rise and fall of Athens tells us nothing about how the mind and the sensitivities of Aeschylus, Sophocles, Euripides, Socrates, Plato, or Thucydides will respond. It tells us nothing of the power of the mind to create its own reality and weave out of the concrete stuff of brute fact dreams and fantasies and imaginative solutions.

The point I am trying to make can be illustrated by the fact that Jews, Christians, and Muslims have responded to

identical external stimuli in a variety of ways. When, therefore, I single out the economic factor for a determinative role, I
am not thereby denying the autonomy of the mind to react
with its own symbolic systems, nor am I advocating a blind
and passive submission to economics; but I do affirm that, because of their fundamental impact on survival, economic balance or imbalance, integration or collapse, equilibrium or
disequilibrium, constancy or change demand a response in
terms of ideas — even as the biological development of the individual demands a psychic response, however private and
distinctive it may be. I also affirm that the degree of pressure
exerted by economic factors, which allow no one to escape
their impact, is greater than the reciprocal pressure that idea
systems make upon economics, though such reciprocal effect
should be neither overlooked nor depreciated. For example,
economic factors played a larger role in the rise of Protestantism than the rise of Protestantism played in the economic
transformation that took place around the same time.

What we observe is a highly complex interaction between economic change and prevailing symbolic systems.
The same economic changes are transformed differently by
different symbolic systems. I come to grips with this interaction between the economic and symbolic realms when I analyze the relationships of Jews and Judaism to the rise and
spread of capitalism (Chapter VI). I break completely with
Werner Sombart, who assigned to Jews and Judaism the creation of capitalism. The first "Jewish" capitalists were not
even Jews but professing Christians, the so-called Marranos.
Instead of cloaking themselves in a Jewish identity, they clung
to their Christian *bona fides* as long as this was more helpful
than damaging. The process of capitalistic development by
which Jews later became entrepreneurs was the same process
that transformed Christians into entrepreneurs.

So much for Sombart's hypothesis. But those of Weber, Tawney, and Marx are also challenged in these pages. In analyzing the role of the Marranos in the development of early capitalism, I have had to cope with the delicate question of identity; i.e., how and why did individuals — the Marranos — who were both professing Christians and entrepreneurs become professing Jews and entrepreneurs? The answer points up the causal connections between religion and the rise of capitalism.

The Marranos as an Example

&❧ The first Marranos, professing Christians but of Jewish birth or antecedents, began operating as entrepreneurs in Lisbon and Antwerp before the onset of the Protestant Reformation. They functioned freely as Catholic entrepreneurs in Antwerp before the threat of harassment by the Inquisition in the 1530's. It was not until the 1550's that the powerful Marrano merchant-banking family, the Mendeses, transferred their center of operations to the Ottoman Empire. Only then did they decide to discard a Christian for a Jewish identity. It was just about then, too, that Catholic entrepreneurs who were not Marranos became associated with the revolt against both Spanish absolutism and the Church. In the process these entrepreneurs chose a Protestant identity.

How do we explain this transfer of identities? The Mendeses and their fellow Marranos had been willing to function as Catholic entrepreneurs for two decades or more and presumably would have continued to do so had not the state and Church threatened them with the expropriation of their wealth. Had such a threat not been forthcoming, there is no reason to believe that the Marranos in Antwerp would have chosen a Jewish identity.

So, too, with the non-Marrano, Catholic entrepreneurs. Clearly, Catholicism per se was not antithetical to the capitalist spirit or to entrepreneurial profit making. The role of Antwerp as the great entrepot of Europe in the first part of the sixteenth century certainly proves this. Religious identity became an issue for these entrepreneurs only when the state and the Church threatened their entrepreneurial freedom — the threat stemming from pro-capitalist dynastic and institutional interests. In order to justify fighting the state, which was backed by the Church, the entrepreneurs transferred identities; they became Protestants.

They did not become Protestants because it was an entrepreneurial religion. They became Protestants because it lent justification to their rebellion against Emperor and Church. Capitalism thus did not create Protestantism, but took advantage of its availability in order to challenge existing authority. Protestantism was thus originally a variation of Christianity in disintegrating societies, which lent itself to any dissatisfied group that wished to challenge prevailing systems of authority. Protestantism was not an economic system but a symbolic transformation of the Christian system of salvation; nevertheless it gave sanction to the transfer of the Church's property and power into new hands.

Thus an analysis of the Marranos reveals the emergence of an "entrepreneurial" identity, an identity that treats religion as a variable. It is in this identity, I argue, that the source of freedom of religion is to be found. So long as the entrepreneurial function was not blocked or destroyed, an individual could have freedom of religious choice. Entrepreneurialism or capitalism is thus not a function of either Catholicism or Protestantism or Judaism, but simply the pursuit of profit. Insofar as a religious system does not exclude the pursuit of profit, it is viable for the entrepreneur. Capitalism thus did not flourish in Protestant countries because they were Protestant but because entrepreneurs had successfully penetrated the country and had removed obstacles to capitalistic development.

Capitalism and the Jews

ॐ Though the Jews were not responsible for launching capitalism, their history from the sixteenth century on has been determined, as has that of no other people, by the vicissitudes of capitalism. I explore this relationship in what I believe to be a highly novel way: I point out evidence for the direct correlation between capitalistic growth and Jewish emancipation; between capitalistic stress and strain and the rise of anti-Semitism; between capitalistic stagnation and decline in Germany and the attempted extermination of the Jews. With the emergence of modern capitalism, anti-Semitism, so I contend, became the weapon of the old regimes or of capitalist societies in trouble, or of Marxist-structured states. On the other hand, developing capitalism always encouraged emancipation of Jews.

Investigating this link between the fate of the Jew in the modern world and capitalistic development, I concluded that prevailing theories of capitalistic development, whether bourgeois or Marxist, are distorting because they are inadequate. The word "capitalism" does not describe repetitive phenomena, but rather dynamic phenomena. Capitalism is not one specific form, but rather all the sequences of forms that its history has revealed. Mercantile capitalism is neither more nor less capitalistic than vast corporations. A corporation producing a single product is neither more nor less capitalistic than a diversified corporation responsible for a wide variety of goods and services. Is David Rockefeller less a capitalist than his grandfather? Is IBM less a capitalistic enterprise than the old Liver Typewriting Company?

Capitalism is thus a developmental economic system that is driven by the lure of profit within a framework of competition to create new forms that render earlier forms obsolete. The new phase of capitalism in which we are now living is evidence of the renovating function of this inner dynamic. Its drive to augment capital through innovating modes of production and forms of business organization makes capitalism the only economic system thus far fashioned by man that has built-in pressures for change and development.

As an economic system, capitalism is committed to profit making. It is thus, in principle, global in its thrust. The world and not the nation-state is its arena. *Indeed, it was not an inherent flaw in capitalism itself but the entrapment of capitalism within the limits of the nation-state that almost destroyed Western civilization.* This neither Marx nor, as far as I know, any other scholar has as yet recognized. Nationalism, though embraced by capitalists, spelled more danger to capitalism than Marxism or the working classes did. The bloodiest struggles of the modern epoch have been between capitalist nation-states, or between capitalist combines against capitalist combines (e.g., the American Civil War), and not between capitalist and Marxist states or between capitalists and workers. Yet, as I shall point out, this was not inherent in capitalism per se, but arose from the fact that capitalism emerged within pre-capitalist societies, and even then did not emerge everywhere in Europe at the same time.

The Rise of Global Capitalism

&⟩ I thus set forth a theory of capitalistic development that on the one hand accounts for the stagnation and collapse of capitalism and the rise of the Soviet Union between World Wars I and II, and on the other hand posits that a new form of capitalism—a form that I call global capitalism—has emerged since World War II within the United States. This form is pressing toward the fashioning of a global community of autonomous, but non-coercive, nation-states. This new globalist form, contrary to widely held beliefs, is anti-imperialistic and committed to individual freedom. It is waging a massive struggle not only against Marxism but also against the older forms of nation-state imperialistic capitalism, both at home and throughout the world, and against the archaic values that these sustain. Far from supporting conservatism and reaction, it is generating an age of permanent revolution. This new form has gone unnoticed largely because capitalism has been identified with a single one of its forms — the nation-state imperialistic — rather than with its inner dynamic that drives it toward the augmentation of wealth and the removal of all obstacles to growth and development.

This developmental quality of capitalism I discovered because I was trying to understand not only the rise and fall of anti-Semitism in the modern world, but also the triumph of Fascist and Marxist totalitarianism. Here, being a Jew afforded insights that might have escaped a non-Jew. No amount of emancipation from Judaism or a Jewish identity was helpful for survival in Nazi Germany, nor did it seem to do much good in the former Soviet Union. Whereas a Christian, or a secularist, or anyone else might have found a way out in Nazi Germany by becoming a follower of Hitler, this option was not available for the Jew. Nor could Jews in the days of the Soviet Union hide behind Communist identities, no matter how sterling their Bolshevik loyalty. Non-Jewish intellectuals may have been attracted to Marxism and may have flirted with Maoism, but the only system that gave the Jew economic, political, and a high degree of social freedom was developmental capitalism. Stagnating capitalism, to be sure, was merciless, but the new form of capitalism emergent today has wiped out in the United States all but vestigial remnants of inequality for Jews; and what it has done for the Jews, I suggest, it is now doing for the blacks and the poor and the wretched of all the earth. As for *operational*, in contrast to *theoretical*,

Marxist systems, these have to show that they can feed their people without capitalistic wheat and grain and rice before their righteous critique of capitalism can be a sufficient promise. A far more radical and effective critique of obsolescent capitalist forms and values is daily being mounted by the transformation of capitalism itself.

   This book emerged out of years of wrestling with the unique phenomenon of Jewish history. I wanted to understand the Jewish past because I was perplexed by it as a Jew and as a human being. And it is this understanding I should now like to share with others for critical evaluation.

My heartfelt thanks go out to all those — my wife, Zelda, and my daughters, Rosalyn and Sharon; Jack Bemporad, Esther Dine, Mark Dine, Michael Dine, Richard Dine, Karen Dine, Jeff Dine, Myron Greenberg, Michael Haas, Michael Howard, Annette Isaacson, Stanley Isaacson, Keith Kilburn, Larry Kogan, Mayer Seligman, Michael Shevack, Connie Yaffe, Martin Yaffe, Herbert Zafren, and Miriam Zafren — who have read the Postlude to *The Unity Principle* and shared with me their critical reactions as I wrestled with how the Unity Principle might be applied to a future which can only be dimly perceived, given that it will be the outcome of a myriad of interactions and interconnections which are continuously in the process of shaping and reshaping through replication, variation, and mutation. As to whether I was wise enough to incorporate all the wisdom that these friends shared with me, only the future itself can render judgment. In the interim, my appreciation for the time, energy, and depth of their insights will surely stand the test of time.

A special word of appreciation is due to Seymour Rossel whose long held conviction that *The Shaping of Jewish History* was — to paraphrase Thucydides, not an essay to win the applause of the moment, but a possession for all time — has, after many trials and tribulations, eventuated in the publication of *The Unity Principle: The Shaping of Jewish History*. Were this not reason enough for my gratitude, his editing of this new edition with exemplary subheadings throughout the volume, along with the stripping of the original text of gender-discriminatory language, has earned for him a *"dayenu" ad infinitum*.

I
Patriarchs and Prophets

One God or Many

༄ Israel's origins in the Ancient Near East are obscure, but its earliest mode of life is known to have been semi-nomadic. The progenitors of the Jewish people appear in the Book of Genesis as patriarchs ruling over a mobile, tent-dwelling, sheep- and cattle-raising society. Abraham is portrayed as a patriarch exercising absolute authority and demanding undeviating loyalty from his followers. This patriarchal structure underwrote the power of a single and absolute God. God's role was to preserve the semi-nomadic mode of life and its system of absolute authority. Just as the human patriarch demanded undiluted loyalty, so did their eternal counterpart. The existence of other deities exercising sovereignty over other semi-nomadic cultures or urban societies was irrelevant for this group.

Once this concept of an absolute deity functioned successfully, it was extended to cope with more complex societies and more complex experiences. When the society dominated by matriarchs and patriarchs was followed by a wilderness society, the notion of divine absolutism proved to be transferable. Since Moses exercised absolute authority in the wilderness, his absolutism was strengthened by the Jews' allegiance to a single deity. Although Moses was not a patriarch and did not seek to establish a hereditary line, he did share with earlier leaders the need for a single deity to underwrite his authority.

When the wilderness phase of Jewish history was followed by the conquest of Canaan and settlement there, the idea of a single God supervising the process was both appealing and functional. The one God who had proved to be a good and sufficient God for the originating Hebrews and for Moses was also a good and sufficient God for a sedentary agricultural society. Just as an individual may have many talents, a single God may have many powers.

God as a Problem Solver

ह God is the eternal problem solver; this is the leitmotif of Israel's history. In the semi-nomadic phase, God was called upon to solve the problems of a mobile society. When the Children of Israel found themselves enslaved in Egypt, this God solved the problem by bringing sufficient pressure to effectuate their release. In the wilderness, God overcame all obstacles. When the problem of Canaanite resistance was encountered, God solved it by encouraging armed conquest. When God was confronted with agricultural and urban responsibilities, God took them over. When the Philistines threatened to overrun the country, God was ready to sanction the monarchy, which could deal effectively with their threat.

The success of this extension of the single God's power is manifest in the biblical account of Samuel's role in launching the monarchy. Samuel's exercise of absolute authority reflects the fact that his God is a single omnipotent deity. Samuel spoke in this God's name and the people listened to him because this was their God. They reaffirmed this loyalty when they accepted Samuel's choice of Saul to be king. When Samuel subsequently deposed Saul and shifted his support to David, the people transferred their loyalty because Samuel spoke authoritatively in the name of God.

Samuel's leadership role thus illustrated how the single God idea could be utilized to solve new problems as they arose. Clearly Samuel's authority testifies to the widespread belief that, as far as Israel was concerned, one God had been adequate for the transition from a semi-nomadic to a sedentary society. Samuel is the leader of a settled non-tribal society, yet he derives his authority from the God of the early Hebrews, of the wilderness, and of the conquest.

Samuel extended this God's power to establish and underwrite a monarchy. He gave divine sanction to a novel institution, because he saw the need for a military leader to cope with the inroads of the Philistines. Since Samuel could not provide this sort of leadership himself, he sought out someone who could. But since he also wished to exercise ultimate authority, he abandoned Saul for David when Saul failed to carry out his instruction to the letter.

Samuel's significance lies in this extension of Yahweh's power. It demonstrates how a single God could master new problems and undertake new functions. It establishes this God as preeminently a problem solver. God's attributes become clear as they become operational. For the patriarchs, the one God was an eternal patriarch. For Moses, God was a skillful and talented leader. For Samuel, the God who ruled a fairly complex agricultural and urban society was confronted by a military challenge to omnipotence and therefore needed a new instrument to illustrate God's omnipotence. By sanctioning that new instrument, the monarchy, Samuel was proclaiming that this God was also a king.

Toward an Absolute Monarchy

ટ࠵ Monarchy, however, created a problem so stubborn and so resistant to the concept of unity that only the destruction of the Jews' country and their exile could resolve it. For the kings sought to free themselves from prophetic authority and assert their independence. The monarchical challenge to the unity idea took time to mature. David was legitimized by Samuel and sustained by Nathan the Prophet. He was not an absolute monarch. When he had Uriah killed so that he might take Bathsheba to wife, Nathan scourged him with Yahweh's curse. When David's son Adonijah sought to proclaim himself king by hereditary right, Nathan stepped in and had David elevate Solomon to the throne.

This precarious situation was incompatible with monarchical absolutism. Solomon, therefore, sought to ground his sovereignty in something more firm than a prophet's oracle. Unlike his father, David, he was in a position to do so. He had a bureaucracy loyal to him, and he had a standing army which could be used, if necessary, to put down rebellion. He carried through measures, such as a vast building program, which demonstrated his ability to extract both wealth and labor from his subjects. He erected a magnificent Temple to Yahweh and placed it in charge of priests whom he, not the prophet, had appointed. But, most brazenly, he challenged prophetic power at its core by giving royal sanction to polytheistic shrines. Yahweh's absolute singularity was thereby undermined. Yahweh was no longer single and omnipotent as the patriarchs Moses, Samuel, and Nathan had proclaimed.

Polytheism now became a real problem to the Jews for the first time. Yahweh, as a single omnipotent deity, had proved adequate for semi-nomadism, for an agricultural urban society, even for a limited monarchy, but God was a barrier to absolute monarchical despotism that sought total independence from prophetic controls. Monarchical absolutism was impossible as long as Yahweh's prophets could seat and unseat kings. Either Yahweh or the king was absolute; hence Solomon saw in polytheism his only hope for an absolute monarchy. Solomon's fathering of polytheism is recounted in the Book of Kings:

> *Now King Solomon loved many foreign women, besides the daughter of Pharaoh, women of the Moabites, Ammonites, Edomites, Zidonians, and Hittites; of the nations concerning which the Lord said to the children of Israel: "Ye shall not go among them, neither shall they come among you; for surely they will turn away your heart after their gods"; Solomon did cleave unto these in love. And he had seven hundred wives, princesses, and three hundred concubines; and his wives turned away his heart. For it came to pass, when Solomon was old, that his wives turned away his heart after other gods; and his heart was not whole with the Lord his God, as was the heart of David his father. For Solomon went after Ashtoreth the goddess of the Zidonians, and after Milcom the detestation of the Ammonites. And Solomon did what was evil in the sight of the Lord, as did David his father, when did Solomon build a high place for Chemosh the detestation of Moab, in the mount that is before Jerusalem, and for Molech the detestation of the children of Ammon. And so did he for all his foreign wives, who offered and sacrificed unto their gods* [I Kings 11:1-8].

Although the writer attributes Solomon's defection to his wives it is clear to us that the king himself must shoulder the responsibility. Indeed, the polytheistic shrines were so securely linked to Solomon that this fact is simply taken for granted by the writer of II Kings 23:11-14, when he recounts Josiah's efforts to destroy them:

> *And he took away the horses that the kings of Judah had given to the sun, at the entrance of the house of the Lord, by the chamber Neth-melech the officer, which was in the*

precincts; and he burned the chariots of the sun with fire. And the altars that were on the upper roof of the upper chamber of Ahaz, which the kings of Judah had made, and the altars which Manasseh had made in the two courts of the house of the Lord, did the king break down, and beat them down from thence, and cast the dust of them into the brook Kidron. And the high places that were before Jerusalem, which were on the right hand of the mound of corruption, which Solomon the king of Israel had builded for Ashtoreth the detestation of the Zidonians, and for Chemosh the detestation of Moab, and for Milcom the abomination of the children of Ammon, did the king defile. And he broke in pieces the pillars, and cut down the Asherim, and filled their places with the bones of men.

Solomon's bid for independence from Yahweh was met with resolute resistance. A prophet urged Jeroboam to rebel against Solomon's legitimate heir, Rehoboam, and sanctioned the establishment of the Northern Kingdom of Israel. Jeroboam, it was hoped, would be more aware of the need for prophetic support. But once on the throne, Jeroboam was no more willing to knuckle under to prophetic king makers than Solomon was. He, and the kings of Israel who followed, chose Solomon's solution: dilution of Yahweh's absolutism by supporting other deities.

The Power of the Prophets

&❧ The prophet Elijah in the first Book of Kings stated the Yahwist position clearly: Yahweh is single, absolute, and omnipotent; hence the king must be subordinate to Yahweh's spokesmen, the prophets. No compromise was possible. Yahweh could not settle for partial sovereignty, since God exercised *all* sovereignty. Yahweh was the God of all economic functions, not some. Yahweh was the God of sheep- and cattle-raisers, of wandering nomads, of the rain and dew, of the soil's fertility. Yahweh was also the God of all political functions.

Prophetic power ebbed and flowed during the years that followed the division of the kingdom. At times, Yahweh's prophets were threatened with extinction; at times, they seemed on the verge of reestablishing their former ascendancy. A novel element was introduced into this basic struggle when, in the mid-eighth century B.C.E., prophets of a new kind made their appearance. These prophets had some new notions as to what it was that Yahweh wanted. They did not merely echo the pristine prophetic teachings that Yahweh was one, omnipotent, and demanding of exclusive loyalty. To this basic theme they added other motifs. Amos proclaimed that the exclusive worship of Yahweh was in itself not enough, and he leveled his most devastating critique against those who venerated Yahweh without comprehension of what God really wanted. Micah, Isaiah, and Jeremiah reiterate his novel insight. Even if Yahweh were worshiped exclusively, and polytheism swept away, Yahweh would not be satisfied. The covenant for these prophets envisioned a people dedicated to righteousness and justice. It was blasphemous to proclaim Yahweh as the only God, offer God generous sacrifices, and build God a beautiful temple yet neglect justice and righteousness. Yahweh's covenant contained for these prophets two provisions: Yahweh was the only God *and* a God of justice, righteousness, and loving kindness.

This twofold message was voiced exactly at a time when both the Northern and Southern Kingdoms faced problems of physical survival. Amos launched the new prophecy during the reign of Jeroboam II, not long before the destruction of the Kingdom of Israel in 722 B.C.E. Amos realized that the destruction was inevitable, for he was convinced that Yahweh would have to punish the people in some decisive way. By allowing the people to get away with the notion that worshiping God alone was sufficient, Yahweh would have violated God's own covenant. Since Amos took Yahweh's omnipotence for granted, he was certain that Yahweh would find a way to wreak devastation on the erring people.

When—not long after Amos's threatening oracles—the Kingdom of Israel was destroyed by the Assyrians (722), other prophets were encouraged to drive home the implication. The issue had become clear-cut. Either Yahweh had allowed the Assyrians to destroy Israel, or Yahweh was not the only God. Since, for prophets such as Isaiah, Yahweh must be the only God, Assyria must be the rod of God's anger. Assyria was an instrument of Yahweh's power, not an independent imperial power. Since Assyria happened to be at hand at that juncture when Yahweh wanted to punish the people, God exercised omnipotence by having mighty Assyria do it. The destruction of Israel demonstrated not how weak Yahweh was but how powerful. God's was the power to reward and punish. When the people kept the covenant, God gave them the land; when they violated it, God took it away. Yahweh was the source of prosperity and well-being; Yahweh was equally the source of terrifying destruction.

Imperialism thus proved to be no barrier to Yahweh's omnipotence. Indeed, Yahweh's power was nourished by defeat. Imperialism could serve Yahweh's ends only if Yahweh was the God of all imperial powers. The implicit belief that Yahweh must be omnipotent had now become explicit. If Yahweh could use the world's most powerful empires to chastise Israel, Yahweh must be the only God in the universe.

Yahweh as the Only God

&⚓ The notion of God as problem-solver was once again triumphant. Pre-committed to Yahweh's power, the prophets explained that even the most negative experience was God's handiwork. Pre-committed to the notion that Yahweh was the only God for Israel, they had to proclaim Yahweh as the only God in the universe. They widened the idea of the one God to bring all phenomena, whether positive or negative, natural or historical, under Yahweh's control. Although this had never been explicitly formulated by the patriarchs, or Moses, or Samuel, or Elijah, it had been there implicitly in the notion of God's omnipotence — Yahweh had all the power necessary to effect Yahweh's will and to preserve Yahweh's people, even if this ultimately required that Yahweh be the only God in the universe.

When the Kingdom of Judah was conquered by the Babylonians in 586 B.C.E., and the Temple destroyed and the ruling elite exiled to Babylonia, the disaster appeared as an awesome tribute to Yahweh's omnipotence. It had been proclaimed by Jeremiah as inevitable and necessary; it had been prophesied as necessary by Ezekiel; it was a prerequisite for the glorious restoration predicted by the Second Isaiah.

> *Who hath measured the waters in the hollow of his hand,*
> *And meted out heaven with the span*
> *And comprehended the dust of the earth in a measure*
> *And weighed the mountains in scales*
> *And the hills in a balance?*
> *Who hath meted out the spirit of the Lord?*
> *Or who was His counsellor that he might instruct Him?*
> *With whom took He counsel, and who instructed Him,*
> *And taught Him in the path of right, and taught Him*
>   *knowledge,*
> *And made Him to know the way of discernment?*
> *Behold, the nations are as a drop of a bucket,*
> *And are counted as the small dust of the balance,*
> *Behold, the isles are as a mote in weight*
> *And Lebanon is not sufficient fuel,*
> *Nor the beasts thereof sufficient for burnt-offerings*
> [Isaiah 40 12-16].

The new prophecy thus solved a problem in the concept of unity. Yahweh transcended appearances. Yahweh was the One behind the many: The contradictory and bewildering qualities of experience were attributable to God's omnipotence, not to God's weakness.

This idea, which was the most enduring achievement of the new prophecy, was achieved only in the face of considerable strain. These new prophets were not at first embraced enthusiastically by other groups faithful to Yahweh. Amos' claim to speak in Yahweh's name collided with the prevailing notion that a prophet had to undergo years of apprenticeship. Spontaneous revelation threatened disciplined revelation. If Amos could speak out in Yahweh's name, then anyone could — and did.

The New Prophets

𝜀𝔞 The new prophets were also frightening to a class that had become quite powerful in Yahwist circles in both the kingdoms of Israel and Judah: the priests. Although the line between priestly and prophetic functions was not always clear, it was nonetheless a line that had come to be respected. But for the new prophets no line existed at all. They flayed the priests of Yahweh as mercilessly as they did the priests of Baal. For them, a sacrifice to Yahweh could be as abhorrent as a sacrifice to other gods. Indeed, in some respects the Yahweh cult was far more harmful because it blinded true believers and misled them as to the provisions of the covenant.

The new prophecy was threatening because it was spontaneous and because it was individualistic. There was no way to control it. The prophet was bound to no one but Yahweh. The prophet could denounce anything displeasing to Yahweh, no matter how sacrosanct it was. And it was difficult to muzzle the prophet since the oracles were proclaimed in Yahweh's name.

The springboard for the new prophecy had been the old. Moses, Samuel, Elijah—all had claimed authority because Yahweh spoke with them. But these early prophets had sought to regulate access to Yahweh's voice. Joshua, for example, is pictured as having been Moses' apprentice, invested with rights of revelation by the master himself. In much the same way Elisha followed Elijah. Prophecy had thus come to be regulated by the prophets themselves. Prophets and would-be prophets had recognized some kind of discipline that seemed to acknowledge that one prophet at a time should hold preeminence. The new prophets recognized no such discipline, however. They were freewheeling spirits, who fearlessly spoke out what Yahweh had revealed to them, caring little for the consequences.

The new kind of prophet could no more be tied down by binding precedent than Yahweh could. The essence of prophetic power was flexibility, the freedom to shape new options. The prophet could not be restricted by rigid past rules. For the prophet, the immutable teachings regarding Yahweh were strictly limited to those claiming God's unity, God's omnipotence, and God's accessibility to the prophets who were Yahweh's instruments. In principle, the prophets were opposed to immutable divine legislation; such legislation curbed prophetic discretion. And the prophet was especially sensitive to claims that Yahweh had accorded some other class, such as the priests, a permanent status; i.e., a status that prophets could not alter.

This open-endedness is reflected in the so-called JE material, which deals with the Exodus, the wilderness wanderings, and Moses. Moses, and no one else, speaks for Yahweh. No authority is granted to a priestly class. Sacrifices are tolerated, but they are not in the forefront of concern. No special class is assigned priestly prerogatives. The question was: *to* whom should the sacrifice be offered, not *by* whom. Nor do these texts acknowledge any monarchical claim. If we further analyze these texts, we also note that the power of Moses is rooted in his continuing relationship with Yahweh. Yahweh was always available. God's ongoing will was made known to Moses. Yahweh solved problems as they arose.

These texts set up a model of leadership, under Yahweh, which is plastic and flexible. It is not rigorously bound by specifics. It is free to move with events. It is problem-oriented, not precedent-oriented. The only binding principles were those that upheld this flexibility. Yahweh would always provide a leader who would make on-the-spot decisions in Yahweh's name just as Moses had done in the wilderness. Moses' wilderness leadership served as the model for the prophetic role.

Moses as a Model

❧ The implications of Moses' role are far-reaching. They reveal a Moses who gave his successors a free hand to make whatever decisions might be necessary to sustain Yahweh's authority. Moses actually did not reveal permanent laws, although our picture of him now is primarily as a lawgiver. Rather, he revealed examples of how a Yahwist leader operated. To promulgate permanent laws in Yahweh's name would have been tantamount to undermining effective, ongoing Yahwist leadership, a leadership dependent on knowing what Yahweh wanted *now*.

The activities of such post-Mosaic prophets as Samuel, Nathan, Elijah, and Elisha confirm this hypothesis. They do not appeal to a fixed body of law. They do not look back to some immutable revelation. These prophets derive their authority from the fact that Yahweh makes them privy to God's will. Samuel seats and unseats Saul; Nathan castigates David; Elijah flays Ahab because this is what Yahweh wants *now*.

This freedom to respond to crises is the essence of prophetic authority. To curb and restrain prophetic freedom was to undermine the function itself. For this reason, no previous prophet, not even Moses, was elevated so far above contemporary prophets as to foreclose their freedom of action. Moses was Yahweh's spokesman during the Jews' sojourn in the wilderness. He listened to Yahweh and led Yahweh's people accordingly. He was a model, rather than a substitute, for the active prophet such as Samuel or Nathan. And just as Elijah felt no need to invoke Samuel or Nathan to justify his dealing with a crisis, he felt no need to invoke Moses. If Yahweh was telling Elijah what to do *now,* what need was there to know what Moses did *then?* Moses, Samuel, Nathan, and Elijah were *all* models of leadership, not legislators or framers of immutable fixed precedents.

Basing prophetic authority on what was going on *now* explains why Moses plays so small a role before the promulgation of the Book of Deuteronomy. Samuel, Nathan, Elijah, and Elisha do not need him; they need Yahweh. It was likewise with Amos, Hosea, Micah, Isaiah, and Jeremiah. Although they challenged the prophetic establishment, they did not challenge the basic principle of prophetic authority; Yahweh's will is revealed whenever Yahweh needs to make it known. The issue was not *whether* Yahweh revealed an ongoing will, but rather to *whom* God chose to reveal it.

If then we turn back to the wilderness texts that appear in the Pentateuch and measure them against subsequent prophetic practice, we would consider as bona fide only those that show Moses solving day-to-day problems with the guidance of Yahweh. Whenever he is depicted as doing the sort of things that Samuel, Nathan, or Elijah are also reported to have done, we may provisionally accept these accounts as reporting what Moses actually did do. When, however, he is reported as doing the sort of acts that these other prophets did not do, i.e., promulgating immutable laws as Yahweh's permanent will, then we must question the age of these texts.

They probably do not come from the time when Moses actually was alive. To cast Moses in the role of lawgiver is to expose prophets such as Samuel who followed him as lawbreakers; for they considered themselves bound by Yahweh's ongoing revelation, not by Moses' immutable laws. For them, Sinai played no role, because Sinai had not yet emerged as the mountain where an immutable law had been given.

The Emergence of Sinai

૨૭ The process whereby Sinai became the mountain of an immutable system of laws and whereby Moses came to be both lawgiver and Yahwist spokesman par excellence is obscure. We just do not know how it happened. Our sources raise the question, but conceal the answer. Neither the books of the Pentateuch nor any other biblical books describe the process by which Moses came to over-tower Samuel, Nathan, and Elijah. Even on the eve of the destruction of Jerusalem and the Temple, Jeremiah puts Samuel on the same level as Moses. "Though Moses and Samuel stood before Me [i.e., Yahweh], yet My mind could not be toward this people" [Jeremiah 15:1].

To align Moses with Samuel, Nathan, and Elijah is to bring the data from the historical and prophetic books of the Bible into some sort of interrelationship, whereas an over-valuation of Moses pits one segment of Scripture against another, without any objective criteria for adjudicating the clashing claims. An alignment such as this has strong scriptural support; for there are any number of Pentateuchal texts which reveal Moses as an ad hoc problem solver, a leader appropriate for the wilderness, a man bearing an uncanny resemblance to Samuel, Nathan, Elijah, and Elisha.

These prophets, like Moses, solved problems confronting Yahweh's people, and taught the same immutable doctrine: Yahweh is one, omnipotent, and always revealing Yahweh's will to a spokesman with ongoing authority like Moses. This *ongoing* authority is confirmed by the activities of the later prophets and it explains why Moses is so rarely mentioned by them. It also accounts for the refusal of the later prophets to be bound by prevailing Yahwist practices, however traditional they may have become. All laws for the prophets were provisional and contingent and could make no claim to immutability, for such a claim would curb Yahweh's freedom of action, and this could not be tolerated. The prophet might sanction a prevailing law or practice, but he could not guarantee its permanency. Only Yahweh's singleness, omnipotence, and freedom to act were immutable.

These prophetic principles frustrated all efforts at establishing enduring Yahwist institutions on secure foundations. Monarchy and priesthood were especially insecure because, unlike prophecy, they were novel institutions. When Solomon's kingdom was split in two, the power of the priests was gravely threatened. Not only were the claims of the emergent Jerusalem priesthood ignored in the Northern Kingdom of Israel, but prophecy proved very vigorous, precluding the establishment of priestly supremacy there too. Priestly institutions were too new, and their Yahwist grounding too precarious. Their connection with Solomon, who had given royal sanction to the shrines of other gods, also weakened their claims. A descendant of Zadok the priest could not speak for Yahweh the way Elijah or Elisha could.

Aspirations for priestly supremacy did not fade away, however. The Temple of Solomon was not dismantled. Its commitment to Yahweh was reaffirmed. Its magnificence drew worshipers and its priests performed their functions with pomp, circumstance, and dependable regularity. Within the sanctuary, law, precedence, and custom reigned. Sacrifices were offered in accordance with unbreakable rules by experienced priests who knew where, how, and why to sacrifice.

The priests claimed that Yahweh abhorred interlopers. They believed that God had chosen a hereditary class—the priests—who pleased God with the meticulous repetition of sacred procedures.

This priestly class thus staked out its claim to be a specially chosen hereditary group, destined to carry out sacerdotal functions in an elaborate cultic system devoted to Yahweh. This class needed precise, tamper-proof laws. It needed a Yahwist barrier, barring even prophets from interfering with cultic procedures. It was important, therefore, for the priests to ground their claims in the remote past, in some Yahwist revelation which would be binding on the prophets and which would deter them from interference with priestly prerogatives.

The wilderness experience of the Jews offered fertile ground for such claims, for it was associated with the Exodus, with the shaping of the people, and with Yahweh's promise to give them the land in which they now lived. And since the wilderness migrations antedated prophetic activity within the land, the prophets could presumably be kept within bounds if there was evidence from the wilderness that the priests were superior to them. Such a solution offered the basis for a modus vivendi with prophecy, and, were the opportunity ever to present itself, could provide a basis for phasing out the prophetic function altogether.

The figure of Moses could be altered to serve this purpose since Moses had been the leader of the people and had been privy to Yahweh's will. If Yahweh's revelation to Moses had consisted of two teachings: (1) Yahweh is one and omnipotent, and (2) Yahweh had singled out Moses as a spokesman par excellence against whom all other prophets were to be measured and as a lawgiver who established the priesthood in Yahweh's name, then the cultus would no longer be insecure.

The monarchy, like the priesthood, needed secure under-girding to enjoy autonomy. It was essential that the laws that regulated the lives of the king's subjects not be at the mercy of prophetic whim and that lines of demarcation would mark off the prophetic to stave off anarchy. The prophets, so the Yah-wist priests and kings believed, should have the right to speak in Yahweh's name, but they should not be permitted to challenge traditional laws and institutions so long as these maintained a connection with Yahweh.

Priest and king thus shared a common need, yet neither had an authentic wilderness tradition to fall back upon. In fact, the wilderness traditions exposed their claims as spurious. Furthermore, prophetic activity inhibited the reshaping of traditions, since at any time the prophets could cry out "Fraud."

Prophetic resistance to stable laws and institutions from the eighth to the sixth century B.C.E. was not easily overcome. The prophet was on solid Yahwist ground when he exposed the monarchy and priesthood and their laws as nonessential. He felt free to regard as blasphemous customs that the priests regarded as sacrosanct. The Sabbath, the celebration of the New Moon, and the holding of holy convocations were all provisional practices to the prophets. These modes of wor-shiping Yahweh may have been *permitted,* but they were not mandatory, and the prophet was ultimately free to reject them. The fact that the people had come to believe that Yah-weh required them was irrelevant. Such widespread beliefs simply revealed that the people had little comprehension of Yahweh's covenant—a covenant calling for absolute fidelity and commitment to righteousness, not to solemn assemblies or sacrifices.

Varieties of Yahwism

ૡ By the time the Assyrians destroyed the Kingdom of Israel in 722 B.C.E., Yahwism had seeded not one but several varieties of Yahwism. There was the Yahwism of the tribal phase; the Yahwism of the wilderness phase; the Yahwism of the pre-monarchical agricultural and urban phase; the Yahwism of cult and priesthood; and the Yahwism of the new prophecy. All these varieties of Yahwism had been spawned by loyalty to the same omnipotent deity, and though each variety of Yahwism differed from every other and often clashed, each shared a pre-commitment to Yahweh's omnipotence. Yahweh was the God of the past, the present, the future. Yahweh was the God of mobility *and* the God of the settled mode of life. Yahweh was the God of tents and of houses; the God of the wilderness and of hills and valleys; the God of the country and the city. Yahweh was likewise the God of sheep and cattle; of agricultural fertility; of industry and commerce.

The rivalry among Yahwist functions was far from trivial, however. Precisely because Yahweh was singular and omnipotent, it was essential to know what it was that God wished and who spoke legitimately in God's name. All Yahwist groups were aligned against polytheism, yet each was competing with every other for supremacy. The fate of the people, the land, and the covenant hung in the balance, for what priests regarded as essential, prophets regarded as peripheral. For the priests, offering sacrifices warded off destruction; for prophets, preoccupation with sacrifices provoked it.

Deuteronomy: The New Compact

ૡ It was in an effort to resolve the crisis arising as a result of this situation that a coalition of priests and prophets promulgated, with royal approval, the first version of what was later to become known as the Book of Deuteronomy, the fifth and final book of the Pentateuch. But when Deuteronomy was promulgated in c. 621 B.C.E., during the reign of Josiah, it was a proclamation in its own right, for the Pentateuch as such was not yet in existence. Deuteronomy was proclaimed to be the long-lost farewell address of Moses to his people, summing up the meaning of Israel's experience in the wilderness. The theme is simple: Yahweh would wreak violent vengeance on the people if they were disloyal to God and failed to obey God's laws, but Yahweh would bless them and cause them to prosper if they heeded God's words.

No Yahwist could quarrel with this simple theme. But Deuteronomy did not stop here. It boldly sought to resolve the inner crisis of Yahwism by making two claims: (1) Yahweh's revelation to Moses was definitive; no prophet like Moses had arisen since and presumably none ever would; (2) Yahweh had revealed to Moses laws that were binding on all subsequent generations. Among these laws were those establishing a mandatory cultus, a specialized priesthood, and a Yahwistically regulated monarchy. Prophetic authority, though recognized, was curbed. It was not permitted to challenge the Mosaic laws, or the legitimacy of the priesthood or the monarchy. The authenticity of a prophet was now to be measured against the Book of Deuteronomy. In case of conflict, the book would prevail.

Deuteronomy was the first major effort to curb prophetic license and to supplant revelation with immutable legislation. Rejecting the prevailing notion that Moses was just another prophet and that the wilderness experience was just another example of Yahweh's singularity and omnipotence, the framers of Deuteronomy sought to elevate both; it raised Moses above all other prophets, singled out the revelation in the wilderness as the definitive revelation, and proclaimed this revelation immutable. Prophet, priest, king—each is assigned his role in Deuteronomy, in a united front of Yahwists against polytheism, to stave off disaster from within and from without and to demonstrate to Yahweh the people's determination to be loyal to God.

To bring about this coalition, the authors of Deuteronomy created a wilderness experience that bore only superficial resemblance to the traditional picture preserved in the so-called JE account. The laws found in the JE texts do not establish a single cultus, or a specialized hereditary priesthood, or a monarchy. Nor do they single out the tribe of Levi for priestly functions or Moses primarily as the giver of laws. In contrast, Deuteronomy demands that a single cultus be established and that an exclusive priestly monopoly be granted to the tribe of Levi. It sanctions a king (so long as he binds himself by Deuteronomy as taught by the Levites), and it limits prophetic freedom by insisting that prophecy be measured against Moses and the laws of Deuteronomy.

The Prophetic Reaction

❧ Although Deuteronomy was promulgated under powerful auspices it failed to attain its objectives. Prophets such as Jeremiah and Ezekiel refused to give up their prophetic freedom. Yahweh and *not* Moses was the one and only omnipotent God. Yahweh had *not* become bound by immutable laws. Yahweh had *not* cut off the possibility of making future decisions. Yahweh's sovereignty had *not* been surrendered to any class or institution. Yahweh remained determined to raise up prophets *like* Moses, with robust prophetic power, and not prophets curbed and hemmed in by an alleged revelation in the wilderness.

Jeremiah and Ezekiel showed so little regard for Moses' farewell address that they ignored it and barely mentioned Moses at all. They did not even dignify Deuteronomy's claims with a refutation. They continued to exercise their prophetic prerogative as though Deuteronomy had never been promulgated. Jeremiah preached that the kingdom, the city, and the Temple would be destroyed. He proclaimed this in Yahweh's name, not in Moses'. And Ezekiel echoed him.

And when the exile to Babylonia did take place after Jerusalem and the Temple had been destroyed in 586 B.C.E. and the so-called Second Isaiah promised redemption, he did so in Yahweh's name, not in Moses'. Even the prophet whose oracles are to be found in the latter chapters of the Book of Ezekiel—who he was or when he prophesied or why his prophecies were attributed to Ezekiel is not ascertainable—sets forth a blueprint for a restored Temple and for a restored priesthood, and he does so by virtue of his own prophetic authority. He does not mention Moses, much less feel himself bound by Deuteronomy. Indeed, he insists that the Levites who have been assigned altar rights in Deuteronomy are to be stripped of these rights and are to subordinate themselves to the sons of Zadok, who alone, so Ezekiel claims, are to offer up sacrifices on Yahweh's altar.

An analysis of all the exilic and postexilic prophets reveals that only one of them, Malachi, seeks to underpin Deuteronomy with prophetic authority. He insists that Yahweh had made an eternal covenant with Levi, and that God had voiced some permanent revelation in the wilderness. Clearly, however, if this covenant and this revelation had to be confirmed by a prophet they were not self-sustaining.

How miserably Deuteronomy had failed is revealed in the malfunctioning society which Nehemiah found when he visited the restored Judea around 450 B.C.E. Following the decree of Cyrus in 538 B.C.E. granting the Jews the right to resettle and rebuild the Temple, an effort had been made to construct some sort of viable society. Such a reconstruction, however, proved to be extremely difficult because of the clash of conflicting interests: the Davidic line wished to restore the monarchy; the Levites wished to make good their claims to altar rights and to have Deuteronomy acknowledged as Yahweh's immutable revelation; the prophets wished to hold on to their role as the spokesmen of Yahweh's will. The failure to resolve these conflicts was quite apparent to Nehemiah during his visit to the community. Though polytheism was no longer a threat, the Yahwist community was anything but a light to the nations or a holy showpiece.

The problem was clear enough but the solution elusive. The problem was prophetic authority. So long as prophets had the freedom to speak out in Yahweh's name, no institution was safe and no authority, other than prophecy, sacrosanct. No society could function on such precarious foundations. Without secure legitimacy, even the most Yahwist institutions could not function effectively. If the worship of Yahweh was to endure and a Yahwist community be established, then prophecy had to go. But how?

II

The Revolution
of the Aaronides

The Creation of the Pentateuch

&❧ How was prophecy to be phased out? Deuteronomy had tried to solve the problem by assigning a preeminent role to Moses, elevating him over all subsequent prophets, and using the wilderness as the setting for revealed immutable legislation. The solution failed because, as we have seen, prophets refused to be curbed. But another reason played a part in its failure: Not one, but three Yahwist institutions—monarchy, priesthood, prophethood—were accorded legitimacy. There was a built-in invitation to clash over the lines of authority.

Faced with the need for a radical restructuring of Judean society, and finding Deuteronomy's blueprint nonviable, a group of gifted, though anonymous, leaders grappled with the core problem and shaped a solution: the Pentateuch. Stirred by the crisis threatening Yahwism, they flung precedent and tradition aside and transferred all power to a priestly class they themselves designed as the solution. This priestly class was to consist of the descendants of Aaron, the brother of Moses, and it was to exercise its authority forever, its rights being grounded in immutable laws revealed by Yahweh to

Moses on Mount Sinai, laws investing the Aaronides with absolute power.

What is remarkable about this transfer of authority is that this priestly class, the Aaronides, was created by the shapers of the Pentateuch. It had never before existed. It was created to solve a problem, and solve it, it did.

Pre-Aaronide Priests

ðɹ There had been priests long before the Pentateuch was promulgated. Eli had been a priest in the sanctuary of Shiloh; the priests of Nob had helped David when he fled from Saul; Abiathar and Zadok, both priests, supported rival contenders for the throne of David; Solomon built a magnificent Temple and put Zadok, the priest, in charge; Amaziah the priest scolded Amos for disrupting worship in Samaria; Hilkiah, the high priest at Jerusalem, played a crucial role in calling King Josiah's attention to the Book of Deuteronomy found in Yahweh's house. Deuteronomy, as we have seen, assigned to the priests of the tribe of Levi — the Levitical priests — exclusive altar rights and charged them with the teaching of judgments to Jacob and the Torah to Israel (Deuteronomy 33:10). Jeremiah was himself of priestly family, and his prophecies castigating the priests testify to their power in his day. Ezekiel, too, was a priest, though prophecy was his calling. And the prophet whose blueprint for a restored cultus is etched out in the latter chapters of the Book of Ezekiel looked to a priestly family, "the sons of Zadok," for dedicated Yahwist leadership.

Priests there had been in abundance, but they were not Aaronides. Priests with impressive genealogies, yes. Priests belonging to the tribe of Levi, yes. Priests flaunting descent from Zadok, yes. But prior to the promulgation of the Pentateuch no priests are Aaronides. This fact is confirmed by the so-called JE texts where Aaron is pictured as Moses' brother and companion, but not as the ancestor of a Yahwist priesthood. The only priestly role Aaron undertakes in these texts is the building of the Golden Calf, a role scarcely calculated to win from Yahweh eternal priesthood for his descendants. Even more striking is the confirmation in Deuteronomy. Deuteronomy is very much concerned with establishing a permanent cultus and a priestly class. Yet Deuteronomy, recalling Aaron's building of the Golden Calf, bypasses him as a candidate for fathering a priestly caste. Instead, it assigns the priestly function to the tribe of Levi.

The same is true in the writings of the post-exilic prophet whose program for the restored cultus appears in the latter chapters of the Book of Ezekiel. In his efforts to strip the Levites of the priestly prerogatives bestowed on them by Deuteronomy, he contrasts their disloyalty to Yahweh with the steadfast loyalty of the "sons of Zadok." He does not challenge them with being non-Aaronides; nor does he turn to the "sons of Zadok" because they are Aaronides. This prophet knew nothing of Yahweh's violent outburst against the Levites' bid for priestly prerogatives under the leadership of Korah, which looms so large in the completed Pentateuch. Had he had any inkling that Yahweh had already exposed the Levites as usurpers, he would have had no need to have Yahweh deliver the *coup de grâce* through him.

More information appears in the prophetic books and in the Book of Kings. Prophets are aware of priests, but they are in the dark about Aaronides. Some prophets testify to the existence of Levitical priests; none testify to the existence of Aaronide priests. Only in the completed Pentateuch, in the so-called P texts of Joshua and Judges, and in Chronicles is Aaronidism rampant.

Shadowy Beginnings

ह‌ How are we to account for this phenomenon? So long as there is no Pentateuch—only the so-called JE texts and Deuteronomy—there are no Aaronides. The moment, however, we have the Pentateuch there seem to be *only* Aaronides. Not only have kings and princes vanished, but there are no longer any prophets. Before the canonization of the Pentateuch, even as late as the time of Nehemiah's visit to Judea about 445 B.C.E., prophecy is still alive. And then, in the fourth century, there is the Pentateuch, and prophecy has evaporated. A class which had spoken out in Yahweh's name for centuries; which boasted of such creatively audacious leaders as Moses, Samuel, Nathan, Elijah, Elisha, Amos, Micah, Isaiah, Jeremiah, and Ezekiel; which had challenged king, priest, and even rival prophets, simply evaporated with the promulgation of the Pentateuch. Exercising authority in its stead is a priestly class of Aaronides, unknown to Moses, unmentioned in Deuteronomy, unheard of by Ezekiel, and outside the ken of even so late a prophet as Malachi!

This is a bewildering phenomenon indeed, and one resistant to clarification. There just is no way of determining how the Pentateuch was finalized. The Pentateuch itself gives no clear-cut answers, for it does not proclaim itself to be a composite work. One God, Yahweh-Elohim, is the source of authority throughout the work. Moses is God's spokesman for prophetic power, for Levitical priestly power, for Aaronide power. The God who has no interest in establishing a priestly class and who is perfectly happy to be worshiped at any place where God's name is remembered is the same God who is determined to have only the Levites make sacrifices and terribly concerned that sacrifice be made in the one place that God has chosen. Yet this God who, in Deuteronomy, so loved the Levites that they were given hegemony over the sacrificial altar is the selfsame God who trampled the Levites down when, in the Book of Numbers, they joined with Korah to challenge Aaronide hegemony.

The Pentateuch is not a self-revealing book. It packs into the wilderness period experiences ranging from the most simple to the most complex. Consider, for example, Yahweh, Moses, and the Tent of Meeting in the following vignette:

> *And Moses would take the tent and pitch it outside the camp, and he called it the Tent of Meeting. And it used to be that whoever sought out Yahweh would go out to the Tent of Meeting which was outside the camp. And it used to be that when Moses would go out to the Tent that all the people would rise up and stand, each man at the entrance of his tent and they would look after Moses until he came to the Tent. And it used to be when Moses came to the Tent that the pillar of cloud would come down and stand at the entrance of the Tent, and speak with Moses. And all the people would see the pillar of cloud standing at the entrance of the Tent, and all of the people would get up and bow down, each man at the entrance of his tent. And Yahweh would speak with Moses face to face, as a man speaks to his neighbor, and then he would return to the camp. And his apprentice Joshua the son of Nun, being a lad, did not depart from the midst of the Tent* [Exodus 33:7-11].

What utter simplicity! How so in accord with a wilderness setting! So plain, so informal, so direct! Yahweh is to Moses what Moses is to the people. Yahweh speaks to Moses face to face; Moses speaks to the people face to face. The people have tents; Yahweh also has a tent. And as for Joshua, he is learning to be *like* Moses, watching him converse with Yahweh and looking after the Tent when Yahweh and Moses leave.

Contrast this scene with the following, likewise purported to have occurred in the wilderness:

> *And Yahweh spoke to Moses saying: "On the first day of the first month you shall set up the Tabernacle, the Tent of Meeting. And you shall put there the Ark of the Testi-*

mony and you shall cover over the Ark with the Veil.

"And you shall bring the table and arrange it properly, and you shall bring the lamp and set up its lights. You shall then set the gold altar of incense in front of the Ark of the Testimony and put the covering of the entrance of the Tabernacle in place.

"You shall put the altar of the whole offering in front of the entrance of the Tabernacle, the Tent of Meeting.

"You shall put the basin between the Tent of Meeting and the altar and put water in it.

"You shall set up the court all around and put in place the cover of the gateway of the court.

"You shall take the anointing oil and anoint the Tabernacle and everything in it; thus you shall consecrate all its furnishings and it shall be holy.

"You shall anoint the altar of the whole-offering and all its vessels; thus you shall consecrate it, and it shall be most holy.

"You shall anoint the basin and its stand and consecrate it.

"You shall bring Aaron and his sons to the entrance of the Tent of Meeting and wash them with water.

"Then you shall clothe Aaron with the sacred garments, anoint him and consecrate him; so he shall be my priest. You shall then bring forward his sons, clothe them in tunics, anoint them as you anointed their father, and they shall be my priests. Their anointment shall be for them as a priesthood forever throughout all their generations. "

And Moses did in accordance with all which Yahweh commanded him, so he did.

And it came to pass in the first month of the second year on the first day of the month the Tabernacle was set up. And Moses set up the Tabernacle. He put the sockets in place, inserted the planks, fixed the crossbars, set up the posts. He spread the Tent over the Tabernacle and fixed the covering of the tent above it, as the Lord commanded *him. He took the Testimony and put it in the Ark and he put the poles in the Ark and put the cover of the Ark above it. And he brought the Ark to the Tabernacle and he put the veil of the covering veil and covered over the Ark of the Testimony as the Lord commanded Moses.*

And he put the table in the Tent of Meeting on the north side of the Tabernacle outside the veil, and arranged the bread on it before the Lord as the Lord commanded Moses. He placed the lampstand in the Tent of Meeting opposite the table, on the south side of the Tabernacle. And he lit the lamps before the Lord — as the Lord had commanded Moses. He placed the altar of gold in the Tent of Meeting, before the curtain. On it he burned aromatic incense — as the Lord had commanded Moses.

Then he put up the screen for the entrance of the Tabernacle. At the entrance of the Tabernacle of the Tent of Meeting he placed the altar of burnt offering. On it he offered up the burnt offering and the meal offering — as the Lord had commanded Moses. He placed the laver between the Tent of Meeting and the altar, and put water in it for washing. From it Moses and Aaron and his sons would wash their hands and feet; they washed when they entered the Tent of Meeting and when they approached the altar — as the Lord had commanded Moses. And he set up the enclosure about the Tabernacle and the altar, and put up the screen for the gate of the enclosure.

Thus Moses completed the work and the cloud covered the Tent of Presence, and the glory of the Lord filled the Tabernacle.

Moses was unable to enter the Tent of Meeting because the cloud had settled on it and the glory of the Lord filled the Tabernacle [Exodus 40: 1-35].

The simple Tent of Meeting has been transformed into an elaborate Tabernacle for the Aaronides, and this transformation is carried out by Moses himself. He personally puts the sockets in place, inserts the planks, fixes the crossbars, and sets up the posts. And all to what end? To make certain that Aaron and his sons will have the perfect Tabernacle for exercising their priestly monopoly: Their anointing by Moses is to establish for them "a priesthood forever throughout all their generations." The Tent of Meeting is no longer to be the Tent where Yahweh and Moses conversed and which Joshua looked after when Yahweh and Moses had departed. It was now to envelop the Tabernacle where Aaron and his sons were to offer sacrifices to Yahweh and from which *Moses himself is to be excluded since he was not one of the Aaronides.* Far from looking upon this as usurpation, Moses is the divine instrument for its fulfillment. He establishes the Aaronide hegemony by transforming a tent into a sanctuary and by transferring to Aaron the symbol of his special relationship to Yahweh, the Tent of Meeting.

How ironic! At one time the cloud of Yahweh settling down on the Tent of Meeting had been the sure sign that Yahweh wished to speak with Moses. Now it meant that Moses was unwelcome.

These texts have been set side by side though they reveal with such clarity the sort of problem the Pentateuch sets for us. Both texts utilize a wilderness setting. Both texts acknowledge Moses' preeminence. Both texts take Yahweh's authority for granted. Yet for anyone who is not pre-committed to Moses' authorship of the Pentateuch, these texts are mutually exclusive. The simple vignette comports well with a wilderness experience; the elaborate Tabernacle does not. The Moses-Yahweh relationship of the vignette is far more believable as a wilderness possibility than is that of Yahweh and Moses devoting all their energies to establishing Aaronide hegemony.

How are we to account for such mutually exclusive claims sharing the same God, the same wilderness, and the same Pentateuch? The historical books of the Bible are of no help, for they do not reveal any knowledge their authors may have had of how the Pentateuch came to be what it is. Nor do the prophets come to our aid. They neither affirm nor denounce the Pentateuch, for it seems that the promulgation of the Pentateuch was itself the occasion for silencing prophecy once and for all.

The literature of the Ancient Near East likewise offers us no way out. There is no book like the Pentateuch in all the extant documents of Ancient Near Eastern civilization. There are myths; there are collections of laws; there are annals; there are psalms, hymns, proverbs, maxims, and parables; there are countless texts, sacred and profane. But there is nothing analogous to the Pentateuch; namely, a concentration of centuries of complex experience within a historical framework. Packed within this framework are laws ranging from the most simple to the most complex; mutually exclusive systems of authority; and contradictory notions, concepts, and beliefs—all attributed to a single omnipotent deity who had revealed them all without firmly guiding followers as to which of the conflicting beliefs should take priority. The Pentateuch has no equivalent in the literature of the Ancient Near East because the commitment to a single deity required a kind of problem-solving unknown to polytheistic systems. Yahweh had to handle all problems, all complexity, all diversity, all contradiction, or otherwise Yahweh could not be both one and omnipotent. Problems could not be broken up to be parceled out among several deities.

The Pentateuch and its Formation

ॐ How, then, is the problem of the Pentateuch to be solved? Critical scholars have perforce been thrown back on their own imaginative resources, i.e., they have been compelled to conjure up conceptual models of how the process of forming the books took place. Since virtually all scholars working in the biblical field have been drawn to it by religious or academic interests, they tend to think in religious and literary categories. Ideas, thoughts, concepts of God, Israel, ethics, morals—these seemed to be the keys for unraveling the Pentateuchal secret. These, linked with tools of literary analysis, enabled scholars to distinguish one source from another. And since so much of the Pentateuch is narrative and since the accounts of the patriarchs in Genesis are cast in story form, the notion of storytellers seemed reasonable enough. There was the J narrative, the E narrative, the integrated JE narrative, the P history, and Deuteronomy D. And since the Pentateuchal texts were highly cooperative in offering literary and conceptual criteria for distinguishing these sources from each other, and since difficulties could be handled by assigning them to redactors, or to additional sources, or to ad hoc exceptions, a strong case could be made for the documentary hypothesis. Especially appealing was the Graf-Wellhausen rendition, for it not only separated the sources, but argued cogently for a chronological scheme among them—first JE, then D, and finally P.

The Wellhausen hypothesis has been challenged in recent years and alternatives have been offered which have appealed to large numbers of highly competent scholars. These involve reordering the documents, utilizing form criticism, and tapping the vast new knowledge of the Ancient Near East that archeologists have placed at our disposal. But what has not altered is the fact that no sources have been discovered which explicate the process by which the Pentateuch came to be the Pentateuch. Scholars today must, no less than yesterday, ultimately fall back on what they visualize as possibility. And, as a reading of the current state of Pentateuchal research will verify, what is imagined by one scholar to be obvious is, for another scholar, absurd. One has only to set down alongside each other the reconstructions of Albright, Noth, and

Kaufman to realize that each pictures the process in a radically different way.

The problem of the Pentateuch is thus not the sort of problem that can be solved by marshaling texts or erudition, for the most benighted and the most learned share a common ignorance: the sources do not tell us how, why, or when. The Pentateuch reveals only that it is a composite; it does not communicate how this composite came to be.

Perhaps a more fruitful line of thinking is to recognize the stubbornness of the problem and experiment with new conceptual possibilities. Religious and literary concerns have obscured the fact that the Pentateuch reveals itself to be a record of conflicting claims regarding authority and power. What can be differentiated with absolute clarity is patriarchal power, prophetic power, Levitical priestly power, royal power, and Aaronide power. There may be other powers as well, but those listed are readily discernible by tutored and untutored eyes alike. And equally discernible is the fact that these powers are buttressed by claims that could not have been simultaneously implemented. Moses could not have had the Tent of Meeting for conversing with Yahweh if it was the exclusive Tabernacle of the Aaronides; the Levites and the Aaronides could not simultaneously have enjoyed a cultic monopoly; the Levites who control the cult in Deuteronomy know nothing of Aaronides, while in the Book of Numbers the Aaronides threaten the Levites with awesome punishment if they dare approach the altar.

These diverse and conflicting powers are confirmed by the Pentateuchal texts. They are concrete and objective data. The fact that they are found side by side in the Pentateuch, the fact that all are authorized by Yahweh and Moses, and the fact that all (aside from the patriarchal authority) are pictured as having functioned in the wilderness beg for explanation. And the only explanation that accounts for these rival claims to exercise power is the existence of rival claimants; i.e., if the wilderness account reveals Moses as exercising absolute power as Yahweh's spokesman, then an explanation is to be found in the existence of a class of Yahwist spokesmen; if Moses shares his power by bestowing cultic rights upon the Levites, then an explanation is to be found in the existence of a Levitical class of priests; if Moses assigns a cultic monopoly to the Aaronides and excludes himself from the Tent of Meeting, then an explanation is to be found in the existence of a priestly class of Aaronides. Since the Pentateuch reveals itself to be an account of powers contending with each other for approval by Yahweh and Moses, then an explanation of how it came to be must be sought in the rise of classes who sought to make good their claims to exercise authority.

The Struggle for Power

ह्ल   We therefore arrive at a self-sustaining hypothesis, that the Pentateuch has preserved within it four phases of authority in Israel: (1) patriarchal absolutism; (2) prophetic absolutism; (3) collaboration among Levitical-priestly, royal, and prophetic powers; and (4) Aaronidism. For each phase we have a set of texts: patriarchal, wilderness, Deuteronomy, and Aaronide. These texts are differentiated not primarily by literary criteria, but by power criteria. There are indeed literary differences, and these literary differences distinguish the JE, D, and P documents. This not only is to be expected but supports the power hypothesis, for each class articulated its claims at a different time and consequently expressed its claims in the language current at the time. There is, however, an essential difference between approaching the Pentateuch from the point of view of literary style and from the point of view of power. Whereas the power hypothesis looks upon literature as an instrument for attaining nonliterary ends, the documentary hypothesis considers literary criteria fundamental.

The Pentateuch was thus the outcome of efforts to solve problems in a Yahwist society. It was not primarily the work of scribes, scholars, or editors who sought out neglected traditions about the wilderness experience, but of a class struggling to gain power. Since the Pentateuch does not spell out any power or authority for scribes, scholars, or redactors, it is gratuitous to assign to them — powerless as they were — the power to decide who speaks for Yahweh. The storytellers or redactors were not free agents but were subordinate to power groupings who utilized whatever communicating means were at hand to make known their claims. The Pentateuchalizers — a name coined to convey the nature of the activity they carried out — were not tradition-seekers, but tradition-shapers. They were problem solvers committed to Yahweh's omnipotence. Their concern was to make Yahwism work. To achieve this they drew on traditions when helpful, negated traditions when harmful, and created traditions when necessary.

The power groups responsible for Deuteronomy had made a valiant effort to solve concrete problems by transferring them back to the wilderness, as it were, and having Yahweh solve them there. We have already seen that this valiant effort failed. But though a failure, Deuteronomy opened up the wilderness experience for problem solving and set up Moses as the instrument for innovating solutions.

The Aaronide Success

இ. The Aaronides succeeded where Deuteronomy had failed. They saw Yahwism threatened unless they wielded absolute authority. They therefore designed the Pentateuch to attain this end, arrogating to themselves not only altar rights but also control over the process of expiation from sin. They broke prophetic authority by having Moses invest Aaron and his sons with the priesthood forever. They had Moses himself build the Tent of Meeting-Tabernacle. They had Moses willingly forgo entering it when the cloud of Yahweh descended upon it. Aaron, not Moses, dispenses expiation. Aaron's sons, not Moses', are to have hereditary authority.

The Aaronides also buried the claims of the Levites by re-counting the rebellion of Korah, the Levite, and his company of Levites against Aaron's hegemony (Numbers 16-18). Never was Yahweh more angered. Not even the Golden Calf had so outraged Yahweh. Korah and his entire company were buried alive. Still burning with anger, Yahweh let loose fire and plague and was calmed only when Aaron interceded. In all of the Pentateuch there is nothing comparable to the annihila-tion of Korah and his fellow rebels. More than one hundred verses are lavished on this episode. No punishment is too harsh; no vengeance too extreme. So momentous indeed was this proof of Yahweh's love for Aaron that the fire pans of the rebels (representing their offering) were to be hammered out and affixed to the altar, so that all Israel would recall how merciless Yahweh could be when Yahweh's Aaronides were challenged.

The shaping of the Pentateuch was thus a deliberate and conscious effort to save Yahwism from disintegration. Its cre-ation was deliberate and conscious, similar to the decision of the founding fathers of the United States to write a Constitu-tion rather than modify the Articles of Confederation. A group of gifted leaders, utterly committed to Yahweh and drawn for the most part from the priesthood, were distraught with Ne-hemiah's report of conditions in restored Judea. They recog-nized that only the most drastic surgery could repair the malfunctioning Yahwist society. They therefore drew on the Yahwist resources already at hand and, subordinating them to clearly visualized goals, designed the Pentateuch to attain their goals.

These were their resources: (1) the one and omnipotent God, Yahweh-Elohim, (2) the pre-patriarchal and patriarchal traditions as recorded in the so-called JE texts, (3) the Mosaic wilderness texts, (4) Deuteronomy, and (5) prophetic oracles. This was their problem: how to consolidate all effective Yahwist power in the hands of a single class and head off counterattacks from those who traditionally had wielded Yahwist authority.

This is how they seem to have done it: (1) All pre-patriarchal and patriarchal traditions already recorded and sacrosanct were left untouched. (2) All Mosaic wilderness texts already sacrosanct and recorded were left untouched. (3) Moses' farewell address in Deuteronomy was similarly left untouched. (4) A framework of Aaronidism was built around these earlier materials so as to nullify their effectiveness and replace them with functioning Aaronidism.

The framework played two roles: (1) it encouraged the reading of non-Aaronide texts from an Aaronide point of view, and (2) it surrounded all texts that endangered Aaronide absolutism with massive Aaronide claims, overwhelming with sheer quantity and repetition the claims of prophets or Levitical priests to exercise Yahwist authority. By judicious insertions, Aaronide pressure on the reader is maintained throughout the Pentateuch.

Overcoming Difficulties

੨੩ The embarrassing account of Aaron's role in building the Golden Calf, found in the Mosaic wilderness texts and also in Deuteronomy, was highly combustible stuff, which might flare up into anti-Aaronidism. How did the Aaronides handle it? Counting up the number of verses devoted to the episode in the two accounts of Aaron's defection will show that they do not number more than a couple of dozen at most. But the account in Exodus of how Yahweh commanded Moses to build an elaborate Tabernacle and invest Aaron and his sons with a priesthood forever contains no fewer than one hundred verses which spell out with meticulous care all of Aaron's prerogatives. This is not all. More than one hundred such verses precede the Golden Calf incident, verses couched in the form of commands. Then, following the Golden Calf incident, almost as many verses are devoted to a detailed account of the carrying out of what Yahweh had commanded. Thus, before the reader reaches the story of the Golden Calf, he has been impressed with Yahweh's determination to single Aaron out for the priesthood. He is thoroughly aware that Aaron is virtually on the same plane as Moses. Then lest the reader be under any illusion that Yahweh had changed his mind about Aaron, he is reassured that everything that had been commanded with respect to Aaron and the Tabernacle was indeed carried out by Moses himself *after* Aaron had built the Golden Calf.

No less vivid an illustration of Aaronide technique is afforded by the account of Korah's rebellion. The claims of the Levites to altar rights were impressively set forth in Deuteronomy. The Aaronides had to find a way of canceling them out and reducing the Levites to a subordinate role. Here the problem was sticky because the farewell address of Moses in Deuteronomy had to remain unaltered and the final blessing to the tribe of Levi had to be retained. The solution was found in the dramatic handling of the rebellion of Korah and the Levites. As already indicated, the episode reveals Yahweh at a pitch of anger unequaled anywhere else in the Pentateuch. The story of God's vengeance is followed by a detailed account of Aaronide prerogatives, in the form of legislation that is to be everlastingly binding. Similarly, the subordinate role of the Levites is made crystal clear. Any misstep on their part is to be punishable by instant death.

But the Korah episode is only the most dramatic of the Aaronide devices for sealing off Deuteronomy from dangerous anti-Aaronide claims. For, in effect, most of Exodus, all of

Leviticus, and most of Numbers serve this purpose too. In these books there are hundreds of verses concentrating on Aaronide prerogatives, Aaronide activities, Aaronide concepts, and Aaronide values—all building up an Aaronide edifice that will not be rocked by Deuteronomy.

These devices and techniques all served a single purpose—the transfer of power from those who had held it to a new class that had never held it before. To effectuate the transfer, the Aaronides had Yahweh express Aaronidism as the will of God. They had Yahweh command Moses to transform the Tent of Meeting into a Tabernacle. They had Yahweh exclude Moses from entry when the cloud of Yahweh descended upon it. They had Yahweh bury Levitical claims. They had Yahweh spell out with precision their monopolistic privileges. They had Yahweh single them out to expiate the sins of the people. They had Yahweh ordain cultic occasions (such as the First Day of the Seventh Month, the Day of the Blowing of the Ram's Horn) for the display of priestly power. But most impressive was their setting aside the Tenth Day of the Seventh Month, the Day of Atonement, for re-consecration of Aaronide absolutism. On that day the Aaronide-in-chief was to enter the Holy of Holies in the Tabernacle and there in Yahweh's presence seek expiation for Israel's sins. Each year when he emerged from the Holy of Holies, still alive after having, as it were, been exposed to the very presence of God, he bore testimony to Yahweh's re-commitment to Aaronidism. The Tent of Meeting had been the site of Yahweh's revelations to Moses; it had been transformed and turned over by Moses himself to Aaron. Year in and year out, commemorating this, the Aaronides celebrated with appropriate expiatory sacrifices.

The Measure of Success

ɐ̀ঌ   The Aaronides were triumphant. The Pentateuch, shaped
to rescue Yahwism from deterioration and extinction, was a
brilliant tour de force. To this day millions of Jews and Christians still believe it to have been the revelation of God to
Moses. In every synagogue and temple throughout the world,
selections from it are read on every Sabbath. Even the most
radical wing of Reform Judaism pays it special veneration.
For more than two thousand years, its devotees have attached
awesome sanctity to every letter. Its authority has been called
upon to buttress the claims of clashing forms of Judaism, and
its verses were drawn upon by Paul and the writers of the
Gospels to prove that Jesus was the Christ. Not until the birth
of modern critical thinking in the seventeenth century did
awareness of the Pentateuch's composite character penetrate
the traditional barriers and provoke minds to question Mosaic authorship. One is awed by the mental ingenuity of a
Rashi, a Maimonides, or a Thomas Aquinas, sufficiently adept and agile to dissolve what they themselves recognized as
stubborn contradictions. Yet dissolve them they did.

This is a remarkable achievement by any standard, but
most biblical scholars have overlooked it. Glance through any
of the most respected introductions to the literature of the Old
Testament and you will be impressed with the incredible
complexity of the Pentateuchal problem. You will be stag-
gered by the erudition that has dismembered into dozens of
units in a book that functioned as a unity for centuries. You
will be bewildered by the array of scholarly options, all in
good standing, sporting compelling arguments and deftly
drawing on a decisive verse here and a telling expression
there. But I doubt that you will come away with any notion of
an Aaronide revolution. You will learn of Aaron and his sons,
but the aggressive and brilliant tour de force of the Aaronides
will be blurred. You will also figure out that there must have

been a time when there was no Pentateuch, and then a time when the Pentateuch became preeminent, but you will not have encountered the concept of the Pentateuchal Revolution.

This concept is obscured by the assignment of the canonization of the Pentateuch to redactors drawing now on one source, now on another; digging up a lost tradition here, reconfirming a vintage tradition there; knitting together a skein from this pattern, a thread from that, and a fully worked-through design from another. The picture you will carry away is that of assiduous redactors and scribes piously selecting, rejecting, piecing and patching traditions together which somehow or other, perhaps through Ezra the Scribe, get promulgated. And then all of a sudden there are no more prophets; no more claimants to David's throne; no more Levites sacrificing at the altar. There are only Aaronides. This cannot be the work of pious scribal redactors who give the Aaronides a power monopoly and do not even mention scribes in the Pentateuch, much less give them any voice or power. There is a transfer of power from classes that had wielded it for years to a class that had not wielded it at all, and all we have is redaction! Can there be Aaronide power and the Aaronides not have fashioned it?

The leitmotif of Aaronidism is preserved most effectively in the very last verses of the Pentateuch: "And there never again arose a prophet like Moses whom the Lord knew face to face." Since there never again was a prophet like Moses, the vast corpus of legislation establishing Aaronide hegemony, which God had revealed to Moses on Sinai, was absolutely binding. Originally, the writers of Deuteronomy had penned this tribute to Moses to underwrite Levitical power. Now it effectively solidified Aaronide power, since in Exodus, Leviticus, and Numbers Moses bestowed supreme authority upon the Aaronides.

Securing a Silent Revolution

ટ♣ The Pentateuchal "All power to the Aaronides" did indeed come through and the Aaronide program did indeed become operative. But how were the shapers of the Pentateuch able to carry off this coup in the face of such strong support for Leviticism in Deuteronomy and for prophetic authority in a thousand or so years of relatively unchallenged prophetic supremacy? For this we have answers no more secure than those we have for the process by which the Aaronides organized themselves into a class and decided on shaping the Pentateuch. But if we stick with this methodology, we can come up with some intelligible hypotheses.

Aaronidism permitted a coalition of Levitical families to join together as a privileged class, the sons of Aaron, against other priestly families. At the same time, by elevating one of the families, presumably the sons of Zadok, to high-priestly status and allocating to the high priest the special privilege of being the Grand Expiator with the right once a year to enter the Holy of Holies, the powerful Zadokite family was allowed to enjoy priestly primacy, although not the monopoly accorded to them by the last chapters of Ezekiel. Such a coalition could easily beat down the claims of the other Levitical families for altar rights.

To gain popular support for the Aaronide enterprise, the priestly coalition offered the peasantry liberation from debt slavery and a guarantee that the land of the peasant could not be sold into perpetuity—in the Jubilee year the land was to revert to its original owner. Along with this promise, the Aaronides themselves forswore any right to land ownership; instead, they and the cultic establishment were to be richly endowed. In return for handsome revenues, the Aaronides were to offer their cultic know-how to seek atonements for sins and thereby assure the peasant abundant harvests.

A restored Yahwist society of expiating priests and prosperous peasants — this was the Pentateuchal program. It appealed to the Persians who ruled over the Jews as just the sort of benign absolutism that also served their interests best. The Pentateuch for them was a reassuring document. It concentrated power in what was, from an imperial point of view, a powerless class. The Aaronides proclaimed Yahweh-Elohim as the one and only God, and themselves as the indispensable mediators of God's will, but they did not call for a military establishment, nor did they call for the overthrow of Persian sovereignty. In the wilderness, the tribes had sent armed levies to defeat Israel's enemies, and had anticipated a hard struggle to win the land; but when the Pentateuch was shaped, there were no longer tribes, armed levies, or enemies to be overthrown in battle. The Aaronides were not a military class; rather they were a class whose effective exercise of power depended on the existence of a benign emperor protecting Judea from external enemies and protecting them from any challenge which might arise from efforts to restore the throne of David in Yahweh's name. And, as for the interests of the Persian emperor, the stronger the Aaronides, the weaker the Davidites; the more absolute Pentateuchal power, the less threatening the discords and disruptions of prophecy. The Pentateuch was thus tailored to serve the interests of a coalition of priestly families, a disgruntled and disillusioned peasantry, and an imperial sovereign eager for an effective and loyal leadership in Judea.

Such a combination of interests guaranteed that the Pentateuch would pass muster as Yahweh's unchallengeable revelation. And as for the inevitable question as to where the Pentateuch had been all these many hundreds of years when there had been no Aaronides, it was sufficient to answer that the Pentateuch had been lost, and had now been found. But however it was explained, of this we are certain: the Pentateuch was accepted as authentic; the Aaronides sat in Moses' seat; the Levites knuckled under; and the prophets faded away. And as for aspirants to David's throne, they vanished with the prophets.

The New Constitution

૪ૐ What had Yahweh wrought? Out of loyalty to Yahweh, the Aaronides had fashioned a new creation. The religion of Yahweh had broken through to new ground. The Pentateuch is not a distillation of traditional Yahwism, but a fresh vintage. Yahweh was now preeminently the God whose will had been proclaimed with such sufficiency that it need never be modified again. It was there—immutable, final, and holy—in the Pentateuch. Not a word too much, not a word too little. Yahweh had revealed commandments, statutes, judgments, testimonies to Moses on Sinai and in the wilderness, and had taken up residence in the Tent of Meeting-Tabernacle, where, daily and on the Sabbath and festivals, Yahweh savored the sweet-smelling sacrifices offered up on the holy altar by the beloved Aaronides. And abiding within the Holy of Holies, God's presence assured the sinful that their sins would be shriven. And, year in and year out, God's presence was confirmed when the high priest, with pomp and circumstance, entered the Holy of Holies and offered incense directly to God to seek atonement for Israel.

This stress on expiation through priestly mediation had not been the religion of Israel prior to the promulgation of the Pentateuch. There had indeed been a cultus; there had been priests; there had been sacrifices. But there had not been the concentration on the expiatory role of sacrifices (the sacrifices in Deuteronomy are not expiation sacrifices); expiation had been a function of the prophet: the prophet interceded on Israel's behalf. And now all had changed. The Temple and the Aaronides are now at the center of the stage. Here, in the Temple, is where Yahwism lives. One now turned to the Aaronides for divine guidance and forgiveness.

Much else was now altered. Whereas at an earlier time the festivals had commemorated either a historical event, such as the Exodus, or a harvest season, or both, now these festivals were overshadowed by the two impressive expiation days: the First Day of the Seventh Month, a day of Memorial of the dedication of the Tabernacle-Tent of Meeting; and Yom Kippur, the Day of Atonement, the Tenth Day of the Seventh Month—a day totally devoted to the demonstration of the efficacy of Aaronide intermediation between the people and Yahweh. Neither the Feast of Unleavened Bread, nor of First Fruits, nor of the Ingathering could so grip the heart and soul of the Israelite. For everything else depended on the power of the high priest to win atonement for the people. The effectiveness of the entire Pentateuchal system—laws, promises, threatening punishments— was re-tested annually when the high priest entered the Holy of Holies. If the system collapsed, Jews were taught, there would be no wheat or barley harvest, no gathering of the first fruits, no granaries stocked high with grain, no dough in the kneading trough, no security.

Everything, however traditional, was now shadowed with the brush of expiation. The historical and harvest festivals now became occasions for massive sacrifices, as much to gain forgiveness as to express thanksgiving. Each day, in the morning and in the evening, the Continual Sacrifice was offered up to seek atonement. On the Sabbath, the New Moon, and the festivals, there were additional sacrifices. For each sin the individual had to bring an appropriate offering. Each moment of the day and night the fire on the altar burned, symbolically confirming that the altar was always ready to offset sin whenever it might occur.

This elevation of sin and its expiation to preeminence was perhaps the most enduring creation of the Aaronides. Sin was no new concept. It was as old as Yahwism, for to be disloyal to Yahweh was to sin. But the idea of what constituted disloyalty and how reparation might be made was always in flux. Sin now took on a new dimension, being defined as the failure to obey scrupulously the Aaronide laws. The most heinous sin was to challenge the expiation system itself. Sin now became a matter of intense individual concern, for the Pentateuch placed a heavy responsibility on each Israelite. Since each sin endangered the security and the prosperity of the entire people, the individual's bringing sacrifice to expiate it was fraught with significance.

The Aaronide fixation on the sinning-expiation process was thus a momentous innovation. It shifted the focus from the economic sphere, i.e., sacrificing to Yahweh in thanksgiving for the fruit of the land, to the personal sphere. It pushed the individual toward introspection. It saddled the individual with subtle responsibility for the welfare of Israel as a whole. It enhanced the individual's own personal contribution to well-being or disaster; for to sin was to expose all of Israel to awesome punishment.

The linking of the individual's sin to expiation had profound consequences. Although the Aaronides served as essential intermediaries between the sin and its atonement, each individual was alerted to *personal* responsibility for observing the Pentateuchal laws. What a person did or did not do was crucial not only for the fate of Israel, but for the individual as well. Each person's life, literally, was on the line, for the Pentateuch promised to the law-abiding person long life, prosperity, and numerous offspring; and to the sinner, death. Each person thus had a vital stake in knowing and obeying the laws, and in introspection and reflection. Was he or she truly loyal to the laws? Did he or she sincerely love God and God's commandments? Were his or her motives and intentions pure? Did illness, suffering, and premature death lessen his or her faith or spur him or her to higher resolve? Would God take note of his or her human frailty, his or her proneness to temptation, his or her loneliness and despair? Would God hear his or her plaint, his or her anguished cry?

The Unity Principle at Work

ào By ushering in a radically new form of Yahwism the Pentateuch reveals the dynamic power of the Unity Principle. The divine name attached to this principle—Yahweh, or Elohim, or El Shaddai, or El Elyon—is of little import. The one God had thus proved capable of underwriting many things and was always able to cope with the novel, the unforeseen, the untried. This was a God who continually became what it was necessary to be. And this is the grand paradox. For God to become the eternal problem-solver, it was essential that those who had faith in God take this problem-solving power on faith. They had to be pre-committed. This pre-commitment is what links the patriarchs with Moses of the wilderness; with the older type of prophets like Samuel and Elijah; with the later type of prophet, like Amos, Isaiah, Jeremiah; with the Yahwist kings; with the Deuteronomist Levites; and with the Aaronides. This pre-commitment connects semi-nomadism with agricultural and urban settlement, with monarchy, with divided kingdoms, with the destruction of the Northern Kingdom, with Exile, and with restoration. The stubborn insistence that Yahweh was one and omnipotent, compelled all who believed this to be true always to be solving new problems in Yahweh's name.

Perhaps we can formulate the significance of the Pentateuch most clearly if we assert that the shapers of the Pentateuch were so pre-committed to Yahweh's omnipotence that they could solve no problem without acknowledging God as the source of the solution. In taking the resolute action that they did, they revealed that Yahweh was preeminently a God of process, of history, and of problem solving. As such Yahweh was the Power enabling the enduring to persist, the obsolescent to wear away, and the not-yet to emerge. Yahweh was the God of replication, disintegration, and innovation. The God of the past that was, the present that is, and the future that becomes. As the eternal ground of shifting appearances, Yahweh appeared to Abraham the patriarch with one set of attributes, to Moses of the wilderness with another, to the prophets with a third, and the Aaronides with still a fourth. To have followed Yahweh was to have ventured into the unknown as much as into the known, to have courted risk as much as security, to have stumbled on new attributes as much as to have clung to the old.

III
The Pharisaic
Revolution

A Decisive Mutation

&⃛ The Aaronide revolution ushered in an age of growth, development, and relative tranquility. Liberated from the cacophony of prophetic urgings and freed from the yoke of Davidic sovereignty, Israel basked in a golden glow of priestly rule. Enjoying the protection, first of Persian then of Ptolemaic kings, the Aaronides ruled firmly and they ruled well. Spurred by promises in the Pentateuch that their land would never be taken from them in perpetuity, that the Aaronides themselves would never lay claim to land ownership, and that the priestly and cultic dues would not be raised, the peasants sowed the soil with confidence and reaped prosperity as their reward. As the peasants thrived so did the priests. And as the economic base became more and more secure, the priestly elite ruled in splendor, and with compassion. The Aaronides did not break their covenant with the peasantry; for though it is impossible to determine whether the provisions of the Jubilee year were ever actually realized — that all mortgaged or lost lands were to revert to their original owners — the peasantry remained throughout the period of Aaronide rule a free peasantry. The priests, seeing their own power rooted in a free and prosperous peasantry, exercised authority in such a way as to retain the loyalty and the affection of the peasant class.

Under the enlightened policies of the Aaronides, Judea was transformed into a prosperous land, and Jerusalem into a city of cosmopolitan urbanity. Since these developments are obscure, we do not know how much of a part was played by the years of Persian hegemony. But it is certain that the process speeded up after the conquests of Alexander the Great.

The priests exercised their authority because God had granted it to them. It was therefore a matter of indifference to them which imperial system ruled the Holy Land. So long as the emperor, whoever he might be, reaffirmed their local autonomy, the high priest could serve him loyally. When Alexander the Great replaced the Persian emperor, the Aaronides were quick to acknowledge his imperial rights. When he in turn was followed by the Ptolemies, the Jews transferred their loyalties. And when the Ptolemies in turn were replaced by the Seleucids, the Aaronides were ready to serve them as well.

The Hellenistic Social Structure

ເ❧ The Hellenistic takeover of the Near East, however, involved far more than a shift from one imperial master to another. The Persians had underwritten, not undermined, the cultural patterns and institutions of the Near East. The Hellenistic intrusion, by contrast, was unsettling. The Greek *polis*, introduced by Alexander and his successors in the Near East, was a radically different kind of societal structure promoting a radically different world-view. The *polis* was a self-governing entity that allowed its citizens to enjoy a considerable amount of legislative autonomy. The *polis* citizens, not the gods, made the laws. Associated with and encouraged by the right to make laws was a high sense of individual independence. The *polis* citizen was schooled in a culture that fostered human individuality and the tendency of individuals to press their powers to their height. In the Near East the *polis* was a different kind of city; its citizen's mind visualized a different kind of reality, and the heart of every citizen throbbed to different kinds of stimuli.

The *polis* civilization encircled Judea. Jerusalem did not become a *polis* and the Aaronides did not seek for themselves *polis* rights. Their power lay in absolute loyalty to a single omnipotent God, and they enjoyed all the autonomy they needed. Nonetheless, the Aaronides had to deal with Hellenistic overlords; widening channels of trade, commerce, and industry invigorated economic growth in Judea; and a leisured class of wealth and learning became stimulated by the universal aspects of Greek wisdom.

The insinuation of Hellenistic motifs was slow and subtle, but effective; at first they seemed to offer no challenge to Aaronidism. Under the Ptolemies, the high priest continued to exercise his hegemony with only occasional intimations of the severe problems that lay ahead. An emperor as grand as Ptolemy Philadelphus (288-247 B.C.E.) showed such keen interest in the Pentateuch that he is reputed to have insisted that it be translated into Greek and deposited in his royal library. The Ptolemies' behavior showed their high regard for Jews and Judaism by bestowing upon Jews living in Alexandria the equivalent of *polis* rights, and at the same time permitting them to exercise a high degree of religious autonomy. To such royal overtures, the Aaronides responded with a reciprocal appreciation of those aspects of Hellenistic culture that were compatible with Pentateuchal monotheism.

The Soferim

๕๏ These conditions nurtured the growth of a new class of Aaronide intellectuals called *Soferim*. Although the term *soferim* is generally translated as "scribes," a more meaningful translation would be "intellectuals." These Soferim were deeply committed to the Pentateuch and the Aaronides, and to the pursuit of "Wisdom." They loved to spin maxims, weave proverbs, conjure riddles, contrive paradoxes, imagine parables, and articulate maxims. They were masters of the sententious, given to wise counsel. They scanned experience and drew helpful generalizations. Sighing over human follies, looking askance on human vices, they sought to lead people by Wisdom's light onto the paths of righteousness. Sustained by their slogan, "The beginning of Wisdom is the fear of the Lord," they venerated the Pentateuch, brought their sacrifices with song and gladness, and acclaimed the Aaronides as God's holy priesthood.

Ben Sira, who lived in the third or perhaps the second century B.C.E., belonged to this class of Soferim, and his book, *Ecclesiasticus*, reveals the Soferic mind. Showing Aaronidism at its height, it is full of maxims, proverbs, riddles, paradoxes, parables, musings, descriptions, and even a psalm or two — all subsumed under the broad designation Wisdom.

But in addition to being an example of Soferic interests, *Ecclesiasticus* actually gives us a portrait of a Sofer far different from the Pharisaic Scribe who was to emerge a short time later teaching a radically different concept of the Law:

> *On the other hand he who devotes himself*
> *To the study of the law of the Most High*
> *Will seek out the wisdom of all the ancients,*
> *And will be concerned with prophecies;*
> *He will preserve the discourse of notable men*
> *And penetrate the subtleties of parables;*
> *He will seek out the hidden meanings of proverbs*
> *And be at home with the obscurities of parables,*
> *He will serve among great men*
> *And appear before rulers* [Ecclesiasticus 39:14].

The Soferim were held in high esteem, but they did not exercise any authority over the Law. They studied the Pentateuch and heeded its teaching: God had given the Aaronides authority over God's statutes and judgments and had enjoined them to enlighten Israel with God's Law. The Soferim loved, honored, and obeyed the Aaronides; they did not compete with them.

Indeed, Ben Sira is a precious source testifying to the effectiveness of the Pentateuchal revolution and of priestly power. For him, Moses is the *revealer* of God's revelation, but Aaron *is* the revelation. Aaron overshadows Moses. In his book, Ben Sira lovingly bestows more verses on Aaron's dress than on Moses' face-to-face encounter with God.

Lest there be any doubt that Ben Sira was being carried away by mementos of a luster long dimmed, consider the hymn he composed to glorify the noblest Aaronide of them all, Simon, the High Priest, who ministered during Ben Sira's lifetime:

The leader of his brethren and the pride of his people
was Simon the high priest, son of Onias,
who in his life repaired the house,
and in his time fortified the Temple.
He laid the foundations for the double walls,
the high retaining walls for the temple enclosure.
In his days a cistern for water was quarried out,
a reservoir like a sea in circumference.
He considered how to save his people from ruin,
and he fortified the city to withstand a siege.
How glorious he was when the people gathered round him
as he came out of the inner sanctuary!
Like the morning star among the clouds,
like the moon when it is full;
like the sun shining on the temple of the Most High,
and like the rainbow gleaming in glorious clouds;
like roses in the days of the first fruits,

like lilies by a spring of water,
like a green shoot of Lebanon on a summer day;
like fire and incense in the censer,
like a vessel of hammered gold... [Ecclesiasticus 50:1–10].

Little wonder, then, that the Aaronides looked upon the Soferim with favor and gave them a free hand to pursue Wisdom. The Soferim in turn led the Pentateuch to the Aaronides. They taught Wisdom itself as a bona fide discipline and did not need to justify their teachings by latching them on to biblical verses, for such devices were unnecessary so long as the priests themselves sanctioned Wisdom as legitimate and compatible with the Pentateuch. A Sofer like Ben Sira who urged the people to bring the sacrifices, study the Pentateuch, and heed the Aaronides could simply assert that Wisdom, like the Pentateuch, was given by God to Israel:

Wisdom will praise herself,
And will glory in the midst of her people.
In the assembly of the Most High she will open her mouth,
And in the presence of his host she will glory:
"I came forth from the mouth of the Most High,
And covered the earth like a mist.
I dwelt in high places,
And my throne was in a pillar of cloud.
Alone I have made the circuit of the vault of heaven
And have walked in the depths of the abyss.
In the waves of the sea, in the whole earth,
And in every people and nation I have gotten a possession.
Among all these I sought a resting place;
I sought in whose territory I might lodge.
Then the Creator of all things gave me a commandment,
And the one who created me assigned a place for my tent.
And he said, 'Make your dwelling in Jacob,
And in Israel receive your inheritance'"
[Ecclesiasticus 24:1-13].

Ben Sira is committed to the cultus as a divinely revealed institution essential for expiation:

He who keeps the law makes many offerings;
He who heeds the commandments sacrifices a peace
offering.
He who returns a kindness offers fine flour,
And he who gives alms sacrifices a thank offering.
To keep from wickedness is pleasing to the Lord,
And to forsake unrighteousness is atonement.
Do not appear before the Lord empty-handed,
For all these things are to be done because of the
commandment.
The offering of a righteous man anoints the altar,
And its pleasing odor rises before the Most High.
The sacrifice of a righteous man is acceptable,
And the memory of it will not be forgotten
[Ecclesiasticus 35:1-9].

and:

With all your soul fear the Lord,
And honor his priests.
With all your might love your Maker,
And do not forsake his ministers.
Fear the Lord and honor the priest,
And give him his portion, as is commanded you
[Ecclesiasticus 7:31-34].

Ben Sira eloquently confirms the spiritual grandeur that Aaronidism made possible. Indeed, though not susceptible to the precise kind of dating possible with Ben Sira, a good number of the most poignant and introspective psalms were composed some time during the golden age of Aaronide hegemony. With prophecy blocked, creative spirits turned to the exploration in depth of the full range of the individual's relationship to God, cultus, and self. Human pain and bewilderment were filtered through sensitive souls who were committed both to Aaronide intermediation between the in-

dividual and God and to an aspiration for a one-to-one relationship with God. For them, loyalty to the Pentateuch and
fulfillment of its prescribed sacrifices elevated the individual
to that plane where direct communion with God became possible. Little wonder, then, that the introspective quality of the
psalms still resonates.

Emerging Dilemmas

2ᴪ But there was a major obstacle to the psalmist's deepest
aspiration for experiencing the righteous life as uniquely precious: There was no convincing proof that the righteous were
fully rewarded in this world, as the Pentateuch and the Aaronides claimed. Indeed, there was persistent evidence to the
contrary. As an answer, the psalmist needed immortality, but
the ideology of the Pentateuch and the Aaronides militated
against it. It is in this light that the dilemma of Job is revealed
in all its agony. The righteous Job confronts Pentateuchal
belief that righteousness is rewarded in this world with the
disturbing evidence of his own tribulation. Job needs immortality to save the idea of God's justice, but the solution evades
him.

Priestly resilience was not sufficient for solving the problems that emerged following the Seleucid takeover of Judea in
197 B.C.E., for the Seleucids consistently utilized techniques of
imperial control that differed from those of their predecessors, the Ptolemies. The Ptolemies had restricted the building
of *poleis*, but the new rulers looked to the *polis* as the most effective means for holding an empire together and for keeping
the native peasantries under effective controls. By according
privileged status to the *polis*, a status marked by a wide range
of autonomous powers, the Seleucids sought to bind the *poleis*
to themselves by ties of self-interest.

So long as the Ptolemies controlled Judea, they were only
too pleased with the Aaronides. Those Jews who were inter-

ested in Hellenism could not have anticipated a favorable response had they appealed for *polis* rights. Indeed, such an appeal might have been interpreted as evidence of disloyalty, a wish for a degree of autonomy that the Ptolemies were not willing to encourage.

All this changed when the Seleucids took over. For them, making the city of Jerusalem a *polis* might be the most effective way to assert imperial control. The fact that the Aaronides had shifted loyalties so easily was not very reassuring. A *polis* structure in the hands of privileged Hellenized Jews who would have a real stake in loyalty to the Seleucids might be more reliable; for they would then oppose a return of the Ptolemies, or a takeover by Rome, which would deprive them of *polis* privileges.

Because the Seleucids were being subjected to increasing Roman pressure, loyalty was now more than ever at a premium, and the Seleucids could take no chances. It is no surprise therefore that, as soon as the Seleucids took over, Hellenized Jews began to press toward *polis* rights. Wishes that had lain dormant under the Ptolemies became aggressive and open under the Seleucids. With the accession to the Seleucid throne of Antiochus Epiphanes in 175 B.C.E., Hellenization of Judea was viewed with favor. Very quickly the usurping high priest Jason, a mild Hellenist, was replaced by the radical Hellenist Menelaus, and a policy of forced Hellenization was activated and supported by Antiochus.

These quickly moving events catapulted the Jews into a crisis for which there was no ready and simple way out. For several hundred years—from the turn of the fourth century till the usurpation of the high priesthood by Jason—the Aaronide-Pentateuchal system had ruled effectively. The high priesthood had been passed on from father to son without serious disruption. This line of succession had grounded its legitimacy on God's revelation to Moses that Aaron was to transmit his authority to his son Eleazar, and Eleazar, in turn, was to transmit it to his son Phineas. God had made a covenant with Phineas in perpetuity, a covenant, so it had been believed, which had never been violated. Zadok the high priest in the Temple of Solomon was said to be a descendant of Phineas. When the Temple was restored after the Exile, the direct descendants of Aaron, Eleazar, Phineas, and Zadok had resumed their role as high priests. Ben Sira calls Aaron, Eleazar, and Phineas the progenitors of the high priest of his day; and his fulsome praise of the incumbent high priest, Simon, confirms the effectiveness with which priestly claims of direct descent had been maintained.

Then, suddenly, Jason, the brother of the legitimate high priest, Onias, usurped the high priesthood for himself by offering Antiochus not only money but assurances that Hellenistic reforms would be carried out. This was blow enough. But when Jason in turn was ousted by Menelaus, and when the latter embarked on a thoroughgoing Hellenization program, the people were shocked, bewildered, and helpless. They were bereft of legitimate leadership. Onias, the descendant of Eleazar, Phineas, and Zadok, had been exiled. Jason was himself a usurper whose only redeeming feature was that he was not as radical a Hellenist as Menelaus, who succeeded him. To support Jason, the lesser evil, may have been preferable to supporting Menelaus, but it could not erase the fact that Jason had violated God's covenant with Phineas and had thereby exposed his contempt for the very Pentateuch on which his priestly claims were based.

The Moment of Crisis

ॐ The Jews thus faced a crisis of leadership. The Aaronide system had bankrupted itself, for Jason and Menelaus were both Aaronides, yet they had violated the covenant with Phineas. Where were the people to turn? Who would make known to them God's will now that prophecy was no more? How were they to face the threat to their very existence posed by radical Hellenists, who not only controlled the Temple but who could call upon the coercive might of the Seleucids to attain their ends: *polis* rights for Jerusalem, which would turn it into a Greek city?

A crisis of such intensity brooked no easy solution. Only desperate measures could forestall chaos. A classic revolutionary situation was at hand, a crisis-laden opportunity for an audacious leadership to vault into power with a stirring proclamation of a constructive and creative solution. And such a revolutionary class did mount the barricades with a solution: the proclamation that God had revealed on Sinai to Moses not one Law, but two. God had given not only the Pentateuch, but the Oral Law as well. This Law promised eternal life and resurrection for the individual who remained loyal to the twofold Law. The scholarly class that proclaimed the revolutionary gospel of the twofold Law called themselves Soferim, but they are better known to us as the Pharisees.

These revolutionary Soferim were not the Soferim whom Ben Sira described, though some may have been drawn from this class. Ben Sira's Soferim had been Aaronide supremacists, devotees of a literal reliance on the Pentateuch, men who had exercised no authority over the Law. Their *metier* had been Wisdom: the proverb, the parable, the simile, the bon mot, the riddle, the paradox. They had praised the Pentateuch, the Aaronides, Wisdom. They did *not*, however, *determine* the Law; nor did they apply exegesis to it. They had known nothing of an Oral Law. For them, the literal Pentateuch was the entire Law, and the literal Pentateuch was preeminently concerned with priestly absolutism.

The Pharisees

ào By contrast, the Pharisees claimed absolute authority over the Law by proclaiming that God had given Moses not only the Written Law, but the Oral Law as well, making the Law twofold. This twofold Law, they stressed, had been transmitted from Moses to Joshua to the Elders, to the prophets, and most recently to themselves. They also claimed that the priests had never been the transmitters of the Law; they were cultic functionaries, not legal authorities, their role being limited to the administration of the cult and the offering of sacrifices. The Pharisees noted that no Aaronide had ever been vouchsafed a direct revelation from Yahweh after the conquest of the land. In the years following the death of Moses and Joshua, God had spoken to judges and to prophets, but never to Aaronides. A Jeremiah and Ezekiel may have been priests, but they had spoken in Yahweh's name as prophets, even when they spoke of priestly concerns.

God's teachings, so these scholars declared, were not confined to the Pentateuch. Although not a letter was to be added to the Written Law, no such restriction applied to the Oral Law. The Oral Law was not so much a body of laws as a principle of ongoing authority, which could solve problems in God's name. The prophet, they pointed out, had ignored Pentateuchal Law whenever the viability of the Law itself was threatened. Prophetic authority had been an ongoing authority. So long as the Soferim did not alter the Pentateuch, they exercised the divine right to determine at any given moment what the Law demanded.

This concept of the twofold Law — open-ended and serving to solve problems — was revolutionary. The concept is nowhere articulated in the entire biblical literature: one looks for it in vain even in the very latest books of the Bible. It was absolutely unknown to Ben Sira. The Aaronides had not drawn upon it during the three hundred or so years of their hegemony. And it contradicts the Pentateuch, which, far from espousing an Oral Law, reiterates that the written laws are to be eternal, and warns against any addition or alteration.

Equally revolutionary was the claim that a scholar class had been vested with authority over this twofold legislation. This, too, was an audacious claim, for no biblical book records a scholar class participating in the process of revelation. Other classes had enjoyed participation: prophets spoke with God; the Levites, in Deuteronomy, received divine sanction to administer the Law; the Aaronides were given hegemony; but nowhere do we find a scholar class granted access to the divine will. The scholars' revolutionary claim, in effect, affirmed that the class which had hitherto ruled, the Aaronides, had been ruling illegitimately, having usurped power by suppressing the Oral Law and by proclaiming the Pentateuch as the *only* law which God had given. The Pharisee scholars challenged the *literal* Pentateuch, which did seem to assign the Aaronides absolute authority over the Law, with an appeal to an unwritten law assigning this authority to them.

A New Source of Power

&b This doctrine was an ingenious innovation, for it made the Pentateuch a handmaiden of the Oral Law, even though it proclaimed the Pentateuch to be the word of God. The focus was shifted from a book to a scholar class. The Pharisees exercised authority; their teachings were not designed for congealment into some fixed and final corpus; their power was to be insulated against obsolescence; their broad mandate would enable them to respond quickly to new situations. To insure fresh and dynamic leadership, the hereditary principle of the Aaronides was abandoned, and proven competence in mastery of the twofold Law became the measure for wielding authority. The scholar class was thrown open to priest and non-priest; it was not to be a self-perpetuating oligarchy. The prophetic principle that God was always making the divine will known was resurrected even though the mode of divine communication was highly novel.

The role of the Pharisees contrasted sharply with that of the Aaronides. Whereas the essential power of the Aaronides had been concentrated in their expiatory role—no one could gain atonement by bypassing the altar or resorting to non-Aaronide priests—the Pharisees laid no claim to altar rights, nor did they offer themselves as intermediaries between the individual and God. They claimed no expiatory powers, as Jesus was subsequently to be reminded (Mark 2:6-12). Their function was to teach the demands of the twofold Law, and to urge the individual to abide by them. The Pharisees undermined the concept of priestly intermediation, by positing the possibility of a direct one-to-one relationship between the individual and God. This they accomplished by stressing the need to *internalize* the system of the twofold Law and to look *inward* to determine our relationship to God. The cultus was considered only one aspect of a larger system of Law, and the Aaronides were transformed into cultic functionaries, who looked to the legislation of the Pharisees for a description of their duties. Eventually this resulted in a situation in which the high priest himself was being briefed, year in and year out, by representatives of the scholar class on how to enter the Holy of Holies on the Day of Atonement. This briefing was saturated with high symbolic meaning, since the ritual prescribed by the Pharisees was different from that which had prevailed during the centuries of Aaronide supremacy. Hence, each time the high priest followed the Pharisaic procedures, he was publicly acknowledging that the effectiveness of his expiatory act was dependent on the Oral Law, rather than the Written, and that power had been transferred from the Aaronides to the Pharisees.

New Principles

ε❧ The Pharisees elevated the individual above the cultic system, even as they preserved the cult. They did not make a direct frontal assault against the Temple, but confirmed the legitimacy of its function at the same time as they were depriving the cultic system of its central importance. They made the cultus less relevant, and dimmed its luster, by focusing attention on the individual and the individual's salvation. For this was the essence of the Pharisaic revolution: God offered the individual, through the system of the twofold Law, eternal life in the world to come, and eventually bodily resurrection; this was the reward for loyalty to the twofold Law. By this shift in sanctions the Pharisees transformed Judaism into a religion of personal, individual salvation.

The twofold Law was the road to this salvation — and it was a road that could be traversed by the individual alone, even though no other Jew might walk with that individual. Revelation was no longer considered as having come primarily for a people, but for the individual, and the Pharisees taught that this had always been the case. Belonging to Israel gave one access to personal salvation, though the fate of the people could not affect one's eternal life, however much it might affect existence on earth. An Israelite who violated the twofold Law was endangering the possibility of personal salvation, while an Israelite who kept it was assured that *that individual* would enjoy the world to come and be resurrected in God's good time, along with all other Israelites who had been loyal to the twofold Law.

The concept of Israel was radically altered, for now Israel meant a community aspiring to salvation through loyalty to the twofold Law. This concept of Israel was revolutionary. Being born into Israel was an opportunity, not a fulfillment. Being born a pagan was a disadvantage, but a pagan could attain eternal life and resurrection by adopting the internalized constitution of the twofold Law. The individualistic bent of the Pharisees triumphed over the exclusivism of the Aaronides, and Israel became a people of salvation-seekers. Any person born a Jew, whether high priest or devout champion of the Pentateuch, could be destined to obliteration—no eternal life, no salvation—by denying the authority of the twofold Law. However, a proselyte who kept the twofold Law and acknowledged the authority of the scholar class would enjoy—along with companion souls—the world to come; and some day would reenter his or her body, never to die again. The Israel of the spirit, not of the flesh, was the true Israel.

Testimony to the New Judaism

&ved;A community of salvation-seekers—this was the Israel shaped by the Pharisees. It was a new creation; but it prevailed. The new Israel became the authentic Israel, while the old Israel withered away along with priestly supremacy.

Josephus testifies to this transformation, though he himself, like the Pharisees whose doctrines he espouses, was unaware that a transformation had occurred. In his forceful and eloquent apologia, *Against Apion*, Josephus portrays Judaism as a system of internalized laws guiding the individual to an eternal life.

> *For those, on the other hand, who live in accordance with our laws the prize is not silver or gold, no crown of wild olive or of parsley with any such public mark of distinction. No; each individual, relying on the witness of his own conscience and the lawgiver's prophecy, confirmed by the sure testimony of God, is firmly persuaded that to those who observe the laws and, if they must needs die for them, willingly meet death, God has granted a renewed existence and the revolution of the ages the gift of a better life. I should have hesitated to write thus, had not the facts made all men aware that many of our countrymen have on many*

occasions ere now preferred to brave all manner of suffer-
ing rather than to utter a single word against the Law
[Against Apion, 11:217-19].

Josephus stresses this faith in otherworldly sanctions with
great force in his desperate plea to his followers to give themselves up to the Romans rather than to endanger their bid for
immortality by committing suicide.

And God – think you not that He is indignant when man
treats His gift with scorn? For it is from Him that we have
received our being, and it is to Him that we should leave
the decision to take it away. All of us, it is true, have mor-
tal bodies, composed of perishable matter, but the soul
lives for ever immortal: it is a portion of the Deity housed
in our bodies.... Know you not that they who depart this
life in accordance with the law of nature and repay the
loan which they received from God, when He who lent is
pleased to reclaim it, win eternal renown; that their houses
and families are secure; that their souls, remaining spot-
less and obedient, are allotted the most holy place in
heaven, whence, in the revolution of the ages, they return
to find in chaste bodies a new habitation? But as for those
who have laid mad hands upon themselves, the darker re-
gions of the nether world receive their souls, and God,
their father, visits upon their posterity the outrageous acts
of the parents. That is why this crime, so hateful to God, is
punished also by the sage of legislators [Moses] [Wars,
III:371-76].

The remarkable powers of the internalized laws to sustain loyalty in the face of external pressures has, so Josephus
claims, no counterpart in the Greco-Roman world.

We, on the contrary, notwithstanding the countless ca-
lamities in which changes of rulers in Asia have involved
us, never even in the direst extremity proved traitors to
our laws; and we respect them not from any motive of
sloth or luxury. A little consideration will show that they

impose on us ordeals and labors far more severe than the endurance commonly believed to have been required of the Lacedaemonians, whose men neither tilled the ground nor toiled at crafts, but, exempt from all business, passed their life in the city, sleek of person and cultivating beauty by physical training; for all the necessities of life they had others to wait on them, by whom their food was prepared and served to them; and the sole aim for which they were prepared to do and suffer everything was the noble and humane object of defeating all against whom they took the field. Even in this, I may remark in passing, they were unsuccessful. The fact is that, not isolated individuals only, but large numbers have frequently, in defiance of the injunctions of their law, surrendered in a body, with their arms to the enemy.

Has anyone ever heard of a case of our people, not, I mean, in such large numbers, but merely two or three, proving traitors to their laws or afraid of death? I do not refer to that easiest of deaths, on the battlefield, but death accompanied by physical torture, which is thought to be the hardest of all. To such a death we are, in my belief, exposed by some of our conquerors, not from hatred of those at their mercy, but from a curiosity to witness the astonishing spectacle of men who believe that the only evil which can befall them is to be compelled to do any act or utter any word contrary to their laws. There should be nothing astonishing in our facing death on behalf of our laws with a courage which no other nation can equal. For even those practices of ours which seem the easiest others find difficult to tolerate: I mean personal service, simple diet, discipline which leaves no room for freak or individual caprice in matters of meat and drink, or in the sexual relations, or in extravagance, or again the abstention from work at rigidly fixed periods. No; the men who march out to meet the sword and charge and rout the enemy could not face regulations about everyday life. On the other hand, our willing obedience to the law in these matters re-

sults in the heroism which we display in the face of death [Against Apion II:328-35].

Josephus pits the power of the internal and the external against each other in two other forceful statements:

> *And from these laws of ours nothing has had power to deflect us, neither fear of our masters, nor envy of the institutions esteemed by other nations. We have trained our courage, not with a view to waging war for self-aggrandizement, but in order to preserve our laws. To defeat in any other form we patiently submit, but when pressure is put upon us to alter our statutes, then we deliberately fight, even against tremendous odds, and hold out under reverses to the last extremity. And why should we envy other nations their laws when we see that even their authors do not observe them?* [Against Apion II:271-73].

> *Robbed though we be of wealth, of cities, of all good things, our Law at least remains immortal; and there is not a Jew so distant from his country, so much in awe of a cruel despot, but has more fear of the Law than of him. If, then, our attachment to our laws is due to their excellence, let it be granted that they are excellent* [Against Apion II:277-78].

The New God Concepts

ε🍐 Committed so strongly to the salvation of the individual, the Pharisees developed new concepts of God, giving voice to a yearning for intimacy long felt, but never, hitherto, fully realized. God, so the Pharisees taught, was preeminently a Father, not only the Father of a people, but the Eternal Father of the individual. God was the Father who was always there, always available, always just, merciful, and understanding. Unlike one's human father, God was not mortal and transient; God was not imperfect; God was only sometimes unavailable. And, unlike one's real father, God could penetrate into one's inner self and evaluate and measure the loyalty to God's Law. There was no escaping God's eye, for as a Father God was personally concerned with every one of his children and with their salvation. The realization that the Father in Heaven had a personal interest in the meanest of individuals, one who was not prophet, priest, or scholar—and that this Father was the very one who had created the entire universe and had wrought awesome wonders for Israel—could hardly have left any individual unaffected. The sense of worth, of self-esteem, of dignity, of equality that it generated must have been intoxicating. To dare think that every I, no matter how seemingly insignificant, was equal to every other I in the sight of the Father in Heaven and that eternal life awaited each person on the same terms that it awaited others was to undergo a psychic transformation.

Once this happens, the external, empirical world ceases to be reality. It is a temporary, transient, and unpredictable realm; callous, cruel, indifferent. How different the reality within! Here one was insulated against the bludgeonings of Fate and the crushing blows to one's self esteem. Here one had communion with the Eternal Father. Here one nourished the expectations of an eternal life aroused by the Eternal Father's promise; here one healed the ego's wounds with the sure knowledge of a resurrection that would blot out temporal pain and suffering.

The concept of God's Fatherhood was reinforced by distinctive appellations that came to be applied to God. The Pharisees called God *Shekhinah*, the Divine Presence, and *Makom*, the Everyplace, to stress God's accessibility. Unlike the Temple, which was a fixed place, God was the Everyplace; God's *Shekhinah* was a presence to be sought not in the Holy of Holies but in one's inner consciousness. God took up residence in one's soul.

Similarly, God was called *ha-Kadosh barukh hu*, "the Holy One Blessed Be He," so as to permit the individual to have a name that would not frighten a person with its awesomeness. The biblical names for God were restricted to Scriptural readings and formalized prayer, while such terms as *ha-Kadosh barukh hu* and *Makom* came to be used in an intimate, almost casual way, as a form of direct address, not circumscribed by any formula.

This coinage of new names for God was itself a revolutionary act. For a millennium or more, Yahweh and Elohim had been freely used. The Psalmist and Ben Sira used them without inhibition. They seemed to have no need to coin new names for God. But with the rise of the Pharisees, we note a studious avoidance of the biblical names for God, except when Scriptures are quoted, or when a formal prayer is uttered. At the same time, new names are conjured up that comport with the Pharisaic ideology. It is as though in drawing a line of demarcation between the Written Law and the Oral Law, the Pharisees declared the biblical names for God out of bounds for non-formal usage.

Among the most dramatic innovations of the Pharisees to bring the individual into direct communion with God was making prayer mandatory. This was a truly revolutionary step, for nowhere in the Pentateuch is prayer obligatory. Although prayer may indeed have been as old as Israel, prayer had never been required by law. The Pharisees were therefore once again going off on a highly original tack when they made mandatory the saying of the *Shema* — "*Hear*, O Israel, Yahweh is our God, Yahweh is one" — in the morning and evening, and when they introduced the recitation of the prayer now called the *Amidah* or *Shemoneh Esreh* as the prayer par excellence; when they required each individual to utter benedictions before meals, after meals, and on other occasions; and when they established fixed readings from the Pentateuch and the prophets on the Sabbath. And although the synagogue may at first have been a place where Scripture was read and only later a house of prayer, the Pharisees were its creators. It had not existed in the period of Aaronide hegemony; it was generated out of the need that existed for a flexible structure through which to carry out the Pharisaic revolution. Its origin must have been analogous to that of such revolutionary gatherings as the conventicles of the Puritan revolution, the Committees of Correspondence of the American Revolution, the Jacobin clubs of the French Revolution, or the soviets of the Russian Revolution.

Institutionalizing the Revolution

〰 The scope of the Pharisaic revolution was total. It left little of Aaronidism unaltered. The Pharisees established an institution called the *Beth Din ha-Gadol*, the Great Legislature, which had no biblical prototype as its model, for legislation in the past had come directly from God alone. This novel institution became responsible for preserving the twofold Law and for legislating oral laws when necessary. These oral laws came to be called *halakhoth*—a freshly coined non-biblical term conveying the notion of roads and pathways to salvation. Halakhoth, along with other oral laws called *gezeroth*, "decrees," and *takkanoth*, "ordinances," had only the most tenuous connection with biblical legislation. The oral laws were not dependent on the Pentateuch, but on the authority of the scholar class. There was no requirement to justify these laws upon proof texts, though such justification was permissible. This independence of the oral laws was so sacrosanct that even centuries later, when the oral laws were finally written down in part in the compilation called the Mishnah (c. 210 C.E.), more than three centuries after the Pharisaic revolution, they were written down as laws in their own right, with only an occasional citation from Scripture!

Equally innovating were the forms that the Pharisees developed to communicate and transmit their laws and doctrines. They broke with all biblical precedent, for they did not draw on a single literary form from the sacred Scriptures as a model. The Pharisees were dead serious when they affirmed that the Oral Law was *oral*. Whereas the Pentateuch sets forth the laws within a historical framework, the Pharisees simply transmitted the laws as units or bits of legislation that might freely be joined one to another. These they never set within a narrative frame. Furthermore, they differentiated laws from pronouncements about doctrine.

Even in phrasing the oral laws the Pharisees departed from the model of the Pentateuch. Gone, for example, is the formula: "When or if X does something, then...." Instead they employed a variety of formulas. Some set out the law explicitly in a generalized form, as "There are four principal causes of damage..." or, "All are permitted to carry out ritual slaughter..."; others introduced the law with a question: "From what time is it permitted to say the *Shema* in the evening?" The Oral Law uses such expressions as "the general principle is" or "logical reasoning demands." Evident throughout these laws is an awareness of the need for coherence and consistency, and of the operation of logical and analytical categories — an awareness alien to the Pentateuch. Nor should one overlook the high level of abstraction attained by these oral laws; their principles and categories reduce the need for casuistic and *ad hoc* legislation and serve to integrate the laws into a consistent system.

The Pharisees even went so far as to allow discussion, debate, and even alternative renderings of the Law. This, too, was revolutionary innovation; the oral laws had the status of divine revelation, yet they were thrown open to scholarly debate. What was immutable was not the laws themselves, but the authority of the Pharisees over the laws. Thus the controversial discussion of laws came to be a divine mandate. Differences over the laws were not considered a derogation of revelation but, in a sense, what revelation had been all about. This is a startling contrast to the Pentateuch's concept that God alone legislated, and that God's legislation was immutable. The Pharisaic notion is not by any means a logical development out of the Pentateuch. It is a mutation, more discontinuous than continuous.

An Absence of History

8 The Pharisees abandoned historical narrative not only for their laws, but for their lore and doctrines as well. The form they adopted, called *aggadah*, "a communication, a telling," was the single unit, be it an anecdote, a description of a historical event, or a paradigm for the righteous life. There is no connective tissue. Every unit of Pharisee lore is freely available for combination with every other unit. Maxims, proverbs, sententious sayings were not bound together, as in Proverbs or Ecclesiastes, in a book, but were orally taught as separate items. Gone is any sense of history as a continuum. Gone is any real concern with before and after. Time has ceased to flow as it does in the Pentateuch, for in the Pharisees' mind the empirical world was not the real world. History was not going anywhere; event jostled event. The real world was not this transient world of pain, suffering, anguish, uncertainty, insecurity, history, but the world to come where life was eternal and free of pain. The terrestrial world was where eternal life was won; but eternal life was the reward for those who were steadfast in their loyalty to the twofold Law, *despite* the pressures of the terrestrial world!

The resurrection of the dead might be visualized as a return to a terrestrial existence, which would have little resemblance to the world of one's earlier existence, for it would be stripped of all that had made life difficult to bear, with the body neither suffering nor wearing out. The day of resurrection would be ushered in by some miraculous divine act. It would not be the outcome of historical development.

The Pharisees thus had no interest in history, even when they used historical personages and events. The crucial concern was salvation, not the petty distinction between fact and non-fact. Whether an event had or had not occurred was not nearly as important as how it served as a paradigm for emulation and as a spur toward attaining salvation. Their orientation towards the individual and the individual's salvation led them to emphasize what the individual alone could do to attain salvation. Since this involved the fulfillment of the internalized twofold Law, there was no need for historical narrative at all — especially in view of the fact that the source of knowledge of what the Law demanded could not be found in a book, but only in the teachings of a scholar class who, as a matter of principle, prohibited the writing down of their laws or teachings. The Pharisees, it must be reiterated, refused to endow their individual teachings with permanency by writing them down.

The Pharisees' break with the biblical stress on historical processes as the working through of God's relationship to his people is dramatically revealed in Josephus' reconstruction of Israel's early history. Although he prided himself on being a historian who prized factuality, and although he regarded the Bible as divinely inspired, he elevates the great heroes of Israel's past above the restraints of time, structure, and process. Abraham, for example, is pictured as more of a philosopher than a semi-nomad, and Moses resembles Solon or Plato more than the leader of a wilderness people. The chasm separating the biblical from the Pharisaic concept of the patriarchs is exposed by Josephus' account of the binding of Isaac:

> *But when the altar had been prepared and he had cleft the wood upon it and all was ready, he said to his son: "My child, myriad were the prayers in which I besought God for*

*thy birth, and when thou camest into the world, no pains
were there that I did not lavish on thine upbringing, no
thought had I of higher happiness than to see thee grown to
man's estate and to leave thee at my death heir to my do-
minion. But, since it was by God's will that I became thy
sire and now again as it pleases Him I am resigning thee,
bear thou this consecration valiantly; for it is to God that I
yield thee, to God who now claims from us this homage in
return for the gracious favor He has shown me as my sup-
porter and ally.*

*"Aye, since thou wast born (out of the course of na-
ture, so) quit thou now this life not by the common road,
but sped by thine own father on thy way to God, the Father
of all, through the rites of sacrifice. He, I ween, accounts it
not meet for thee to depart this life by sickness or war or by
any of the calamities that commonly befall mankind, but
amid prayers and sacrificial ceremonies would receive thy
soul and keep it near to Himself; and for me thou shalt be a
protector and a stay of my old age — to which end I above
all nurtured thee — by giving me God instead of thyself."*

*The son of such a father could not but be brave-
hearted, and Isaac received these words with joy* [Antiq-
uities I:228-32].

Josephus does not simply take liberties with the text, but
fashions an account out of some other source, a source that
was deemed by him more authoritative than the Pentateuch.
Since Josephus' deviation inserts a belief in the immortal soul
and in its immediate access at death to God the Father, his
source must have been an oral teaching that took precedence
over the literal meaning of the text. Josephus was drawing
upon the lore of the teachers of the twofold Law, and was giving preference to an *aggadic fact* over a biblical fact, even
though the biblical fact was written, older than the twofold
Law, and believed by Josephus and the teachers of the aggadah to have been actually dictated by God.

History has thus become only a record of event jostling event; it is not headed anywhere. The individual's life should be shaped by adherence to the twofold Law and by taking for models the great spiritual leaders of Israel who never deviated from virtue, goodness, and righteousness despite the pressure of historical circumstance. One was no closer to or farther away from eternal life or resurrection *now* than Isaac had been *then*.

Revelation through a New Lens

&. The shift in time perspective had other profound consequences. The entire corpus of Holy Scriptures came to be looked upon as expressing the divine will. Although the Pentateuch was still accorded a certain kind of primacy, it was not the only source of God's revelation. The historical books, the prophets, and the canonical hagiographa—all were repositories of God's word. As such, they could not be considered to contradict one another. Not Moses, nor Elijah, nor the Psalmist could be considered to have ignored (1) the principle of the Father God, (2) the twofold Law, (3) eternal life and resurrection for the individual. Every verse was believed either to presuppose these principles or witness to them. Holy Scriptures thus could be drawn upon freely to confirm, amplify, and enrich them, but never to challenge them. When David, for example, composed the Psalms, it was felt that the Law he praised was the twofold Law, the God he addressed was the Heavenly Father, and the hope that sustained him was of the world to come and of the resurrection.

The assumption that these three principles were the leitmotif of revelation encouraged the exploration of biblical writ for appropriate verses to support them. Interest no longer centered in the book itself, but in the sentence. What was needed was scriptural proof to clarify a situation, illumine a teaching, underwrite a law, inspire an act. The larger context was irrelevant and could not stand in the way of finding supporting evidence for the new ideas. Combining verses drawn from different biblical books to drive home the identical lesson came to be far more crucial than context. The fact that a verse in the Pentateuch was reinforced by a verse from the prophets and confirmed by a verse from the Psalms was the most powerful proof one could bring for the essential unity and timeless quality of the revelation.

The reawakening of Scriptures thus went hand in hand with its subordination to the new principles. With a technique that paralleled that of the Aaronides, the Pharisees used the historical, prophetic, and hagiographical writings to underwrite their authority. For them, Scripture was a confirmation of the twofold Law system of salvation for the individual, not a challenge to it.

As part of their break with biblical literary models the Pharisees shunned poetry. Not a single Pharisaic teaching has been transmitted in poetic form. This is astonishing when we recall that the Pharisees not only made prayer mandatory, but formulated prayers and benedictions; not a single one of these is poetry. A scholar class, heir to psalmody, but creating not a single psalm of its own!

The Pharisees' abandonment of poetry was to have long-range effects. More than five hundred years of creative activity were to go by in Palestine and Babylonia before poetry was to be revived as the normal mode of religious expression. In that time all new prayers were in prose.

Interpretation through Exegesis

&ℰ Exegesis, with its awareness of logical deductive principles, was another Pharisaic contribution. Unfortunately, because the Pharisees did not write down their teachings we cannot be certain when exegesis first came into use. Perhaps it arose when the new scholar class pointed to specific verses in the Pentateuch to demonstrate their ambiguity, or to juxtapose one text with another, or to counter priestly arguments. It is very likely that from the first the Pharisees pointed out flagrant contradictions in the Pentateuch to attack Aaronide hegemony. Contradictions demolished the illusion that the Pentateuch was consistent. A careful reading of the text revealed several conflicting authorities, each given authentic power by God.

Moses grants authority to both Joshua *and* Eleazar, Aaron's son and successor as high priest. As to who was to hold the ultimate authority, the text is ambiguous: on the one hand, it affirms that Joshua is rightfully entitled to inherit the power wielded by Moses, and on the other hand, it makes Joshua dependent on Eleazar, who is put in control of the divine oracle. So long as the Aaronides held undisputed power the literal meaning was unambiguous: Eleazar was to hold ultimate authority. The Pharisees, however, by pointing out the ambiguity, maintained the supremacy of Joshua, setting for the path of transmission of the twofold Law a line moving from Moses to Joshua to the Elders and to the prophets, completely bypassing the Aaronides.

Exegesis and the use of logical deduction were tools fashioned by the Pharisees in the very first stages of their revolution. More elaborate hermeneutics did not come into use until the time of Hillel (c. 30 B.C.E.-C.E. 9). The formal commentary—a line-by-line exegesis of the biblical text—did not develop until after the destruction of the Second Temple, C.E. 70. The Pharisaic revolution was responsible for the exegesis and logical-deductive hermeneutics, which were to play a vital role in medieval Judaism, Christianity, and Islam.

The Sources of Pharisaic Thought

From whatever angle we look at the Pharisees, we can see that they struck down the old and shaped the new. They turned Judaism upside down, all the while claiming that they

were setting it right side up. They viewed themselves as re-
storers, not revolutionaries. In their own eyes, they were
counterrevolutionaries—ousting the Aaronide usurpers, who,
they alleged, had grasped power from the legitimate transmitters of the twofold Law.

Where did the Pharisees' innovating ideas come from?
Once again we are at a loss for contemporary records to answer this question; for the Pharisees, as we have already
pointed out, had no interest in chronicling any history, least of
all their own. We must therefore fall back upon an analysis of
Pharisaic institutions, forms, and concepts, and compare
them with institutions, forms, and concepts of the biblical and
Hellenistic worlds.

The Pentateuch and the prophetic books of the Bible were
major sources of the Pharisaic system, even though the Pharisees rejected biblical concepts and biblical literary forms. The
Pharisees never challenged the biblical claim that God was
one, omnipotent, and omniscient. They believed, along with
the Aaronides, that God was a person, and that God had
revealed to selected individuals—Moses being preeminent—
revelations of the divine will. Indeed, it was this unquestion-
ing belief that served as the formative principle guiding the
thrust of their innovations. Like their predecessors, the Pharisees were pre-committed to the unity idea. What the Pharisees
did, however, was read the Pentateuch and the other sacred
books through the prism of the twofold Law, restructuring
the elements within these books, shaping them into novel
forms, and redefining their meaning. They activated passive
ingredients, and subdued elements that had previously been
highly charged. The very books which had for centuries confirmed priestly power now reduced the priests to mere functionaries, depreciated cultic expiation, and underwrote the
supremacy of the twofold Law.

This dramatic transformation can be illustrated by the shift that took place in the meaning of the *Shema*. The Pharisees ordained that the *Shema* prayer — "*Hear*, O Israel, Yahweh is our God, Yahweh is one. And thou shalt love Yahweh thy God with all thy soul and all thy might. And these commandments which I command thee this day shall be upon your hearts..." — be said by every Jew twice daily — morning and evening. Since the *Shema* was the only Pentateuchal text elevated to so high a status, its teaching must have been viewed as summing up the essence of God's revelation: that God was one; that Israel was committed to proclaiming this unity; that God demanded love and obedience. With such a formulation, the Aaronides did not quarrel. But when it came down to what law was to be obeyed, the Pharisees insisted that this be the twofold Law; the Aaronides, the written Law only. Following the Pharisaic revolution, those calling for a return to absolute Aaronide hegemony came to be known as Sadducees because they maintained that divine authority should be exercised by the high priest, a descendant of Zadok and Aaron. The *Shema* for the Pharisees was a daily reassertion of their authority and a rejection of Aaronidism — a statement that following the Pentateuch literally was defying God's revelation, not upholding it. Thus, proponents of two mutually exclusive systems of law and authority could invoke the same text with fervor.

The Pharisees altered the whole mindset of the Jews. The Aaronides had counted on the sheer weight of repetition proclaiming priestly supremacy to overwhelm the few revelations that undermined these claims. The Pharisees erased priestly power by focusing on the non-Aaronide verses of the Pentateuch. The choice of the *Shema* for frequent repetition by Jews was thus sheer genius; it was general enough to give the Pharisees a completely free hand. The Pharisees also strengthened themselves by ordaining that portions of the Pentateuch be read on every Monday and Thursday, and on every Sabbath. The more the Pentateuch was read under Pharisaic guidance, the more Pharisee power grew.

So caught up were the Pharisees in the certainty of a revealing God, that they canonized the historical and prophetic writings and elevated them to a status only a little lower than that of the Pentateuch itself. Here were to be found sacred items of inestimable worth and *written* proof that Joshua, the Elders, and the prophets, rather than the priests, had been the teachers of Yahweh's revelation throughout Israel's history. They ransacked biblical writ for material to support their ideas. But whatever was written and sacred was considered only raw material to be processed to conform to patterns laid down by the Pharisees themselves.

The Pharisees also shaped Hellenistic materials to build their novel form of Judaism. Impressed with the law-making process exemplified in the Greek cities' *boule*, or legislative body, they created the *Beth Din ha-Gadol* (Great Legislature) as the lawmaking, law-transmitting, and law-confirming body of the scholar class — an institution with no biblical prototype, but one that does resemble the *boule*. Indeed, the Greek translation of *Beth Din* was "Boule."

The Pharisees also found in the Hellenistic world lawmakers who were not priests, kings, or prophets, but rather statesmen, philosophers, or scholars. They were struck by the student-teacher relationship, alien to Israel but commonplace in the *polis* world and especially stressed by the Stoics. They were impressed with the flowering of personality all about them and the high evaluation placed on the individual and on individual autonomy. The Stoic teaching of an inner standard — a reality impervious to the buffetings of the external world and to the vagaries of chance and fortune — was especially impressive to them. The concept of unwritten laws, so widespread in the *polis* world, may have influenced their notion of the twofold Law.

Polis elements such as these affected the Pharisees in any number of subtle ways; drawn upon and restructured, they served monotheistic ends. But the Pharisees did not simply take over *polis* models. They were no more passive here than they were with biblical material. The notion of a scholar class, of unwritten laws, of a legislative *boule*, of an internalized standard, of logical-deductive modes of thought, of the scholar-student relationship, of the tremendous significance of the individual, may all have come from the *polis* world, but the end product was a novel form of Judaism. The Hellenistic elements were so sublimated that they can be reconstituted only through highly developed analytical methods.

Thus the Pharisees were scholars of revealed, not human, law. Their *Beth Din ha-Gadol* grounded its authority in God, not in the constitution of a *polis*. If the Pharisees introduced new legislation they did so only as legitimate successors of Moses. Unlike the Greeks and their imitators, the Pharisees did not regard written laws as more binding than the Oral Law. The internalized standard that the Pharisees set up for the individual bore little resemblance to that conceived by the Stoics: it was enjoined by God, not established by philosophical reasoning. The very laws of marriage, divorce, property, business, etc., that in the *polis* related externally to the individual, were internal laws in the Pharisaic system. Salvation could be obtained *only* if one were law-abiding in both thought and deed. The *politeuma*, the constitution that regulated the *polis*, was for the Pharisees an internalized constitution, binding the individual regardless of any external laws that might be imposed. A violation of God the Father's twofold Law was a transgression against God, not humanity, and therefore ought to invoke inner discomfort and gnawing guilt driving the individual to repentance. What was at stake here was, to paraphrase Josephus, not some public reward—a sprig of parsley—but one's eternal life.

And this internalized twofold Law, with its promise of individual immortality, was not a system that was meant to appeal only to a small class of philosophers. It was available to every individual, irrespective of economic, social, political, cultural, ethnic, or racial status. The poorest of the poor reaped the reward for keeping the laws; the most learned scholars could not escape the penalty for transgressing them. The scholar class may have been the legal authorities, but God the Father alone looked into the conscience and measured a person's fulfillment of the Law.

Creative Novelty

ﻸ   Creative novelty is the hallmark of all the great revolutions. Creative novelty emerges when a problem has reached such intensity that the mind must innovate or surrender the hope of resolving the problem. If the proponents of monotheism could have offered nothing more than the literal Pentateuch to deal with the crisis of confidence, they would not have been able to rally the masses of people for the kind of sustained effort necessary to wage decades of warfare against the armies of Antiochus. Similarly, if an outright Hellenistic solution had been offered, it would have appeared to be a surrender to the enemy. The Pharisaic scholar class emerged with an innovative solution. They were thoroughly committed to monotheism, steadfast in their faith that a revelation had taken place, appalled at the collapse of priestly leadership, versed in the sacred writings, nurtured in an urbanized, highly individualistic society, and exposed to the Hellenistic *polis* culture on all sides. When they saw monotheism trampled underfoot they looked in vain to Scripture for guidance; they had to leap into the unknown, where they mastered the problem through creative insight.

The consequences of the Pharisaic revolution are immeasurable. There can be no danger of exaggerating their import. Indeed, they are even now by no means fully spent. The triumph of the Pharisees gave birth to a form of Judaism with generative powers exceeding those of the Pentateuch itself. Those forms of Judaism that were simply an outgrowth of, or an adaptation to, literal Pentateuchalism did not survive antiquity. The Aaronides (now called the Sadducees) were able to hold on so long as the cultus remained alive under Pharisaic sponsorship, but they quickly withered away once the Temple was destroyed (C.E. 70). The Hellenistic Diaspora, communities of Hellenized Jews that had emerged in such *poleis* as Antioch and Alexandria before the Pharisaic revolution, disintegrated with the collapse of the Hellenistic monarchies. The Hellenistic form of Judaism that they developed proved viable only so long as the Hellenistic society, which had called them forth, remained secure. This is tellingly illustrated by the fate of Judaism in Alexandria. Although Philo (c. 25 B.C.E.–C.E. 50) articulated a philosophy of Pentateuchal Judaism geared to life in the Hellenistic *polis*, it did not survive the onslaught against Jewish rights and privileges in Alexandria.

Pharisaic Judaism, on the other hand, seemed to thrive on breakdown and disaster. It was itself a child of one phase of the disintegration of Hellenistic society, having come into existence in response to a crisis that had been set in motion by the Seleucids' effort to retain their empire against mounting Roman pressure, and it had traversed a history marked by wars for independence, civil strife, the extension of Roman power, and the ruin of the Jews' country and Temple. Pharisaic Judaism weathered all these storms because it shifted the arena of life from the external world to the internal world; from the nation to the individual's striving for salvation; from an empirical to a spiritual reality. The external world might collapse, but it could not cut off the road to eternal life. Indeed, such a collapse only makes this road more alluring. Because the standard of the Father God was always secure and reassuring, Pharisaism was tailored to serve the individual in a troubled world. Assurances of immortality consoled the people as their life became ever more precarious. The collapse of the great and proud Hellenistic monarchies shattered the faith of even the most privileged *polis* citizen in a secure external world.

Only Pharisaic Judaism offered a viable alternative to the individual. Unlike the gods of the Greek world, Judaism's God had unrestricted power to save. God did not have to share omnipotence with rival gods, or have to engage in competition with other gods for the love and loyalty of human beings. The individual was a one; and God was *the* one. There was no escape from God's watchful eye or loving concern. The individual was spared dashing about, to this deity for one's hates, to that for one's loves, to a third for one's immortality, and was spared gnawing doubt about whether one had wasted prayers, entreaties, and sacrifices on gods whose potency was limited by the potency of other deities. In contrast to the mystery cults, Pharisaism affirmed that one God and one God alone could save. Polytheism ultimately lost its struggle with monotheism because it could not offer a *single* divine power to resonate with *single* mortal individuals. The individual was aware of being a unity, and yet had to seek reassurance of immortality from many gods, compelled to ground personal unity in many persons. Polytheism, far from offering a satisfying solution to the anxiety that arose from the chaos of the world, threatened to engulf the individual.

The spread of the *polis* and of Hellenistic culture had brought to Eastern Mediterranean lands an awareness of unity, of shared institutions and values transcending the political boundaries that separated one Hellenistic monarchy from another. These boundaries were largely the artificial consequence of military power; they rarely disturbed the autonomous *polis*. An Alexandrian and an Antiochene shared a Hellenistic *polis* identity that distinguished them from unassimilated subject peoples. This *polis* elite belonged to an *ecumene*, a world community, which stamped the variety of human experience with the imprint of Hellenism. An idea imposed unity on diversity. When this unity was threatened by the collapse of the Hellenistic monarchies, the individuals who had shared it could not simply fall back on antecedent loyalties; their new identity had created a high sense of individuation that they could not readily surrender. Here, too, polytheism was disappointing; multiple gods only served to emphasize the disorganization of the Hellenistic world. Pharisaism, however, was different, proclaiming that a single omnipotent creator—God—sustained all phenomena, even those that were disturbing and seemingly shot through and through with irrationality and evil. Nothing was out of control. We might not understand the world, but it was, nonetheless, on the leash. After all, this world need not be good for a person to attain a good eternal life in the world to come.

Historical Consequences

૨૭ This, then, was the transmutation Pharisaism wrought. Yet its revolutionary character has not hitherto been appreciated, because the Pharisees did not write down their teachings. Since they strictly forbade the writing down of the Oral Law and lore, and since they rejected the historical narrative as a matter of principle, it is impossible for a historian to reconstruct the Pharisaic revolution as one might the French or American revolutions. A narrative and chronological history of Pharisaism is out of the question. Even Josephus offers us only hints, since he did not look upon the emergence and the development of the Pharisaic scholar class as relevant for the kind of history he was trying to write.

We can therefore only trace the main outlines of its historical genesis and development. Power over the law was transferred from the priests to the scholar during the Hasmonean revolt; the scholars never relinquished their power however severe the pressures may have been at times. After the Hasmonean revolt, political affairs became ever more complex and bewildering, and the Pharisees became less and less interested in exercising political power within the state. Increasingly they became willing to enter into a simple quid pro quo arrangement: the state giving the scholar class complete freedom to teach the way to salvation, and the scholar class in turn acknowledging that the political authority was separate from religious authority. After a generation of bloody war between the Hasmonean Alexander Jannaeus and the Sadducees on one side, and the people at large led by the Pharisees on the other, this principle was implemented for the first time. When a compromise was worked out with Alexander's widow, Salome, the Pharisees legitimized her right to rule, even though she was not a descendant of David, and she in turn accorded them the right to teach the twofold Law. This line of demarcation, separating Pharisaic from state authority, irrespective of whether Hasmoneans, Herodians, or Roman procurators ruled, operated for more than a century, until the revolt against Rome in C.E. 65.

This decisive rejection of the external world for internal concerns was fraught with consequences, for it led the Pharisees to adopt a neutral attitude when the Romans took over Palestine. This neutral posture stirred disaffection with Pharisaic leadership and set the stage for the emergence of Christianity. When the Pharisees advised the people to submit to the census ordered by the Roman governor, Quintinius, a radical revolutionary group, angered by this decision, sprang up, denounced it as ungodly, and called for armed rebellion against the Romans. At the same time, other voices of dissent proclaimed that Yahweh was about to usher in the Kingdom of God through a Son of Man, or Messiah. The Pharisees, adhering to their concept of an internalized kingdom and otherworldly salvation, denounced both the radical revolutionaries and the apocalyptic-messianists as brazen misleaders.

Jesus and the Pharisees

ટ♣ The clash between Jesus and the Pharisees revolved around two basic principles: authority and internality. Did the Pharisees sit on Moses' seat or did Jesus? Did the Pharisees determine the authenticity of a messianic claimant or did the claimant himself? Jesus refused to knuckle under to Pharisaic authority, and he gave the impression that the Kingdom of God was indeed about to be ushered in. He gave priority to external proofs of God's activity, while the Pharisees continued to stress internality. Echoes of clashing confrontations between them have been preserved in the Gospels. The Pharisees rejected Jesus and his claims. A political council, a Sanhedrin, presided over by a high priest, Caiaphas, appointed by the Roman procurator, concluded that Jesus was a dangerous troublemaker, and turned him over to Pontius Pilate. The ultimate decision to crucify Jesus was made by Pilate. The Roman imperial system was thus responsible for the crucifixion. Its quarrel with Jesus was not that he denied the authority of the Pharisees, but that he had kingly ambitions of his own.

The Pharisees rejected Jesus, but in one sense it was they who resurrected him. For what gave life to the crucified Messiah was the Pharisaic belief in the resurrection of the dead. Agonizing, despairing, and stunned, the grief-stricken disciples clutched at the core hope of the Pharisaic system: the belief that the Heavenly Father would reward the righteous with eternal life and resurrection. Every true believer in the

twofold Law had faith that all the righteous would be rewarded, and it dawned on Jesus' followers that the proof of
his claim to be Christ was his resurrection. The disciples had
been misled; the Messiah had not proved himself while alive
but by the awesome fact of his resurrection. Only the stubborn could deny such a sign. Jesus had been crucified and he
had risen. Just as the disciples had been witness to the first
fact, they were now also witness to the second. For them, to
deny that they had seen the resurrection was as inconceivable
as to deny the crucifixion.

Here now was a problem the Pharisees had not anticipated. The Pharisaic belief in the resurrection was being called
upon to confirm Jesus' claim to be the Messiah. The Pharisees
could hardly deny the possibility of this resurrection, when
they daily proclaimed that resurrection was to be anticipated
for everyone.

The Response of Paul

೭ఽ   Paul attests to the turmoil of a Pharisee who wrestled
with the possibility of Jesus' resurrection. By his own testimony, Paul had been a Pharisee, and a precocious one at that,
priding himself on his commitment to the Oral Law and able
to boast that he had been blamelessly righteous under the
Law. He had not known Jesus when he was alive, and the
claim that Jesus had been resurrected stirred him to persecute
the Church zealously. From the outset, the only Christ Paul
had known had been the risen Christ.

"For you have heard of my former life in Judaism," Paul
writes, "how I persecuted the Church of God violently and
tried to destroy it." His hostility to the Church goes hand in
hand with his loyalty to Pharisaic Judaism: "And I advanced
in Judaism beyond many of my own age among my people, so
extremely zealous was I for the traditions [the *paradosis*, i.e.,
the Oral Law] of my fathers" [Galatians 1:13-14].

Why this persecuting zeal? Was it not because Paul's personal salvation was at stake? Resurrection was the reward for loyalty to Pharisaism. No one could be resurrected who had been disloyal. Yet the disciples of Jesus preached Jesus the resurrected Christ, the very Jesus who had, in his lifetime, set himself up as a law unto himself, challenging and defying the Pharisees. His disciples were proclaiming that this challenger of Pharisaic authority had risen from the dead. This could not be, since resurrection was the reward for obedience, not rebellion. So pernicious, false, and dangerous a teaching had to be rooted out, and so zealous a champion of the twofold Law as Paul had to take the lead in exposing this fraudulent gospel.

But doubt lurked behind Paul's righteous determination. What if Jesus had risen? What if his resurrection were a fact? What if the proof of Christ was the resurrection? This doubt gnawed and gave him no rest. The more he persecuted, the more fragile became his certainty. Surging from the deepest recesses of his being, powerful passions threatened to break through the dikes of the internalized Law. The pressure of sinful impulses began to batter away at the carefully constructed defenses barring them from consciousness. He began to perceive another law at war with the law of his mind, making him captive to the sin dwelling in his senses. And suddenly there came a moment of wretched doubt; the dikes would no longer hold; the internal defenses were overwhelmed; and Paul collapsed into Christ and was revived.

Jesus, Paul now knew, had risen from the dead. He was the Christ. He was the Son of God. He sat at his Father's side. Now it was clear: The Law does not lead to salvation, to eternal life, and resurrection. Nor is it the way to overcome the power of sin. The Law is a delusion; behind it, sin lurks. The Law does not vanquish sin. It merely holds it off, blocks its overt activity, screens it from consciousness, serves as a defense. But the power of sin persists through the very com-

mandments themselves. Every "Thou shalt not" is a provoca-
tion, stirring sin to activity and stirring awareness of its power
in human impulses and senses. Law is a defense, not a solution. Unaided, a person cannot master the power of sin. God
the Father, aware of human helplessness, had sent his Son as
an act of grace to deliver the individual from the power of sin
and death. Christ had come to redeem human beings from
sin, not from Roman rule. Jesus had come to Israel with the
gospel of eternal life and resurrection. Resurrection was the
free and gracious gift of God the Father, and not, as the Pharisees taught, the reward for obedience to the twofold Law.

Paul's solution was profound. His gospel of Christ as the
redeemer from sin freed the messianic idea from the shackles
of time and space. Although Paul anticipated that Jesus would
shortly return, and although there are apocalyptic sections in
his gospel, his core teaching was not dependent on Christ's
imminent return. He saw the redemptive power of Christ as
continuously active in every individual who had faith in Jesus. One did not have to wait for Christ to return, because
Christ had not really gone away. He was inside the believing
individual no less than he was outside. He could be internalized so securely that the individual lived in Christ, because
Christ lived in that individual. Secure of his internalized presence, the individual was released from the fetters of the external world. Space and time lost their reality. Slave or free, man
or woman, Greek or Jew, the individual was threatened by sin
now, and Christ was there to help the individual now.

Paul's Christ is parallel with the Pharisaic system of the
twofold Law. Each was believed by its devotees to be the creation of God the Father. Each promises to deliver from sin and
each offers eternal life and resurrection for the individual believer. Each preaches that reality is within, not without. Each
denies the outer world power over the certainties of an *internalized* faith. And each acknowledges that the Messiah will

come—or come again; but, until that unknown and perhaps unknowable day, salvation is at hand: for the Pharisees in the twofold Law; for Paul in the ever-redeeming Christ.

The Christianity that fell heir to the Roman world proclaimed Paul's good news that the Father, by sending his Son to conquer sin, had opened the way to eternal life for those who internalized Christ. One took Christ within oneself as the assurance of God's unbounded love and grace. The internalized Christ was now the shield against the blows of external fate and fortune. The internalized Christ was now reality. The world within was the only real world, the arena where salvation was either won or lost. The external world was transient, storm-tossed, seductive, random and haphazard; the internal world reassuring and rich with hope. Little wonder, then, that the lure of a world within grew as the external power of the Roman Empire disintegrated. The triumph of Christianity was thus, in essence, the triumph of Pharisaism, a victory of reality within over reality without. The Christianity which conquered the pagan world retained two of the three major concepts of the Pharisaic revolution: substituting Christ for the Law; but stressing the idea of one God who was omnipotent, omniscient, and the personal Father of each individual; and the attainment of eternal life and bodily resurrection as a reward for faith.

Paul and the Pharisees

ৰ৶ Though radically breaking with a core teaching of Pharisaism, Paul was operating with its basic revolutionary principles: the centrality of the individual, an internalized standard made known by the Father God, and eternal life.

Paul was not reacting to or transmuting Pentateuchal Judaism. The Pharisees had already transformed the Pentateuch, the prophets, and the other books of the Bible for him. Paul read Genesis in a Pharisaic way, even though he drew anti-Pharisaic meanings from it. He did not read the promise of God to Abraham in Genesis the way an Aaronide would have read it, but after the manner of the Pharisees. His Pharisaic teachers had imprinted belief in salvation and resurrection on Paul's conscience. Paul had no need to discover them in the Pentateuch, in the prophets, in the Greek mystery religions, or in Hellenistic philosophies. The notion of a direct relationship, unmediated by priesthood, between the Father God and his children had been nurtured by Pharisaism. But above all, the introspection, the tense inner struggle with sin, the dread of eternal loss, the realization that one's inner self was laid bare to God the Father and that one had to answer to God directly — all these were Pharisaic.

To look elsewhere for the sources of Paul's creation is to look in vain. His concept of the redeeming Christ is not drawn from the Hellenistic world. The savior gods of the mystery cults were neither his model nor his inspiration. Paul was neither a philosopher nor the intentional founder of a new religion. He was a terror-ridden Pharisee who feared that his impulse to break the twofold Law would bring down upon him the eternal wrath of an omnipotent Father God. He clutched at Christ's grace out of a deep inner need for forgiveness and reassurance. Whatever is not original in Paul is Pharisaic, not Hellenistic. Much that Paul said appealed to pagans because it resonated with elements that were already known to them through the mystery cults, but this does not mean that Paul based his thinking on the mystery cults.

Paul becomes thoroughly intelligible the moment we recognize that he carried through a transmutation of Pharisaism. Christianity, like Pharisaism, became a primal generative force in its own right; it has demonstrated its power time and again to spin off highly original and creative new forms. Yet Christianity is interlocked with Pharisaism, even as Pharisaism is interlocked with Pentateuchalism. Pentateuchalism itself is linked with all those earlier forms, which ultimately reach back to the semi-nomadic concept of a single patriarchal deity. The definitive generative power thus lay in the demonstrated power of the Unity Principle to widen, elaborate, and mutate. This quality of the Unity Principle to develop through problem solving must be the irreducible surd. If the concept of unity were static, it could no more have weathered the novelties and perplexities of changing historical conditions than polytheism did.

The Unity Principle and Problem-Solving

ૐ The truth of this generalization can be illustrated by several examples. The Samaritans, who recognized the authority of the Pentateuch and thus acknowledged that God was one, never expanded the Pentateuchal concept to draw in the Hellenistic world; as a consequence the idea literally stayed put with them. Even more telling is the fate that befell the Sadducees, those tenacious supporters of literal interpretation of the Pentateuch and advocates of a return to priestly hegemony. They persisted in affirming that only the written Pentateuch was God's revelation, and they withered away as soon as the destruction of the Second Temple put an end to the sacrificial cult. Similarly, the various forms of Judaism in the Hellenistic Diaspora that remained fixated to concepts of unity that were not resilient disappeared in the general disintegration of the Hellenistic world.

It is not the idea of one God that is essential, but the idea that the one God can be called upon for innovation, and for creative problem solving, and that *God always has powers and attributes not yet revealed*. Only a concept of unity that tolerates the affixing of novel attributes and powers to the one God can cope with process and change. Sooner or later it proves more functional than polytheism in setting into order complex and novel experience.

The Pharisaic revolution assured the triumph of the Unity Principle for both Judaism and Christianity. The opposing principle, exemplified by polytheism, proved no match for Christianity once the disintegration of the Roman Empire became irreversible.

Philosophy was equally impotent in dealing with the collapse of the Roman Empire. It could, like Pharisaism and Christianity, speak to a reality that was separate from the body and its suffering. But its teachings reached at most a tiny minority. The philosophic schools appealed to an intellectual elite, hardly touching the population at large. Furthermore, their concept of reality undercut belief in a personal deity, with human attributes, who was concerned for the salvation of each individual. They did not look forward to personal immortality or to the resurrection of the body. Indeed, for them the body was an obstacle, not a goal. The philosophers thus could not offer either a personal Father God or eternal life.

Like Pharisaism, Christianity could operate multi-dimensionally. It preached of a personal, omnipotent, and gracious Father; it spoke of this Father's Son, who was even more personal, for he had actually become human; it pictured the Son as having been resurrected and rejoined the Father; it urged that the Son be internalized as the ego-ideal, as the hope and the faith of the individual that the individual would be granted eternal life. At the same time, Christianity was susceptible to philosophic explanations identifying Christ with the reality of the philosophers. The monotheism of Christianity enabled it to accommodate to every sort of diversity.

The power of Christianity thus lay in the basic formula of Pharisaism, supplemented by its own unique elements. Pharisaism, to be sure, could not compete with Christianity in a struggle for the pagan soul—the internalization of the twofold Law was far too high a price to pay for salvation when an internalized Christ could bring this about through faith alone;

and the lack in Pharisaism of a divine figure who had undergone human suffering and death weakened the potential for personal identification. But Pharisaism did manage to maintain its own identity vis-à-vis Christianity. Whereas some Jews were drawn to the historical Jesus and even believed that Jesus had been resurrected, few, if any, were drawn to Paul's concept of the Sonship of Christ. This is striking in view of the inroads that Christianity made in the pagan world. Pharisaism must therefore have had what was essential for surviving the collapse of an external world. Paul had failed to internalize the twofold Law as his means for salvation. Few, if any, other Pharisees, shared his failure. For them, the twofold Law within was reassurance enough; for Paul, it was the breeding place of doubt.

This paradox is striking. For the followers of the twofold Law, Paul's denunciation of it was out of joint with their experience. The pagans, on the other hand, who could have had little inkling of what Paul was talking about since they had never internalized the Law, were excited by Paul's replacement for the Law—the idea of Jesus' Sonship, with its rich connotations of a concerned and gracious Father God.

The Centrality of the Individual

ॐ The Pharisees made the *individual* the ultimate concern of Judaism. It is no longer the people, no longer the land, no longer even the Temple. Paramount is the individual and the individual's personal salvation through the laws. The people are now those who internalize the laws; the land, an object of the laws; the Temple, the place where sacrificial laws are obeyed. The individual was spurred to keep the laws foremost in mind in order to secure personal salvation in the world to come and be raised from the dead. The dicta "Everyone in Israel has a share in the world to come" and "The Holy one Blessed Be He desired to benefit Israel and He therefore multiplied the laws for them" express this concept.

The centrality of the individual is nowhere more strikingly revealed than in a passage in the Mishnah dealing with the admonishment of witnesses about to testify in a trial involving the death penalty:

> *You should be aware that judgments involving property are not the same as judgments involving life. In property matters an error in testimony can be atoned for through a money payment, but in a matter of life and death, his blood and the blood of his descendants depend upon it, to the end of time.... For this reason man was created one, to teach you that anyone who destroys a single human soul is reckoned by Scripture as having destroyed the entire world. And anyone who preserves a single soul it is as though he kept the entire world alive...* [Mishnah, Sanhedrin 4:5].

God is thus pictured as concerned with every human being, whether the person is of Israel or a Gentile. A Jew about to testify in a Jewish court of law is reminded that every human life is precious.

And but a few lines further on God is portrayed as being committed to diversify mankind by the nature of God's creative powers:

> *The greatness of the Holy one Blessed Be He is attested by the fact that whereas a human being in making coins from a single stamp can only impress upon them the same likeness, the King of Kings, the Holy one Blessed Be He, stamps every individual with the form of the first man, yet each individual is different from every other.*
>
> *For this reason everyone is obligated [bound by law] to say, "It was on my account that the world was created"* [ibid.].

Pharisaism forged its Judaism out of the crucible of *polisification*. It fought resolutely against Hellenism, while absorbing its most distinguishing features — in a subtle and creative way. It took over the concept of the primacy of laws from the *polis* world, and developed the halakhah system for the individual, with the constitutions of the Hellenistic cities as models. It originated a legislative body, the *Beth Din ha-Gadol*, which bears far closer resemblance to Greek and Roman lawmaking institutions than to anything in the Pentateuch. The concepts of oral laws as distinct from written laws, of law as distinct from non-law, of logical deductive modes of reasoning and exegetical devices — these came from the *polis*, not the Pentateuch. The Pharisaic revolution was thus a novel form of Judaism fashioned by men of genius out of raw materials from both the *polis* and the Pentateuch. And its most significant accomplishment was an internalized system of laws for the individual.

Earlier, when discussing the impact of the *polis* revolution on the individual, I placed considerable emphasis on the desperate need to find an identity. Often, especially in the golden age of *polis* growth under the early Hellenistic monarchs, this identity was achieved through the status of citizenship. One belonged to the *polis* and one was protected by the constitution, the laws of the *polis*. Laws were held in high esteem in the Hellenistic cities, and the great lawgivers, like Solon and Lycurgus, were deeply venerated. Indeed, the very heart of the *polis* form of government was its constitution.

The constitution of a city surrounded the individual. As long as a person was a citizen, and as long as a person lived in his or her city, the *politeia* gave a sense of belonging, of identity, of self-esteem. Once a person left the city, however, either voluntarily or by force, the system of laws was no longer operative. He or she had severed connections with that city's laws. They no longer applied.

The Pharisees solved the problem of the laws and the individuals in a unique way. They built a system of laws, the halakhah, but instead of surrounding the individual with the laws of a single city or country, they had the individual surround the laws. They erected a constitution, a *politeia*, to be put inside and not outside the individual, a system of law that the individual carried inside wherever he or she went, and to which he or she was always and everywhere to be faithful. The giver of this constitution was the one cosmic Father God who was the *Makom*, the All-Present, and the *Shekhinah*—a God who was with one everywhere—in Jerusalem, in Corinth, in Athens, in Rome, in Ephesus. God was always watching with a discerning eye the individual's fidelity to the laws, keeping an exhaustive record of every personal thought and deed, and calculating the ultimate distribution of reward and punishment.

An internal city engraved on the soul of the individual— this was the crucial achievement of the Pharisees. Citizenship was available to all who internalized the halakhah system. It was a city fashioned for "all who came under the wings of the *Shekhinah*," a constitution for living persons, and not for a fixed place. All who accepted it were linked together in collegiality and fellowship, and the place for affirming their loyalty to the internalized laws was the synagogue, a novel institution created by the Pharisees that emerged spontaneously in the course of the Pharisaic revolution. Once in existence, the synagogue spread rapidly through Palestine and the cities of the Diaspora. It was an institution that was especially appropriate for the city. It was a place that could be set apart in *any polis*. In contrast to the Temple, it was not limited to a specific *city* or dedicated *to* sacrificial worship. Rather it was a decentralized gathering place where each individual could listen to the reading of the Law and the Prophets, pray to a personal God and Father directly, and renew a personal allegiance to the internalized halakhah along with like-minded citizens. The Pharisees never sought to destroy the Temple or to challenge the efficacy of sacrifices, but in developing the synagogue they made both irrelevant. A religious institution had been born where neither priest nor altar intervened between the individual and the individual's God. The synagogue, in underwriting an unmediated relationship between the single soul and the single God, became the *patria*, the concrete symbol of one's commitment to an internalized constitution transcending spatial boundaries. God and not a fixed Temple had become the *Makom* — the Place, the All-Present.

The Pharisaic revolution thus proved to be the decisive mutation of Judaism. It created the one and only form of Judaism that proved viable in coping with the Hellenistic-Roman world, the destruction of the Temple and the abolition of sacrifices, the disintegration of the Roman Empire and the triumph of Christianity, and the rise of Islam. As such, Pharisaism became a primal force in its own right, for every subsequent form of Judaism was either a variation or a mutation of the Pharisaic form.

IV
Heirs of the Pharisees

The Paths of the Twofold Law

&. Pharisaism gave birth to the medieval world view of salvation. Its three principles—a single omnipotent Father God, the internalization of God's revealed will, and the promise of eternal life and resurrection—sustained Judaism, Christianity, and Islam throughout the Middle Ages. The formal structure is identical in all three religious systems, though the mode of its expression differs. For the Pharisees, God's will was expressed in the twofold Law as taught by a scholar class; for Christians, Christ was the embodiment of God's will; for the Muslims, God's will was expressed in the inspired teachings of Mohammed.

The Pharisaic version of the unity idea spawned a bewildering variety of shapes and forms. Far from cutting off further development, the Unity Principle seemed to encourage it.

The Diversities of Response

&. The Pharisaic revolution evinced concepts that enabled Christianity and Islam, no less than Judaism, to respond to changing economic, social, and political conditions. The resiliency of these concepts is nowhere more manifest than in the kaleidoscopic history of the Jews during the Middle Ages. Christianity and Islam may have shared the same principles, but they did not share the same history. The Jews had no single medieval history. They had no territorial center to expand from and contract into. They exercised no independent sovereignty. Judaism was never the dominant religion within any territory. Judaism had to meet the challenge not only of novel historical experience, but of highly diverse societies structured in radically different ways, and within which Jews lived simultaneously. Jews were living at one and the same time in different societies within the Muslim and Christian worlds; they could survive only if they adapted creatively to each of these diverse systems; they had to forge a distinctive variation of Judaism as a counterpart to each society within which they lived. To survive they had to shape and reshape communal structures that could function in radically different environments. They had to develop what might be called a Sassanian Judaism (in the Sassanian Empire, which lasted from the third to the seventh century), a Muslim Judaism, and a Christian Judaism.

These variations, far from stripping Judaism of its distinctive identity, enriched it; there was continued pressure for creative innovation, and the development of a rich variety of distinctive Jewish forms, not one of which duplicates an earlier structure or one functioning simultaneously elsewhere. Yet, however original, each form is connected to every previous form and to every contemporary form by virtue of its link to the Pharisaic tradition.

Changes in the Diaspora

֍ So long as Aaronidism had held undisputed sway, the Diaspora was overshadowed by Jerusalem, with its Temple cult, even though large and significant settlements emerged during the Hellenistic period in Alexandria and Antioch. The Hellenistic forms of Judaism emerging in the Diaspora were not taken as models for the Judaism of Palestine. Though the Jews of the Diaspora may have freely left the land and been happy to live permanently abroad, they recognized Jerusalem as their mother city.

The triumph of the Pharisees was the triumph of universalism. Now the vital issue was salvation, not the land and the cult; since salvation was an individual concern, attainable through the internalized Law, one really did not need the land of Israel at all. It made no difference where the lawmakers were; authority was lodged in them, not in a place. The Pharisaic revolution thus made it possible for the Diaspora to become a generating force free of the dependence on the land of Israel and even capable of creating laws to be applied there.

The Pharisees' influence on the Diaspora was not clearly discernible at first. The scholar class had risen to power within Palestine and in response to Palestinian problems. The *Beth Din ha-Gadol* had its seat in Jerusalem, not Alexandria or Antioch. The obligations of the Jewish peasant in Palestine had been a vital concern of the Pharisees and continued to be one. But Pharisaism primarily appealed to Diaspora Jews as a form of Judaism addressed to the individual. It gave the individual the links with the land even as it freed the people from the land. The idea that resurrection and eternal life were attainable even without a visit to Jerusalem or the offer of a personal sacrifice was exhilarating. Diaspora Jews also found appealing the Pharisees' efforts to win proselytes from among the pagans; indeed, some outstanding Pharisee leaders were reputed themselves to be of proselyte descent. The spread of Pharisaism in the Diaspora was encouraged by the synagogue, which was a meeting place not for Jews in general, but for Jews drawn to the teachings of the Pharisees. Jews such as the Sadducees, who affirmed only the Written Law, did not seek it out.

After the Destruction of the Second Temple

❧ The universalist seeds of Pharisaism, however, did not burst into bloom until after the destruction of the Second Temple in C.E. 70. The Pharisees had carried through a revolution, but their revolution had not been total. They had held back from destroying the cultic system, and had undercut but not eliminated the primacy of sacrifice. They had made the priests mere functionaries, without stripping them of all privilege. Had the Romans not destroyed the Temple, a decisive break with the sacrificial system might not have come about.

Nevertheless, sacrifice had lost its original power. Christianity's rejection of animal sacrifices, a rejection stemming from the Pharisaic stress on internalization, is most significant; for it reveals how nonessential sacrifices had really become. The Christians retained the concept, but sublimated it. Sacrifice became an internal experience, with Christ as the paschal lamb.

The destruction of the Temple gave the Pharisees the opportunity to develop fully the anti-sacrificial implications of their revolution. Though there was mourning for the destruction of the Temple, mourning was not overindulged. Indeed, the Pharisaic teachers prohibited morbid grief over the destruction of the Temple. Henceforth the cult was to be preserved and venerated as a memento of an earlier age and not as a necessary institution. There was contemplation of its former glory, an academic concern with the legal minutiae of its operation, and pious verbalization of the hope for its restoration in the messianic age. But no steps were initiated to restore it. Pharisaism had already stripped the cultus of an *essential* role in Judaism.

With the Temple gone, the scholar class could put finishing touches on its revolution. The great cultic holidays were transformed. The first day of the seventh month, the day of the blowing of the ram's horn, which so long as the Temple stood was primarily a day devoted to displaying the expiatory efficacy of the cult, was now proclaimed preeminently as the New Year, Rosh Ha-Shanah, the day on which God had created the world and the day on which each individual was judged and the fate of the individual was determined for the coming year. Yom Kippur, the Day of Atonement, which while the Temple stood had been the occasion for the high priest's entry into the Holy of Holies to make atonement for the entire people, now became devoted to the individual's personal pleading to God the Father for expiation, the day on which God made final decisions as to the individual's fate during the year to come. These two days, which had once served to underwrite priestly intermediation between God and humanity, became days of direct confrontation with God – and so they have remained.

Other sweeping reforms were introduced. Shavuoth, which had been primarily the Festival of the First Fruits and, as such, a holiday of the land, was transformed into the day for commemorating God's giving of the twofold Law to Israel. The Feast of Unleavened Bread, which had hitherto commemorated primarily the exodus from Egypt, was now renamed Passover and made to symbolize God's redemptive power, which was extended to all who joined themselves to Israel. Similarly, the term *Judean*, with its ethnic connotation, was now abandoned; used in its stead was *Israel* – with its overtones of an association of like-minded believers. The marriage contract, which had read "in accordance with the Law of Moses and the Judeans," was now altered to read "in accordance with the Law of Moses and Israel."

Thus the Pharisaic revolution underwent two major phases. The first involved the transfer of authority from the priests to the scholar class and the triumph of the principle of internalization and personal salvation; during this phase the cultus was preserved and Jerusalem and the land were assumed to be the permanent center of the scholar class. The second phase witnessed the collapse of the cultus; thus, legal authority lost its permanent attachment to the land of the Jews.

The Pharisees and Political Power

ȥ The shift did not immediately follow the destruction of the Temple. Indeed, the loss of the Temple and Rome's repression of the Jewish rebellion only enhanced the authority of the scholar class. Such Pharisaic spokesmen as Johanan ben Zakkai had all along considered the rebellion devoid of religious sanction and had hoped for a negotiated peace. When this hope was dashed by the determination of the radical Zealots to fight to the bitter end, Johanan managed to escape the besieged city of Jerusalem by having his pupils carry him out on a bier. He then made his way to the Roman camp; there he was well received by the Roman commander, Vespasian, who permitted him to reconstitute the *Beth Din ha-Gadol,* recognizing it as the Sanhedrin, i.e., a council authorized by the Roman emperor to exercise a high degree of autonomy. Previously the Sanhedrin had been presided over by the high priest appointed by the procurators and had no relationship to the Pharisaic twofold Law; now it was to be presided over by Johanan ben Zakkai and be identical with the *Beth Din ha-Gadol,* the Great Legislature of the twofold Law.

This decision was not taken lightly; it reflected Vespasian's astute assessment of Pharisaism as a system with little interest in political power. Vespasian was well aware that the Pharisees had made every effort to hold the people back from rebellion, and had only reluctantly joined the revolt when there seemed no other way to maintain leadership. The example of the Pharisee Josephus, who had sabotaged rebel efforts to put up a strong fight in Galilee and had openly collaborated with Rome, confirmed Vespasian's assessment of Pharisaism. By reconstituting the *Beth Din ha-Gadol*, Vespasian reassured the scholar class that Rome had no designs on Pharisaism. So long as Jews concentrated on the world to come and did not insist that political sovereignty was a prerequisite for salvation, the Romans would hold their scholar-leaders in high esteem. On this understanding, the scholar class and Rome got along handsomely for approximately half a century. Then, in C.E. 132, the Jews, led by Bar Kochba and supported by a respected leader of the scholar class, Akiba, made a desperate and for a time successful effort to regain independence. This revolt, unlike the previous one, was sparked by messianic hopes, which, partly in response to Christianity, had gained some legitimacy among the scholar class itself in the years following the destruction of the Temple. Despite Akiba, the revolt failed, crushed by Roman power and by the unwillingness of prominent members of the scholar class to acknowledge Bar Kochba as the Messiah.

The war was bitter and its scars were deep; it brought intense persecution of the scholar class. Nevertheless a harmonious relationship was worked out again, based on the original understanding of mutually exclusive jurisdictions. This understanding proved especially fruitful during the years that Judah ha-Nasi (C.E. 170-217) exercised hegemony over the scholar class.

Instituting Structural Changes

֍ Judah ha-Nasi played a role in the evolution of the two-fold Law that cannot be overstated, even though he had little idea of how crucial that role would be. As the *Nasi* ("Prince" or "Patriarch") Judah was primarily concerned with bringing the scholar class under the tight control of his office. This was not easy, for the scholar class had gained a large measure of independence through the development of ordination. (The origin of ordination is obscure, like virtually everything else about the development of Pharisaism.)

From the outbreak of the Pharisaic revolution in the middle of the second century B.C.E. until around the beginning of the Christian era, the scholar class was headed by a Nasi and an *Ab Beth Din* ("Father of the Legislature"). These two were designated *Zugoth,* or "Pairs." Presumably the Nasi presided over the *Beth Din ha-Gadol* and represented the majority position, while the Ab Beth Din was sort of the leader of the opposition. The names of the Zugoth are known to us during the years when they exercised authority; the names of other scholars were not preserved. The Zugoth, though bearing the honorific title Nasi and Ab Beth Din, are not called either *Rabban* ("our teacher") or *Rabbi* ("my teacher"). The Zugoth phase in the development of the Pharisees came to an end with the death of Hillel and Shammai. In its stead we find the descendants of Hillel serving as Nasi by hereditary right and being called by the honorific title Rabban. Other scholars are anonymous as before; but they are now enrolled in two schools—the School of Shammai and the School of Hillel—advocating different legal principles, but each committed to the twofold Law.

After the destruction of the Temple (C.E. 70) a significant structural change appears. The Nasi is still called Rabban, but now individual scholars are called by name, and each bona fide scholar of the twofold Law is called *rabbi,* "my teacher." It is at this point, I suspect, that ordination became significant. For the right of an individual to teach the twofold Law in his own name and to attract young scholars around his person and his teaching would seem to follow from some grant of authority. Ordination meant that a bona fide scholar might ordain another scholar, and that each ordained scholar was as authoritative as any other. Thus there was a proliferation of independent scholars after the year 70—a proliferation that permitted one scholar, Akiba, to look on Bar Kochba as the Messiah and other ordained scholars to ridicule the notion.

Judah ha-Nasi sought to limit ordination to the Nasi and to confer on other scholars, *minui*, authorization by the Nasi, rather than ordination, hoping thereby to cut down the proliferation of conflicting positions.

The Mishnah

ð•　To reduce the large number of opinions circulating, Judah promulgated an authoritative codification of the twofold Law called the *Mishnah* ("Repetition" or "Learning"). By putting his seal of approval on the laws in the Mishnah, Judah in effect reduced the authority of opinions that were not included. At the same time, he abrogated other well-known opinions, including them but negating them either by the anonymous law of the majority or by his own opinion.

Ironically, however, Judah's effort to curb the development of the Oral Law was frustrated by the very book he had promulgated. By making available a codification of the twofold Law, and by preserving within it the conflicting opinions of scholars, Judah opened up undreamed of possibilities for the expansion of the twofold Law. For the Mishnah, like the Pentateuch, marked off a line of demarcation, becoming for the Oral Law what the Pentateuch had become for the Written Law. Opinions recorded in the Mishnah enjoyed an authority that no other opinions enjoyed, even those by the very same teachers. The scholars who taught prior to the promulgation of the Mishnah were elevated above scholars who taught afterwards. They were called *Tannaim*, an honorific title meaning "teachers of the twofold Law," which set them off from the generation of scholars who followed them, called *Amoraim*, meaning "exponents of the teachings of the Tannaim."

The promulgation of the Mishnah freed the scholar class from binding ties to the land. Before that, authority was vested in ordained scholars who taught orally in Palestine, and aspiring scholars living in the Diaspora had to travel there to hear the twofold Law. But when the Mishnah was promulgated, it was readily available to Diaspora scholars.

Two other factors besides the promulgation of the Mishnah helped shift authority to scholars outside Palestine, a shift that made the remarkable Diaspora history of the Jews possible. The first of these was the breakdown of the Roman Empire sometime after Judah ha-Nasi's death and the triumph of Christianity in the Roman world. The second was the result of unusually favorable conditions opened up for a creative Jewish community in Babylonia under the Sassanians in the third and fourth centuries.

The Triumph of Christianity

ﻉ The disintegration of the Roman Empire and the triumph of Christianity can be dealt with briefly. Economic and political breakdown in the third century had devastating effects in Palestine and left much of Palestinian Jewry impoverished. The harmonious collaboration between the Nasi and the Emperor was disturbed as the instability of the imperial system became ever more manifest. And after Constantine, early in the fourth century, desperately sought to stave off collapse by aligning Rome with Christianity, Judaism lost its protected status; the security of the scholar class was jeopardized; ultimately, in the fifth century, the office of Nasi was liquidated. The Palestinian scholar class had striven to retain its primacy—its efforts to use the Mishnah as a base for its own authority is attested to by the Palestinian Talmud—but its authority was undercut by the disintegrative processes which impoverished and depopulated the Jewish communities in the Roman Empire. Under such conditions, laying claim to authority over a prospering Jewish community in Babylonia was an exercise in ever-growing futility.

The Babylonian Community

ใจ The second factor requires somewhat greater elaboration, for it involves the process by which authority came to be exercised in the Diaspora. The development of the very large Jewish settlement in Babylonia before the third century is very obscure, but its flourishing after the Sassanians came to power in the third century is a matter of record. Whereas before the Sassanian takeover the Jewish scholar class in Babylonia enjoyed no independence, after the takeover it steadily increased in prestige, power, and assertiveness. This increase the Sassanians encouraged. The Sassanians originally had drawn strength from the crusading zeal of Zoroastrianism, but they were quick to follow a pragmatic policy once their power was consolidated. At war with Rome and confronted with a vast Jewish population dependent on scholars residing in Palestine, a Roman province, the Sassanians cultivated the loyalty of their Jewish subjects; they gave the Jews' leader, or Exilarch, high esteem and extended to their scholars the tax-exempt privileges enjoyed by the Zoroastrian priesthood. Sassanian kings included leaders of the Babylonian Jewish scholar class, such as Samuel, in the royal entourage. In turn, the Jewish scholar class urged loyalty to the Sassanian rulers, payment of taxes, and recognition of Sassanian law as binding in civil matters. *Dina de-malkutha dina* — "the law of the realm is the law [for Jews]" — was the classical dictum formulated by the scholar Samuel.

The need of the Sassanians for a loyal Jewish community and their encouragement of an indigenous Jewish leadership emerged at a most propitious time for the development of the

Jews. The Mishnah had been circulating for several decades; Judah ha-Nasi had effectively drawn a line between the ordained scholars who had taught before the publication of the Mishnah and the non-ordained scholars who taught afterwards; the Roman imperial system was displaying symptoms of disintegration. Thus, when Judah died, the two foremost Babylonian scholars, Rav and Samuel, who had studied directly under him, were on the same plane as Palestinian scholars; all were equally bound by Judah's Mishnah.

The Scholars of Babylon

ﻪﺑ   The scholars in Babylonia were now freed to develop the twofold Law in a highly original and creative way. They took as their point of departure the text of the Mishnah. The Mishnah was not a simple code of laws. Judah had preserved in it a wide variety of conflicting opinions testifying to the wide range of disagreement among the ordained Tannaim about the specifics of the Law and about some fundamental legal principles. For the Babylonian Jews this was tantamount to an invitation to draw on these authoritative differences to justify perpetuating debate rather than foreclosing it. This was contrary to Judah's intentions, but he was no longer alive, while the Mishnah was very much alive with conflicting views prominently displayed. For the Amoraim, the Tannaim, who expressed divergent views, were authorities whose every word carried greater weight than their own. The Babylonian scholars thus found in the Mishnah a wide range of opinions that enabled them to develop oral laws responsive to the unique needs of the Babylonian Jewish community and to the Zoroastrian-Sassanian environment.

The Babylonians drew on a vast repository of tannaitic teachings called *beraitot,* which, though excluded by Judah ha-Nasi from the Mishnah, were nonetheless saturated with the high esteem attached to every opinion uttered by one of the ordained Tannaim. These *beraitot* might be less authoritative than the Mishnah, but they still carried far more weight than *any* opinion of *any* scholar who lived after the last generation of the Tannaim.

The dependence of Babylonian scholars on the teachings of the Tannaim served as the secure foundation for their *real* independence. They were relatively free to take the law wherever their ingenuity led. Seeking to clarify the Mishnah, they found it bristling with contradictions, and in striving to harmonize and justify these contradictions, they came up with highly original opinions of their own. Searching for principles underlying the laws, they came up with notions that were their own creation, not those of the Tannaim. Needing to cope with novel situations, they compelled the texts to yield novel meanings.

The Mishnah also encouraged the development of individualism among the scholars. The Tannaim served as models. Since the Tannaim held conflicting views, the Amoraim merely followed in their footsteps when they cultivated the art of controversy. They engaged in vigorous debate as to what the Mishnah really meant, challenging each other by adroitly juxtaposing Mishnaic and *beraita* texts, and controverting each other with subtle dialectical arguments based on hermeneutic principles discovered within the tannaitic texts themselves. To hold a contrary view was a sign of learning and a mark of scholarly distinction. To be loyal to the Mishnah was to dredge out every argumentative possibility; to be loyal to the twofold Law was to expose its multifaceted prisms; to gain salvation was to cultivate an independent point of view.

The Mishnah is preeminently a collection of laws. The Tannaim's non-legal teachings—aggadah (lore), as opposed to halakhah (law)—are only sparsely represented in the Mishnah. The Mishnah sets down the halakhoth with brisk authority. Although biblical verses are called upon from time to time to underwrite, reaffirm, or embellish a halakhah, the Mishnah is a self-verifying, self-sustaining, and self-confirming corpus of oral legislation.

The Amoraim dissolved the tight partition between law and lore, and opened the sluice gates for the free flow of biblical texts to underwrite, sustain, reaffirm, clarify, enrich, embroider, and exemplify both halakhah and aggadah. The Amoraim freely intermixed halakhah with aggadah. And they went a step beyond. Whereas the Tannaim, even when engaged in debate, kept the controversy crisp and concise, the Amoraim indulged in controversy as a great sport. They leisurely spun out long lines of controversial opinions that each generation extended and embellished. The *process* of getting to the law was far more precious to them than the law itself. The Amoraim sharpened the mind to serve as a tool for fashioning new legal forms and shapes. And by continuously intermingling law with lore, they used the prim, proper, and orderly Mishnah as rich soil for wild, extravagant, and undisciplined growth.

The Babylonian Talmud

ই. The end product of more than two centuries of Babylonian activity was the Babylonian Talmud. Here it is all revealed: the triumph of the *nominally* inferior Babylonian scholar class over the *nominally* sacrosanct Palestinian, of the non-ordained Babylonian Amoraim over the ordained Tannaim. The Mishnah, in a sense, spins off an anti-Mishnah—not in the literal sense but operationally. The meaning of the Mishnah becomes an amoraic meaning. The operative laws were what the Amoraim decided, not what the Mishnah decided. The literal text of the Mishnah was no more binding on the Amoraim than the text of the Bible had been binding on the Pharisees or the Tannaim. The principles underlying tannaitic law were principles proclaimed by the Amoraim. The Amoraim determined which tannaitic doctrines would be activated and which left to lie dormant. Angelology played little role in the tannaitic aggadah, but it flourished in the amoraic. The messianic idea is barely mentioned in the tannaitic texts, but it enjoys luxuriant growth in the amoraic. Demons cannot be found in the Mishnah, but one has only to leaf through the tractate of *Berakhoth* in the Babylonian Talmud to find them in abundance.

The venerators, the Amoraim, sat themselves in the seat of the venerated. The teachings of Moses were now mediated through the Amoraim; the teachings of the Soferim-Pharisees, the Tannaim, found in the Mishnah and in the *beraitot,* were now refracted through the Amoraim. An upstart scholar class in the Diaspora, lacking ordination and meticulously refraining from using the honorific title of Rabban or Rabbi, exposing their lowly status by settling for the titles *rav* ("master") or *mar* ("mister"), had vaulted themselves into Moses' seat. They reigned over the meaning of the Mishnah and *beraitot.*

The irony is preserved by the text of the Babylonian Talmud itself. There one finds the sacred Mishnah texts set down first. The line of demarcation is kept sharp and clear, for the discussions of the Amoraim which follow the Mishnah text are marked off from the Mishnah by a prefatory title *gemara* (literally, "completion"), the name given to amoraic discussions of the Mishnah. The combination of the Mishnah and Gemara comprises the *Talmud* ("Learning"). But though the lines are kept distinct, the ultimate authority for operational law and operational lore resided with the Amoraim. Amoraic Judaism superseded tannaitic Judaism; Sassanian Judaism succeeded Palestinian; a scholar class confronting the *now* took precedence over a scholar class that had confronted the *then.*

The fruits of the amoraic takeover are still being harvested. The Babylonian Talmud, which was compiled in the fifth century by the assiduous efforts of Rabina and Rav Ashi—two foremost spokesmen for the Babylonian scholar class—came to be venerated as the repository of the twofold Law and lore. The Mishnah retained only nominal preeminence, for the scholar class never again studied it without reference to the Gemara. Even when, in the Middle Ages, such renowned scholarly commentators as Maimonides and Obadiah da Bertinoro wrote learned and distinguished commentaries on the Mishnah, they brought to bear vast knowledge of the Babylonian Talmud to elucidate its meaning. Just as the Bible was never again read literally by Jews loyal to the twofold Law, but only as seen refracted through the Pharisaic, tannaitic, and amoraic prisms, so too the Mishnah was never again read as an independent legal corpus by tradition-committed Jews. And just as the Bible has never ceased to be venerated as God's immutable revelation by Jews whose way of life and whose mode of thought were shaped by the twofold Law, even though the literal text of the Bible ceased with the Pharisees to be in any way determinative, so the Jews throughout the ages reaffirmed the higher sanctity of the Mishnah even as they were subordinating its meaning to the Gemara.

A Continuous Tradition

&❧ Nonetheless, the triumph of the Babylonian scholar class and the emergence of a Babylonian form of Judaism was not a mutation. Though superficially it was reminiscent of the Pharisaic triumph over the Aaronides and the elevation of the twofold Law over the Pentateuch, it was not equivalent. The Babylonian Amoraim represented a variation on a theme of Pharisaism, while Pharisaism was not simply a variation of Pentateuchalism. With all their radical reshaping, the Babylo-

nian scholar class reaffirmed the triple leitmotif of Pharisaism: (1) the one omnipotent Father-God so loved humanity
that (2) God revealed to Israel the twofold Law to be internalized within each person so that (3) human beings could attain
eternal life for their souls and resurrection for their bodies.
Whatever changes the Babylonians effected were to enhance
the authority of the twofold Law, not to derogate it.

It is a striking fact that the Mishnah, despite its authority,
did not serve as the prototype for the work of the Babylonian
scholars. Sassanian society was very different from that of the
Greco-Roman world. The two economic systems, political structures, and intellectual worlds had little in common. In particular, the role of the Zoroastrian priesthood, the *magi*, had no
counterpart in the Greco-Roman world. The Sassanian monarchy did not rule over a network of *poleis*. The spiritual principles that bound this empire together were not the civic,
philosophic, or legal concepts of the privileged classes of the
Roman Empire or the paganism of the common people. The
dominant theme of the Greco-Roman world had been rationality and order — the primacy of logical and deductive modes
of thinking; the dominant theme of the Zoroastrian world was
the eternal struggle between light and darkness, order and
chaos, a conflict which could be resolved in the interests of order only by the mediation of the priesthood. This idea was
dominant even though an effective imperial rule of more than
two centuries maintained economic, political, and social order in the Sassanian realm.

In such a radically different society the Jews could not
build their communities along Greco-Roman lines. Dupli-
cating the communities of Palestine would have courted
disaster. Instead, the Jews shaped communities that were
congruent with the Sassanian world. Their scholar class constructed a system of authority that could function effectively
in a society where a religious class, the magi, enjoyed prestige

and privilege. Since the Mishnah had been the product of Jews living in the Greco-Roman world, it could not simply be transferred to Sassanian Babylonia. The fact that it was sacred collided with the fact that it was out of joint. The Amoraim of Babylonia therefore did not hesitate to develop a form and style uniquely their own.

Just as the intellectual world of the Sassanians was non-rational and disorderly when compared with that of the Greeks and Romans, so the Babylonian scholars appear non-rational and disorderly when compared to the scholars of the Mishnah. And just as disorder in the realm of ideas was compatible with economic, social, and political order in the Sassanian world, it was compatible with orderly reasoning in the world of Jewish law.

The Babylonian Talmud reveals the radical transformation the Sassanian world effected for Judaism. In the Mishnah, an orderly code of laws, the Sabbath laws, are grouped together and distinguished from laws of contracts. There is relatively little intermixture. Furthermore, the law is set down in a simple categorical way. Differences of opinion are noted, but legal debate is rare.

By contrast, the Babylonian Talmud is characterized by disorder. Differentiated categories of law simply disintegrate. Ritual laws intermingle with laws of property and marriage and divorce. Mishnah law in one category provokes a minute analysis by the Babylonians of its implications for every other category. Casuistic debate takes priority over final decision. Drawing non-legal materials, aggadah, into the legal debates further heightens the sense of disorder. To swim in the sea of the Talmud is to swim in eddies and currents springing from the intellectual disorder of the Sassanian and Zoroastrian world.

I am not saying that the Babylonian Talmud was a Sassanian and Zoroastrian creation. And I certainly am not saying that the Mishnah is not compelling. Nor am I saying that because the form is disorderly the legal thinking is illogical. What I am maintaining is that if we want to make intelligible the reason why the Babylonian Talmud is so different in form and structure from the Mishnah, we must look at the form and structure of the Sassanian-Zoroastrian world. The Babylonian Talmud is not a logical outgrowth of the Mishnah. It is, rather, the response of the Jewish scholar class to the problem of a Sassanian-Zoroastrian world in which the literal Mishnah was inadequate. The Babylonian scholars simply followed in the footsteps of their predecessors who had found novel and original ways of drawing the essentials of a civilization into Judaism and had created a new form of Judaism. In this sense, then, we can speak of a Sassanian Judaism, but always with a caveat in mind: the interweaving of the two systems is so natural that any attempt to separate the strands is futile. It is not a Jewish form drawing in Sassanian-Zoroastrian content, so that if one removes the content one is left with the Jewish form. The form itself is an amalgam of the previous Jewish form, in this instance the Mishnaic, in conjunction with the Sassanian-Zoroastrian form. The amalgam itself is the new Jewish form. To separate out the Sassanian-Zoroastrian form of the Babylonian Talmud is to make a shambles of the distinctively Jewish quality of historical experience within the Sassanian Babylonian world. This capacity for form creation and for form amalgamation, generated by the operation of the Unity Principle, is an essential dynamic of Jewish history.

The Process of Interaction

The creative accomplishment of the Babylonian Jewish scholar class was thus a consequence of an intense interplay with a challenging, vigorous, and creative non-Jewish environment. The fact that Judaism was different from Zoroastrianism did not necessarily imply disintegration or destructiveness. Although the rise of Sassanian-Zoroastrian hegemony was accompanied by considerable intolerance for the Jews, the consolidation of power was followed by benign tolerance. The differences did not disappear, but their hostile potential was muted. For more than a century, Jews enjoyed economic freedom and relative prosperity; they had considerable autonomy and were placed under the sovereignty of their twofold Law in all matters pertaining to their relationship with other Jews. Academies for the teaching of the twofold Law flourished, and the scholar class was given a free hand to teach, exhort, and adjudicate.

The fruitful interaction, however, could not be sustained. The Sassanians were no more successful than the Romans in unlocking the secret of sustained economic growth and development. Disintegrative forces began to cut down the Sassanian structure; in the process, the benign link connecting the Jewish and Sassanian systems snapped. The hostility that had lain dormant in Zoroastrianism was now brought to life. The incompatibility between the two intellectual worlds was stressed. The difference once again made a difference, and the Jews were set upon as dangerous outsiders. The scholar class was hounded and their academies were shut down. The Jews, stunned and demoralized, suffered a precarious existence until rescued by triumphant Islam.

This ambiguous experience with Sassanian-Zoroastrian society was to be repeated again and again with other societies in the centuries that followed. At times the difference with the larger society made little difference, and at times it made all the difference in the world. This syndrome is another unique feature of Jewish history that is fraught with meaning, because in each instance the fundamental cause is the same: economics. *Economic growth diminishes the power of contrasting ideologies to provoke hostility; economic breakdown increases the power of contrasting ideologies to provoke hostility.*

The Unity Principle in Operation

&. I have focused attention on the process by which the Babylonian scholar class made good its bid for independent authority because it exemplifies so crisply a process that was never to end. Throughout the Middle Ages and into the modern era, each differentiated Jewish community, in the Diaspora or in Palestine, exercised whatever authority was essential for creative adaptation to its environment, irrespective of any previous claims by anyone of a right to exercise immutable authority in perpetuity. Veneration and awe never paralyzed clear-sighted leaders. They innovated radically whenever new problems resisted traditional solutions. Time and again Jews simply did what the Amoraim had done: they elevated their predecessors to an honored pedestal high above themselves, and then, in their name and in their spirit, built new structures, developed new concepts, launched new institutions, and thought hitherto unthinkable thoughts. What they refused to do was to stand by and allow Judaism to disintegrate, become dysfunctional, and wither away into obsolescence, simply because the Amoraim, the Tannaim, the Pharisees, the prophets, and Moses himself had not fashioned a Judaism for every time, or every season, or for every historical vicissitude.

Indeed, this process occurred simultaneously in both Babylonia and Palestine. Like the Babylonians, the Palestinian scholars were faced with problems that required flexible and open-ended solution. The disintegration of the Roman Empire, the impoverishment of Palestine, the decline in Jewish population, and the linking of Christianity with the Roman imperium demanded reactions highly different from those of scholars basking in the benign favor of Sassanian emperors. The outcome was quite a different kind of Talmud, called the Palestinian, compiled at the end of the fourth century. It accords authoritative status to the Mishnah, but its

Gemara is not nearly so involved with long, spun-out dialectical debate, and it contains far less aggadic material. As a consequence, the Babylonian Talmud overshadows it in sheer quantity.

The Palestinian Talmud lost out in influence to the Babylonian. Its loss cannot be attributed to its smaller size or to any intrinsic inferiority. Its teachings were binding on Palestinian Jewry, and it probably enjoyed higher authority than the Babylonian Talmud throughout the Roman Empire. For several centuries there existed, theoretically at least, two options: one could follow the Palestinian Talmud or the Babylonian, or any viable mixture of the two, as a secure guide to the world to come. The variety of opinions that flourished simultaneously throughout Babylonia was extended to include the teachings of the Palestinian scholars. From all indications, rivalries between the Amoraim of Babylonia and those of Palestine seem to have been no more intense than rivalries within each group. In this they followed the tradition of the Tannaim, whose differences had been based on ideas, not on place of origin.

With the spread of Islam, and especially with the rise of the Abbasid dynasty, the Babylonian Talmud finally triumphed over the Palestinian. With the reorganization of the Middle East under Muslim hegemony, Palestine came to be overshadowed in the eighth century by Babylonia, where the Abbasids based their power. The Abbasid rulers recognized the leaders of the Babylonian scholar class, now called Geonim, and the Exilarch, who resided in Babylonia, as the spokesmen for all their Jewish subjects. These Geonim based their opinions on the Babylonian Talmud and gave it priority over the Palestinian. So effective were they that the Palestinian Talmud fell into disuse. Even today it is hardly studied in academies of Jewish learning — not even in those in Israel — in the intensive way that the Babylonian is. Symptomatic of its

low status is the fact that, whereas a first-rate English translation of the Babylonian Talmud was launched in the 1930's,
only a preliminary translation of the Palestinian Talmud has
been undertaken, and that as late as the 1980's.

The fact that to this day the Babylonian Talmud still
reigns supreme among Jews, even in the State of Israel, is
sturdy proof that the road to salvation was wherever the loyal
and believing Israelites happened to be. The map was a system of laws, not a territory. The triumph of the Babylonian
Talmud thus made explicit what had heretofore been largely
implicit in Pharisaism; namely, that the authority of the scholar
class was within the class itself and was not dependent on the
Pentateuch or on residence within the Holy Land.

The Place of the Land and the Book

૨ঌ This did not mean that either the Book or the land faded
into insignificance. Far from it. Nor did the scholar class ever
depreciate the cultus. Long after the Temple lay in ruins, the
Tannaim and the Amoraim addressed themselves lovingly to
the task of spelling out with exactitude the precise procedures
to be followed by the priests and the Levites when offering
sacrifices, lest a misstep nullify the efficacy of their sacrifices.
Similarly, the scholar class concerned themselves with all the
laws that would be binding in the land, even though they
were irrelevant for the vast majority of the Jews living in the
Diaspora. The notion of the Book and the notion of the land
thus did not wither away, but were preserved as opportunities for vicarious re-identification with the revelation on Sinai,
with the conquest of Canaan, with the Davidic monarchy, and
with the Temple in all its pomp and glory. The Holy Land re
mained the Holy Land. It flourished as fantasy, and it was the
stuff out of which dreams of some resplendent restoration
could be fashioned. Nonetheless, the Torah came forth from

the living scholar class, not from Zion; from the authoritative teachers of the twofold Law, and not from Jerusalem.

As far as legal authority was concerned, the Palestinian scholar class lost its vitality after the compilation of the Palestinian Talmud, after the abolition of the Palestinian Patriarchate (C.E. 425), and following its loss of control over the religious calendar. Nonetheless, in the non-legal realm creativity burst forth. First under Byzantium and then under the Muslim caliphate, scholars in Palestine expanded the aggadah in a highly original way, lifting biblical verses and their aggadic explications out of tannaitic and amoraic teachings, adding novel interpretations of their own, and intermingling the two to spin out homilies for edification and instruction. Some collections of these homilies survive; from them we can derive little secure knowledge of how the homilies were communicated by live preachers to live listeners. It does not seem at all likely, however, that the compilations were simply academic exercises. What is striking is the fact that these compilations all seem to have a Palestinian, not a Babylonian, provenance — which suggests that the encircling Christian environment may have been the prime mover. Once Christianity became the imperial religion, Judaism was put on the defensive. The gospel of Christ was justified from Hebrew Scriptures, and Paul had proclaimed the Christians to be the real Israel.

Palestinian Jewish Creativity

Encircled, harassed, and challenged, the Palestinian Jewish scholars had to mount a counterattack that centered on the true meaning of the biblical text. They had to counter Christian homilies, designed to convert, with Jewish homilies, designed to strengthen the Jews' determination to remain steadfast. Drawing on the rich store of tannaitic and amoraic exegesis, and giving rein to their own imagination and fantasies, these gifted preachers taught that God had chosen the Israel of the flesh to be for all time the Israel of the spirit; that God had given the twofold Law and lore to Moses, and this twofold Law had been preserved with absolute integrity by Joshua, the Elders, the prophets, the men of the Great Assembly, and the successive generations of bona fide teachers. God had selected Israel to proclaim the good news of eternal life. When the Messiah did finally appear, he would confirm Israel's mission, not deny it; reconfirm the twofold Law, not abrogate it. The road to salvation was not meant to be easy, however. The sufferings of Israel aroused all kinds of doubts and winnowed the true believer from the false. But those who remained steadfast, God would save.

Not every Jew may have been sufficiently fortified by these homilies to withstand the eloquence of the great Byzantine preachers and the allure of a life free of persecution, but Jews in very large numbers remained loyal to their own system of salvation. For Christian preachers merely urged Jews to shift from one system of internalization to another. The ultimate value system of Christianity was almost identical with that of Judaism. Both Judaism and Christianity asked the Jew to make a decision affecting eternal life, a decision resting on which of the two systems of salvation had read Scriptures aright.

The Palestinian scholar class was thus compelled by its Christian environment to concentrate on the text of Scriptures in order to parry and expose Christian exegesis. Both parties struggled for control of Scriptures with Pharisaic concepts and Pharisaic tools. Both used the midrashic method; i.e., a biblical text was proof of a non-biblical concept, not a literal communication. They also freely indulged in aggadah, using an imagined fact, an original paradigm, an instructive figment of the imagination shaped to edify, strengthen, defend, and convert without regard to factuality. The Pharisees' shattering of worldly time, structure, and process, their consignment of historical fact to irrelevance, their severance of internal from external reality—all sustained and nurtured both Jewish and Christian preaching. Jewish midrash was developed to block Christian midrash; Jewish aggadah was expanded to offset Christian aggadah.

This concentration on preaching from Scriptures was a Palestinian preoccupation. Babylonian scholars were not challenged in this way since the Zoroastrians did not recognize the Bible as a sacred book, and the Muslims did not root their claims in allusive prophecies within the Old Testament.

The decline of the Palestinian scholar class in the legal sphere was thus offset by its shaping of the homiletical *midrash*. The commentative method of explicating Scripture, i.e., the explanation of one biblical verse after another, was developed in contrast to the method used in the Mishnah, in the Babylonian Talmud, and by previous Palestinian scholars in the Palestinian Talmud. This method drew on biblical verses as the situation demanded, using them as texts to prove a point. The Babylonian scholar class therefore largely ignored the novel commentative mode during the heyday of Islamic hegemony, but it flourished among the Jews in Palestine and in Byzantium and attained a sacrosanct status in Christian feudal Europe when Jewish scholars saw in it and in homiletical *midrash* a strong buttress for Judaism in a Christian environment.

Shaping and Reshaping Forms

ﻉ۹ The rise of the Babylonian scholar class alongside the Palestinian scholar class; the simultaneous utilization of the Mishnah by each as the authoritative text of the twofold Law and the tannaitic *beraitot* as authoritative corollaries; the ultimate triumph of the Babylonian Talmud over the Palestinian Talmud; the emergence in Palestine under Christian pressure of the homiletical *midrash*—all these reveal the dynamic, problem-solving quality of Pharisaic ideas. Both the Babylonian and Palestinian scholar class were spun off by the Mishnah, yet the two shaped its meaning to solve problems set by two highly differentiated environments. The need to function in the Sassanian Diaspora took precedence over the wish to replicate the teachings of the Palestinian Tannaim. The Jew shaped new forms to solve problems, rather than replicate forms that were no longer functional.

This shaping and reshaping of forms reveals a penchant for innovation and a highly pragmatic orientation toward tradition. When traditional forms, motifs, and concepts provided a solution, they were invoked. When they blocked a solution, they were reinterpreted or bypassed and consigned to pious veneration. To preserve the integrity of the Unity Principle, and of the Pharisees' interpretation of it, virtually any change was deemed legitimate. So long as the scholar class affirmed that the Law might be reinterpreted so that it might be preserved, and that the Father God had revealed it to give human beings eternal life and resurrection, scholars were free to spell out the specifics as their situation dictated. Pharisaic concepts thus proved to inspire innovation rather than repetition. They preserved through change, instead of destroying through preservation.

V
Medieval Ways
to Salvation

Diversity in Unity

&. Islam, unlike Zoroastrianism, had an umbilical relationship to Judaism. Mohammed created a distinctive variation of
the Unity Principle as it had been transformed by the Pharisees. Although it was no more reducible to Pharisaism than
Christianity was, Islam nonetheless reaffirmed the threefold
principles of Pharisaism: (1) a single Father God, (2) internalization of God's revealed will, and (3) individual salvation
through eternal life.

Islam, like Judaism and Christianity, proved to be a developmental religion. It continually generated form after form
as it confronted problems of organization and control that
had not been envisaged in the Koran. Mohammed had proclaimed his message in the Koran for a relatively simple society; his followers conquered societies that were highly diverse
and complex and resistant to the literal teachings of the Koran. As each new problem was solved with a new variation of
Islamic teaching, Islam revealed itself to be a generative system. The history of Islam is thus the history of multiple
Islams, even as the history of Judaism and Christianity is the

history of multiple Judaisms and Christianities. Yet each distinctive form of Islam is within Islam; each is interlinked with every other because each was generated out of a single primal form; each is, in its distinctive way, a variation on the theme of unity.

I cannot do justice in this book to the complexity of the interrelationships between Jews and Muslims and between Judaism and Islam. Their beginnings stretch back to the time of Mohammed himself; their end is not yet in sight. There was never a time from the birth of Islam to the present when large numbers of Jews did not live under Muslim rule. There is no phase in Islamic history that does not resonate through Jewish history and no form of Islam that does not have its Jewish counterpart. And though during many periods the differences between Islam and Judaism were stressed to rationalize hostility, these differences also were responsible for catalyzing some of the most creative Jewish achievements of the Middle Ages.

To comprehend the dynamics of Jewish history in Islam, one must distinguish between eastern and western Islam — between the Islamic societies of the Near and Middle East and the societies of Andalusia, i.e., southern Spain.

Eastern Islam

ह♣ First let us consider eastern Islam. Despite Mohammed's hostility toward Jews, and despite the fact that this hostility was incorporated into the Koran, both the Umayyad and Abbasid dynasties proved to be very tolerant toward the Jews. Even though the discriminatory land tax imposed upon non-Muslims effectively drove the Jews out of agriculture, this was offset by the widening of opportunities afforded Jews by the expansion of commerce and industry, and by urbanization. By breaking their last tie to agriculture, the Muslims stamped the Jews permanently as an urban people.

Until the rise of the Zionist movement at the end of the nine-teenth century, most Jews remained urban dwellers. Sever-ance from agriculture fostered mobility. Like every other major development in Jewish history, this economic shift was to have consequences that were both tragic and creative.

Under the Umayyads and the Abbasids, Jews prospered and found their way to virtually every part of the Muslim em-pire. Thriving communities sprang up in North Africa and Spain. The Abbasids, particularly, encouraged Jewish enter-prise, with the result that by the tenth century a small but sig-nificant class of large-scale merchants and bankers had come to play a prominent role in the finances of the caliph. The poli-cies of the caliphs were pragmatic, following from a reading of their own interests, not from a reading of the Koran.

The Gaonate and the Unity Principle

è♣ This pragmatism is seen not only in the economic sphere, but in the sphere of religion and ideas as well. The caliphs be-stowed virtually complete autonomy upon the Jews. The of-fice of the Exilarch, already in existence under the Sassanians, was now given new life. In addition, the authority of the two-fold Law was accorded official recognition in the form of a novel institution called the *Gaonate*, so called because the heads of the Mesopotamian academies of Sura and Pumbe-dita bore the honorific title of *Gaon* ("Excellency," pl.: *Geonim*). Each Gaon was selected by an oligarchal elite; between them they exercised control over the legal system of Judaism throughout Islamic lands, claiming exclusive rights to deter-mine the meaning of the Babylonian Talmud, i.e., to decide which laws were applicable. Since the Geonim determined not only ritual law but economic and social law as well, they wielded great power. And though each consulted the other scholars in his academy, he was in no way bound by their views. The Gaonate was a new institution, and its claims to power were novel. It had not existed during the Sassanian period, nor was its structure modeled after that of the Babylonian scholar class. It did not hark back to an institution prevailing in tannaitic or Pharisaic times. Although the Gaonate venerated the Talmud, the Mishnah, and the Bible, it acted independently, with full power to solve problems, to decide what the twofold Law meant *now*.

The Sassanian Jewish scholar class had been loosely structured, with each scholar expressing his own legal and doctrinal opinions and having his views preserved in the completed version of the Babylonian Talmud; but the Gaonate was a tight oligarchical system. Membership in the academies of Sura and Pumbedita was restricted to seventy oligarchs, plus the Gaon. Seats were hereditary, with the exception of that of the Gaon, who was elected for life almost always from among a limited group of aristocratic families. As Gaon, he alone had the authority to render a final decision on the Law. He listened to the opinions of his colleagues, but decision was rendered in his name, and it did not necessarily reflect majority opinion.

Where was the Jewish precedent for this? In the tannaitic period, the position of the Nasi had been hereditary, but not that of other scholars. The case of the Gaonate reverses this situation. In both the tannaitic and amoraic periods, the names of individual scholars are associated with recorded opinions, but under the Gaonate for a period of about three centuries scholars other than Geonim are rarely mentioned.

Here once again we find the Unity Principle operating. A new form of Judaism was created to cope with the novel problems that the caliphal system and the teachings of Islam posed for the Jews. The Gaonate's models are to be sought in the surrounding Islamic institutions, as well as in some earlier Jewish forms. The structure of the Gaonate looks more like absolutism of the caliphs than individualism of the earlier

Jewish scholar class. Yet, the new Jewish form is not simply mimicking the non-Jewish; it is, rather, the end product of participating in a society that has itself been restructured, and it is no more nor less Jewish than the Patriarchate, the *Beth Din ha-Gadol*, the priestly system. What we observe is an amalgamation of forms. Though the structure of the Gaonate is no replication of anything Jewish that preceded it, the Gaonate still grounded its claim to authority in what had come before. One cannot identify the Gaonate, with all its novelty, without simultaneously exposing its linkages to previous Jewish forms and concepts.

The Karaites

֍   The oligarchical structure of the Gaonate and the dynastic structure of the Exilarchate provoked a highly creative schismatic form of Judaism, Karaism, which emerged in the eighth century and reached its apogee in the eleventh century. Since this movement made considerable headway against the establishment, the Gaonate, and the Exilarchate, it provides an especially luminous example of the range of possibility inherent in the Unity Principle as it had been transformed by Pharisaism. Here was an heretical movement seemingly committed to the extirpation of the twofold Law. Karaism claimed that the Gaonate and the Exilarchate had no legitimate grounds for their authority because the Oral Law, found in the Mishnah and Talmud, was not divine in origin. The Karaites called for a return to the Bible. But they did not advocate that the Bible be read literally. They too recognized the need for at least some interpretation, which they regarded as equivalent to the literal meaning of the biblical text, unlike the interpretations of the twofold Law, which the Karaites denounced as falsifying God's word.

Thus the Karaites did not return to the Pentateuch. Not only did they interpret it, but they were also firm believers in immortality and in the coming of the Messiah. Indeed, some of their most violent attacks denounced the Jewish establishment as the pillar of the Exile, and thus a major obstacle to the liquidation of the Diaspora and the onset of the messianic age. Furthermore, the Karaites were drawn more to the prophetic books of the Bible than to the Pentateuch, seeing similarities between the prophets and their response to their own contemporary situation. The sanctity they assigned to the non-Pentateuchal texts was itself an inheritance from the very system of Judaism they were combating. Among the Karaites, scholars exercised leadership. Here too they were following in the footsteps of their antagonists. The Karaites had no more biblical sanction for the right of their scholars to explicate Scripture than the Gaonate did. The freedom of the individual Karaite scholar to interpret the text as he read it was anathema to the Pentateuch that the Karaites claimed as their guide.

When we analyze the religious practices and doctrines introduced by the Karaites, they show an uncanny resemblance to Rabbinic and Muslim prototypes, but none, except symbolically, to the practices and doctrines of the Pentateuch. Thus the Karaites could no more do without their place of prayer than other Jews could do without their synagogue, or the Muslims without their mosque. The Karaites' seventy-day period of fasting looks more like the Muslim Ramadan than like any of the fasts described in the Bible. Karaism thus developed according to the same rules as the established form of Judaism, basing itself, however unconsciously, on the Pharisaic model, committed to the same Unity Principle.

Were there time, we could follow Karaism through a history that, for a time at least, reveals a great capacity to adapt to new situations. But this would take us too far afield. Karaism proved very viable in the Near East, but it won only a foothold in the Christian West, and we have no way to test whether it could have adapted to the unique problems which Western

Christendom set for Jews. The fact that it could no longer develop viable new forms in Islamic lands after the sixteenth century seems to indicate that it may have lacked the capacity essential for infinite adaptation.

The Abbasid Empire

ào Although Karaism was born in the middle of the eighth century, its heyday was in the tenth and eleventh centuries, for these were the years that witnessed the dissolution of the Abbasid Empire. These were rough days for the Jews living in Baghdad and nearby lands. The Gaonate and the power of the Exilarch, wracked by corrosive rivalry, shrank gradually to become of only regional significance. The Gaonate no longer evoked awe and reverence, and the Exilarch's power practically disappeared. Relations between Jews and Muslims were no longer as cordial or as enriching as they had been. The expansion of the Abbasids had opened up creative possibilities for the Jews; their collapse spread stagnation among the Jews and atrophy within Judaism. Only Karaism was creative, for its doctrines of asceticism and gloom sacramentalized its adherents' experience of disintegration and breakdown. This was neither the first nor the last creative response to social decay among Jews. Early Christianity had been one; Hasidism in the eighteenth century would be another.

As empires rise they integrate areas gained by conquest in such a way as to give impetus to economic growth. This was true of the Abbasid Empire. Once an empire is consolidated and ceases to draw in new areas, economic growth alone proves insufficient to compensate for the loss of new tributaries, and a process of economic disintegration sets in. In the past this process was inevitable, for the ruling classes were concerned with dynastic and political power, not economic growth. They demanded a steady flow of wealth to support their power, without regard to the development of an economic infrastructure that could nurture sustained growth. So long as plundering through conquest continued, the illusion would prevail that the sources of wealth were unlimited. This illusion was fed by the initial surge of economic growth that attended the unification process. By bringing separate territories under a single rule, many economic opportunities were opened up; with no basic change in the mode of production, there was nevertheless a temporary burst of economic growth.

The Abbasid Empire, like the Roman, is a classic example of this process. By spreading the mantle of protection over a territory sprawling from India to North Africa, the Abbasids encouraged a surge of economic activity, particularly in the areas of international trade and finance. By the tenth century, however, the economic demands of the imperial center at Baghdad had outstripped the rate of economic growth. Only some significant breakthrough in the mode of primary agricultural and industrial production could have reversed the trend; but the Abbasid state was geared to wealth consumption, not to wealth production. The failure to solve this basic problem let loose disintegrative tendencies.

Paradoxically, the splitting up of so grand an empire frequently frees regional economic possibilities from constraints. Once severed from the imperial center, economically productive areas, no longer drained by taxation to support the huge demands of the imperial ruling groups, flourish. As a rule, this heightened economic well-being tends to be of short duration, because steady economic growth is not sustained and capital is not augmented. A decline sets in, weakening the structure of the regional society and making it ripe for conquest by some new imperial system. The dialectic of unification and disintegration begins all over again.

The collapse of Abbasid hegemony did indeed release viable societies in North Africa, and, as might be anticipated, in such thriving centers as Kairouan in Tunisia, Jewish communities emerged with their own independent scholar class. A period of heightened creativity ensued, even as the vitality of the Gaonate in Baghdad was wasting away.

Andalusia and The Golden Age

෬ These North African communities are of considerable interest, but I prefer to center attention on Muslim Spain, on Andalusia, for there a distinctive Jewry emerged that exemplifies most clearly the dynamics we are investigating. The creative accomplishments of the Jews in Muslim Spain attained such extraordinary heights that their time is still looked back to longingly as one of the greatest of the golden ages in Jewish history. But it must be stressed that their achievement was possible only because Islam served as the catalyst.

Although Spain had been free of direct Abbasid control, it had nonetheless acknowledged a kind of dependence by recognizing the caliph of Baghdad as the legitimate spokesman for Islam. In the tenth century, this tie was sundered and the Cordovan caliphate revealed itself in all its splendor.

Andalusia was the jewel of Islamic civilization, fresh, unmarred by the clutter and debris of the long-lived cultures of the Near East. Here, Islam could build cities expressing its genius undistorted. Here, sensuous beauty evoked admiration, not fear. Here, economic growth bordered on the miraculous: fields yielded abundance; workshops, a delightful array of wares; commerce and wealth were unbounded; the spirit gave birth to joyful song; the mind, to incisive thought. For Jews Islam braided a garland of freedom.

Hasdai ibn Shaprut

෬ Never before in the Diaspora had the Jews enjoyed horizons so expansive and a soil so fruitful. Their well-being during the height of Abbasid rule in Baghdad was pale in comparison. Abd ar-Rahman III (912-61) appointed a Jewish physician, Hasdai ibn Shaprut, to carry out the foreign policy of his regime. Nothing quite like this had developed in eastern Islam. Jewish bankers may have lent money to the caliphs, but they had never been appointed to any post of authority over Muslims. Indeed, the Koran and the sacred traditions of Islam were in accord: only a Muslim could exercise rule in a Muslim state. But Abd ar-Rahman III proved to be his own exegete.

As the court favorite, Hasdai ibn Shaprut was endowed by Abd ar-Rahman with authority over the Jewish communities of Andalusia. He was given a free hand, and he used his hand freely, demonstrating his independence of the Gaonate by establishing an independent school for the study and mastery of the twofold Law. On his own authority he appointed judges to administer this law. He set the style for the Jewish upper classes by patronizing generously every kind of intellectual and spiritual enterprise.

Hasdai broke the Geonic hegemony, but he did not break with the sources of Geonic authority, the Mishnah and Talmud. Nor did he depreciate the Geonim or hold their decisions in contempt. But he did affirm the right of Andalusian Jewry to chart its own course.

And this they did, creating a novel structure, independent of any previous Jewish structure. Hasdai ibn Shaprut was called *Nasi*, a prince, not Gaon or Exilarch. He was the ruler of the Jewish community and the founder of the academy, but he was not himself the head of the scholar class. He appointed judges, but he was not himself a judge. For his role and function, there was no Jewish precedent. Judah the Patriarch, the promulgator of the Mishnah, had also been called the *Nasi*, but his title meant he was head of the scholar class. The title conferred on Hasdai, in contrast, was meant to convey the notion of sovereign. Hasdai was for the Jews what Abd ar-Rahman was for his Moslem subjects — the caliph.

The Court Jews and Samuel ha-Nagid

&❧ The pattern set by Abd ar-Rahman III and Hasdai ibn Shaprut was adhered to even after the collapse of the united Cordovan caliphate. In the various independent emirates which replaced it, a court Jew like Hasdai was usually appointed who both gave counsel to the emir and presided over the Jewish communities within the emirate. Just as the title emir displaced caliph, his title was now *Nagid*, not Nasi. Again it should be noted that there was no Jewish precedent for this office, even though the term *nagid* is found in the Bible, referring to kings.

One of these court Jews, Samuel ha-Nagid of Granada (993-1056), outshone even Hasdai. He was appointed vizier — an office that, in effect, made Samuel the power behind the throne. But Samuel's talents were not confined to statesmanship. He was a warrior of no mean ability, leading the troops of Islam into battle against the enemies of the emir. He was also a poet, a grammarian, and, according to traditional scholarship, an eminent authority on Jewish law. Samuel not only ruled the Jewish community, but he was also the foremost spokesman for the scholar class and the head of the academy.

New Vistas of Creativity

&❧ With such leaders, talented Jews were spurred to emulation. Every nook and cranny of the mind sprang alive. The Talmud ceased to be the only intellectual preoccupation. Scholars were drawn to study the Hebrew language scientifically. Biblical texts were analyzed to extract their grammar, and to discover the meaning of words in context. The results were stunning, particularly in grammatical research. The crucial role and nature of the verb in the Hebrew language was discovered.

The interest in language was accompanied by the pursuit of philosophy. A rare mind, Solomon ibn Gabirol (1021-69), excited by Neoplatonism, wrote a purely philosophic treatise, *Fons Vitae*, "Fountain of Life," and interwove his platonic ideas with the idiom of Judaism in a masterpiece of liturgical splendor, "The Royal Crown." His philosophic interests were shared by many of his fellow Jews.

The poet was the fairest fruit of this breakthrough, able to utilize an unspoken language, Hebrew, to vie with a spoken language, Arabic, in the shaping of truly great poetry. To have imitated the Psalmist in Hebrew poetry might not have been difficult, but to bend Hebrew to Arabic verse forms could hardly have been accomplished without a thorough awareness of the structure of the Hebrew language. Secure in their mastery of the language, the Jewish poets left no realm of experience unsung. Philosophical treatises were written in verse, and even grammar was elevated to poetic heights. But it was their reaching into the depths of experience that made the poets the crowning glory of this golden age. For the first time in centuries the individual was able to break out from the constraints of a tight religious ideology. Pharisaism had spurned poetry. Even when poetry served as text, as when a psalm was studied, the form of explication was prose.

The Golden Age in Spain unleashed a poetic revolution, but the revolution was spun off by Islam, not by the Judaism of the Mishnah and the Talmud. Yet this revolution was not a revolt against authority, for the greatest poets of this age were themselves the authorities. It was not a revolt against the Talmud, but a novel mode of expressing its most enduring teachings. In some respects it was a translation back into poetry, poetry that had been frozen into prose; for the finest creations of the poets of the Golden Age are liturgical gems. God as Father and King; the human as frail and helpless; the soul yearning for immortality; sin foreshadowing eternal doom — these themes were the warp and woof of Pharisaic Judaism. But it was not only the poetic form that infused worn motifs with life. Now the soul was free to respond to nature and to the senses in a non-stereotyped way. The selfsame poet who filtered life through the senses could also experience the depth of a personal relationship with God.

A final achievement should not be overlooked. The Jewish poets regained the capacity for laughter — a capacity in remarkably short supply in the Bible, the Mishnah, the Talmud, and the homiletical *midrash*. They not only found humor, but they shared it with other Jews in the sacred tongue.

Judah haLevi

೩ಖ Highly responsive to the Islamic environment was Judah haLevi (1075-1140). His love for the people of God and for the land of God was so intense that he left Spain to journey to the Holy Land, where he died. Yet his great philosophical work defending Judaism and the uniqueness of the Jewish people, the *Kuzari*, was written in Arabic, in a dialogue form, with such philosophical sophistication that his most cogent anti-philosophical arguments could be grasped only by another philosopher. The form, the structure, the language, the mode of defense are not patterned after biblical, Mishnaic, or Talmudic models, but are Hellenic and Islamic in inspiration. Even more telling is haLevi's *Ode to Zion*. The yearning and love for the Holy Land is unmatched, even by the Psalmist. But the poetic form does not derive from the psalms or from any other Jewish source. Rhyme, meter, and structure throughout are indebted to Islamic modes. A love for God, Judaism, and Zion expressed in poetic forms made available by Islam!

The Golden Age did not last. The economic growth that had made it possible was not sustained. The rise of the emir-

ates did overcome the disintegration of the Cordovan caliphate. They were buoyed up by economic resources that they
did not replenish; their accumulated capital went a long way,
but it was not inexhaustible. When the fanatical Almohades
swept into Andalusia from North Africa in 1148, the gold was
transmuted to dross and creativity to despair. The Almohades ushered in the new era by giving the Jews the option of
becoming Muslims or getting out.

Maimonides

ﻚ   Among the refugees was a remarkable and gifted young
man, Moses Maimonides (1135-1204), who in so many ways
epitomizes Muslim-Jewish interaction that I shall single him
out before drawing certain conclusions about this epoch.

Born in Cordova when the Golden Age was coming to an
end, Maimonides was the heir of some of its most gleaming
facets. And since he went from a persecuting Islam to a region
of Islam that nurtured Jews, his creative endeavors fall within
the scope of both Western and Eastern Islam.

The genius of Maimonides reveals itself in two realms,
Jewish law and philosophy. Few Jews have achieved such heroic stature. His commentary on the Mishnah is still highly regarded. His code of Jewish law, the *Mishneh Torah*, is found
wherever there is a synagogue. His philosophic treatise *The
Guide to the Perplexed* is held in the highest esteem as the greatest philosophical achievement of a Jewish thinker, ranking
with the work of Averroes and Thomas Aquinas. There can be
no question that most Jews today would grant him rank as
one of their great spiritual heroes.

Yet his towering genius owes as much to his Islamic envi
ronment as to any previous form of Judaism. This is evident
not only in his philosophic treatise, the *Guide*, but in his great
works on Jewish Law. For Maimonides organized the whole
corpus of Jewish Law by applying principles derived from

Aristotelian concepts of logic, hierarchy, and order. He did not follow preexisting Jewish models, not even the Mishnah, even though the orderly character of the Mishnah impressed him more favorably than the disorderly quality of the Talmud, and its seeming awareness of broad general principles attracted his admiration. In the *Mishneh Torah*, he had the opportunity to spell out at the very outset what he considered to be the metaphysical foundations of Judaism. He thus begins not with laws but with first principles.

This was a radical departure from all precedent. No previous scholar of the Law had ever begun with first principles. No previous scholar had ever posited a metaphysic so universal that he did not even use one of the traditional names for God. Maimonides, however, boldly affirms in his very first paragraph that the foundation of knowledge is the awareness that there is a *matzui*, a Being. Not Yahweh or Elohim or Shaddai, but *matzui*, Being. He identifies this Being with the traditional names of God only after he has defined the Unmoved Mover in nontraditional terms. Maimonides begins not with an historical revelation, but rather with a metaphysical one. *Matzui* was always accessible to the refined active mind, whether Jewish or not.

Whence this notion? Surely not from any preexistent Jewish model. The source is Aristotle. Maimonides filtered Judaism through Aristotelian categories and modes of thought. Aristotle represented order, logic, rational hierarchy, first principles. The authoritative texts of Judaism were in logical disarray, and lacked a clear and precise philosophical formulation of what was meant by God, revelation, and immutable laws.

Maimonides was a revolutionary, but he did not give birth to a schism, even though for some decades it seemed that perhaps he had. He claimed that he had made explicit what had always been implicit. He insisted that the Law in all its minutiae had to be obeyed. Even his philosophical treatise, the *Guide*, made clear that the philosopher had to set an example for the masses by meticulously observing all the concrete laws. The upshot was another form of Judaism, created out of the philosophic ideas spread before Jews by Islamic thinkers.

Islam and the Jews

દૈ» This remarkable age of Jewish creativity had been catalyzed by Islam. It was Islam, especially in Andalusia, that had created the climate conducive to innovation and experimentation. The society was Islamic. The Jews were a minority, living on the sufferance of their Islamic rulers. When these were hostile, Jews were forced to flee. When they were benign, Jews reaped the fruit of Islamic excursions into grammar, philology, philosophy, and poetry.

The Jews responded by enriching Judaism, braiding the threads of an Islamic civilization into Jewish designs. They were no slavish imitators. Jewish grammarians were intrigued primarily by the riddle of Hebrew, not Arabic. Jewish philosophers were concerned with the Father God of the two-fold Law, not with Mohammed's Allah. The rhyme and the meter were Arabic creations, but they were not artificially imposed upon the Hebrew language. Rather were these techniques employed to blend numberless biblical allusions and idioms into exquisite poetic compositions. Maimonides' *Mishneh Torah* and his *Guide to the Perplexed* were offered as solutions to problems facing Jews, not Muslims. Yet without Islam there would have been no Jewish poetic awakening. Without Islam, Judaism could not have enjoyed this Jewish Golden Age.

Before turning from Islam to Christian Europe, I should like to underscore a crucial generalization. The relationship of Jews to Islam was complex, at times positive, at times negative. During the tenth century, Jews living under the Abbasids in the east were experiencing a major breakdown, while Jews in Andalusia were embarking on a golden age. In the twelfth century, Maimonides fled from a hostile Islam in Andalusia, tarried briefly in hostile Islamic North Africa, only to become welcome in Islamic Egypt, where he became physician to the vizier of Saladin. Islam created climates favorable to Jewish creativity and climates altogether inimical to Jews. The record is clear: the differences setting Islam apart from Judaism did not always generate hostility. The anti-Jewish passages in the Koran did not keep Hasdai ibn Shaprut from handling the foreign affairs of his caliph or Samuel ha-Nagid from serving as vizier in Granada.

Christian Europe

ે Medieval Christendom was no less complex than medieval Islam. Christian Europe can no more than Islam be treated as a single entity, nor can the configuration of one epoch be made congruent with another. Germany, France, England, Spain, Italy, Poland — each had a history of its own. Jews, drawn into these histories, likewise had Jewish histories of their own. The history of the Jews in Germany is not the same as the history of the Jews in Italy. Not only did the Jews undergo different experiences, but they organized their communities differently. Nor should it be forgotten that the history of the Jews in Christian Europe was going on simultaneously with the history of the Jews living in Islamic lands. Or that Jews had different histories in different Islamic lands.

Here then is a palpable uniqueness of Jewish history. The history of Christian Europe may be kaleidoscopic, but it does not include the history of Islam as an essential experience. The Christians of Europe were related to Islam externally, not internally. Christian princes fought the Muslims, and at times in Spain or the Near East, Christians ruled over Muslims and Muslims over Christians; but these moments do not add up to much, given the range of both Muslim and Christian history. But the situation is different with the Jews. Their history is simultaneously Muslim and Christian history, even though they experience this history as Jews and refract this history through Judaism. The complexity of this experience has no counterpart in Christian or Islamic experience.

Though the various parts of Christendom differed from one another, they do appear to share a basic unity when compared with Islam. The Church stands out sharply against the mosque, and the feudal system against the various forms of political rule in Islamic lands. The manorial system functioning in Europe was unique to Christendom, as was the system of fealty. Equally distinctive was the European town with its self-governing character. Feudal kings, barons, knights, popes, and bishops are types unduplicated in the Islamic world.

The Jewish Community and Its Structure

→ The first Jewish communities that emerged by the tenth century in the Christian-feudal world are not replicas either of the Jewries of Sassanian Babylonia or of Islamic Baghdad. They appear as integral elements of the feudal system. They sport a charter, enjoy considerable autonomy, and carry out their economic activities as befitting itinerant merchants, sedentary burghers, or large-scale moneylenders to kings, barons, and bishops. Already their Judaism mirrors their total involvement in a Christian feudal society.

This is strikingly apparent in their system of self-government. Because within the feudal structure each town had an independent relationship to the overlord, no town had any legal authority over another. Towns might agree to cooperate, but no town surrendered its internal autonomy. As a consequence, each Jewish community was independent of every other community, since each community received its charter separately from the overlord. Each community was thus free to have its own scholar class determine the law without interference from the scholar class of some other community.

The training of such a scholar class therefore had very different goals from the training of a scholar class in Sassanian Babylonia or in the Abbasid realms, or even in Cordova and Granada. The latter societies functioned under a highly centralized authority, whether emperor, caliph, or emir; and their Jewish scholar class legislated for all Jews living under the same ruler. Judges were appointed from above. Even when, as in Sassanian Babylonia, individual scholars enjoyed considerable freedom to determine the Law, their opinions were authoritative throughout the Sassanian empire.

In Christian-feudal Europe by contrast, the scholar class had to be prepared to handle Jewish law in an independent way, in a small self-governing community jealous of its prerogatives. Furthermore, the scholars had to determine the law in a Christian-feudal society out of the Talmud, a work which had developed in response to problems raised by Sassanian society, problems far different from those they now faced. The Talmud could be used effectively, therefore, only if the scholar was trained in casuistry and dialectics; it had to be searched for possibilities, not fixed decisions. Each community chose a scholar, who enjoyed a large measure of autonomy, but had to function effectively as the legal and religious authority of that community. Mastery of the texts enabled the scholar to be flexible, innovative, and creative.

The Scholar Class of Medieval Europe

ঽ❧ The scholar class of Christian-feudal France, Germany, and, after 1066, England thus had to function in a novel way. They venerated the scholar class of the Talmud and the Mishnah and respected the work of the scholar classes of the Islamic world, but they developed their own unique personality. Perhaps nowhere is their audacious originality more evident than in their reintroduction of the concept of ordination and along with it the title of *rabbi*. Both had evaporated with the codification of the Mishnah by Judah ha-Nasi. In Babylonia bona fide scholars were called by the honorific title *rav*, teacher, but not rabbi. Even the compilers of the Babylonian Talmud bore only this title, while the Geonim who wielded vast power and reduced all other scholars to virtual anonymity did not restore either ordination or the title rabbi.

The scholars in Andalusia were called either *hahamim*, "sages," or, when appropriate, *dayyanim*, "judges." Therefore, when Maimonides systematized the laws of the Talmud in his *Mishneh Torah*, he made it clear that ordination could be revived only after the restoration of the Sanhedrin in an independent Palestine. So long as Jews lived in the Diaspora, there were *hahamim*, who were learned in the law and philosophy, and *dayyanim*, judges, who handled litigation—but not ordained *rabbis*. Maimonides even went so far as to affirm that the Exilarch, a descendant of David and not necessarily himself an outstanding scholar, had the regal prerogative of appointing judges anywhere in the Diaspora with or without the consent of the individual communities.

Rashi

ਵੈ What no scholar class had dared to do since the time of the Mishnah, the Jewish scholar class of Christian-feudal Europe did, with seeming disarming naiveté. Confronted as they were with the problems of a decentralized feudal system and a network of autonomous Jewish communities, they, under the leadership of their most brilliant exemplar, Rashi (Rabbi Solomon ben Isaac, 1040 1109), recognized the need to secure their position to offer leadership by virtue of an authority which could not be challenged by laymen. By restoring the concept of ordination, by resurrecting the title rabbi, Rashi, in effect, issued *carte blanche* for limitless development of the legal potential lying dormant within the Talmud and awaiting dialectical exploitation.

Rashi not only pointed the way but developed the tools. Here the contrast with Maimonides is striking. Whereas Maimonides was irritated by the disorder, the confusion, the dialectical gymnastics, cluttering the Talmud and making it difficult to use for determining the final law, Rashi reveled in the freedom of option that its endless debates and contradictory opinions offered the independent scholar. Since he wanted to widen the room available to the scholar class for flexible decision-making, he wrote a commentary on the Talmud, not a code. Seeking to make the Talmud operational, he explains, interprets, draws the threads of reasoning together, explicates the dialectical method; he makes the Talmud a repository of legal possibilities, a spur to independent reasoning. And here too we find a startling contrast to Maimonides, who also wrote a commentary, but to the Mishnah, not the Talmud. The Mishnah attracted him because it was code-like, orderly, and relatively free of debate. By writing a commentary on it he hoped to reorder the Talmud, subsuming its basic legal principles and final decisions under the appropriate category within the Mishnah. To accomplish this end, he appended introductions to the basic segments of law and doctrine so that the more detailed comment would be held together by overarching principles.

Rashi, however, commentated on the Mishnah as an integral part of the Talmud. He did not use the Mishnah to supplant the discussions and the debate that follow it in the Gemara. Maimonides' commentary on the Mishnah and Maimonides' code, the *Mishneh Torah,* were the product of Islamic Judaism; Rashi's commentary on the Talmud, was a product of Christian-feudal Judaism.

Contrasting Worlds

❧ The differences between the two Jewish worlds are no
less striking in the realm of doctrine. Once again, Rashi and
Maimonides exemplify the contrasts. The latter was the son of
a highly urbanized, highly sophisticated, highly centralized
type of society. A wide gap separated the wealthy class from
the poverty stricken, the intellectual elite from the masses.
The Jewish population in the cities of Islam was large and its
class structure complex. Maimonides' mind inhabited a different world from that of the masses. For him, the literal
meaning of the Pentateuch was absurd, fit only for the untutored. Indeed, the *literal* meaning of all sacred literature, be it
Bible, Mishnah, or Talmud, was an affront to his philosophical mind. Since he could not believe that his spiritual heroes,
particularly Moses, could possibly have meant what they
said, he assumed that they spoke in as many tongues as there
were gradations of mind, compelled to adopt this method, so
he thought, because they were not simply philosophers communicating with other philosophers, but statesmen as well.
They were leaders of a highly differentiated society, peopled
by a hierarchy of minds, and if they were to fulfill their roles
as statesmen they had to adopt a multidimensional system of
communication. Maimonides reveals this system in the *Guide
to the Perplexed,* providing a glossary of corporeal, concrete
words that simultaneously have a noncorporeal, abstract and
metaphysical meaning. In this way he can rescue Moses for
the philosophers, even as he spares Moses for the masses.

Rashi, however, lived in the feudal-Christian world,
where the towns were not really cities and the Jewish population was never very large. Each community was largely self-
contained and on its own. The class structure was relatively
simple, with no wide gap yawning between the Jewish patri-
cian class and the so-called "lesser ones." Moreover, all classes
shared the same world of ideas. The intellectual elite was pre-

eminent for dialectical casuistry, not for philosophical sophistication. The literal meaning of the Pentateuch did not distress Rashi any more than it distressed his Christian neighbors; its naiveté charmed him. Far from being disturbed by the miraculous, he adds a miracle or two of his own. After all, he lived in a society where belief in miracles was widespread. God for him, as for the Pharisees, is a Person, a Father, an omnipotent King. God willed, and a world came into being. God was angry at Pharaoh, so God hardened Pharaoh's heart. God loved Elijah, so God whisked Elijah off to heaven. And if God so willed, God could in a twinkling of an eye transport all of Israel back to the Holy Land.

All of this and more is to be found in Rashi's commentary to the Bible. Here is a treasure of feudal-Christian Judaism. The simple stories in the Bible, the simple aggadic teachings of the Pharisees, Tannaim, and Amoraim, the simple teachings of the *midrash* are blended with the simple views of denizens of the feudal world. Metaphysics are as distant and alien to Rashi as Troyes and Mayence are from Fostat or Baghdad. Indeed, in those rare instances in which a sacred text might convey a metaphysical notion, Rashi offers a view of reality hardly distinguishable from that of the less learned.

Rashi's commentaries on the Bible and Talmud became templates for all Christian-feudal Jewries. Rarely does one find such absolute congruence between a structure and its mode of thought. Rashi had solved all the basic problems for the Jewish Christian-feudal mind. The scholars who followed him in similarly structured societies were free to sharpen the tools that he had prepared. They did not have to fashion new ones.

The so-called *Tosaphists*, ardent admirers of Rashi, who flourished in the twelfth century, demonstrated how this sharpening was accomplished. These scholars, spared the need of writing additional commentaries to the Talmud by the brilliant work of their teacher, Rashi, devoted their energies to heightening the dialectical potential lying within the contradictions of the Talmud and Rashi's own commentary. An aspiring scholar could now be schooled for independence by exercising his dialectical talents.

Responsa

৵ The scholar class latched on to a literary form—the *responsa*—that encouraged independence. The form itself was not new; its origins trace back to the Geonic period, when communities throughout the Umayyad and Abbasid empires sent questions on law and doctrine to the Geonim, whose response was an authoritative answer. Since Geonim brooked no rivals, they did not have to defend their reasoning, and their answers tended to be short and sometimes curt.

The responsa form was exactly what the Jewish scholars in Christian-feudal Europe needed. With their commitment to the process of legal reasoning, the final law for them was not nearly as crucial as the method by which one came to a decision. Each individual scholar was independent. To gain a reputation in juristic circles, to keep one's casuistic tools sharpened, to justify a legal decision, the responsa were made to order. The scholar's independence only whetted his interest in how other scholars reasoned about similar cases. Some scholars obviously were more brilliant than others, and their reasoning frequently won considerable support from other scholars.

The responsa literature thus developed an inner dynamism that made for vigorous growth. Scholars who published responsa had to consider not only the Talmud, Rashi, and the Tosaphists, but fellow responsists too. As a consequence, the responsum could not be terse and authoritative; it had to weigh and measure the reasoning of all scholars who had dealt with the same issue.

The responsa form thus came to play a highly creative role. Laws simply could not become congealed, even when efforts were made from time to time to codify them. Even the most respected code became another legal source for the responsists to reason about. No code succeeded in curbing the flow of responsa.

The transformation of the responsa form from an authoritative pronouncement to a forum of dialectical reasoning and criticism was one of the distinctive achievements of the Jewish scholar class of Christian-feudal Europe. From its birthplace in France and Germany the form migrated, along with the feudal type of Jewish self-governing communal structure, into Provence, Spain, Italy, the Ottoman Empire, and Eastern Europe. And along with it came seminal works of independent jurists who turned to the Talmud as a repository of dialectical reasoning and not as an archive of fixed and immutable laws.

The Impetus for the Responsa

೩➫ Whence the source of this Jewish original? The answer by now will come as no surprise. Christian-feudal Europe is imprinted on both form and content of the responsa. Self-governing, independent, decentralized Jewish communities were a mirror image of the town society. The restoration of ordination and the emergence of the rabbi as an independent voice and power within the community was a Jewish refraction of the independent status and power of the Christian clergy sustained through ordination. The simple, even naive, picture of reality was a Jewish rendition of the dominant Christian world view. Without Christian-feudal society there would have been no Rashi, no Tosaphists, no rabbis, no proliferating responsa literature. Without Christian-feudal society Judaism would have been diminished. The pious Jew of today, who religiously studies Rashi and takes pride in being a loyal devotee of authentic tradition, would be startled indeed (assuming that he or she would either listen or comprehend) to learn that Rashi's holy commentary refracts the Christian-feudal world and that this venerated teacher was an audacious innovator, and not simply a passive transmitter of vintage law and doctrine.

This Christian-feudal form of Judaism proved to be flexible and resilient, capable of generating subforms and subsystems in response to the diverse types of Christian-feudal societies and in response to the complex changes that characterized the history of medieval Europe. Consider, for example, what happened when the Jews, expelled from France and England, were welcomed by Christian princes in the newly conquered cities of Christian Spain. These Jews brought along the self-governing type of community to which they had been accustomed. They likewise brought along a scholar class nurtured on independence, tutored in dialectical reasoning, and habituated to the responsa mentality. As the Jews of the conquering Christian princes, they transferred *their* system to Spain, superimposing *their* mode of Jewishness and Judaism on the Jewries whose roots were in Islam—Jewries structured along centralized lines of authority and with intellectual leaders who were philosophically, not dialectically, minded.

The Struggle for Authority

The superimposition was not welcomed. A bitter struggle raged for a generation or more in the thirteenth century, as feudal-Christian Jewry and its world view waged a relentless struggle against a Jewry and a Judaism that had been shaped by a Muslim environment. This warfare has been preserved in the records of the controversy between the supporters and opponents of Maimonides that broke out in the thirteenth century. Maimonides had become the intellectual and spiritual hero of the sophisticated Jewries of Provence and Spain.

The intellectual elite of Provence and Spain could not take the sacred literature literally; for them, Judaism could be meaningful only if grounded in a universal metaphysic. They supported a centralized system of authority to maintain class differentiation, and preferred a fixed law code to the potential anarchy inherent in the dialectical method.

The two systems first jostled each other in Provence; in its wealthy urban centers, such as Beziers and Perpignan, an amalgam of both systems forestalled violent collision. When, however, the Crusaders early in the thirteenth century remorselessly crushed the Count of Toulouse, making a shambles of enlightened Provençal society, the feudal type of Jewish leadership was encouraged to open a barrage against the Maimonidean heresy.

The details of the struggle need not detain us. Its meaning, however, ought to be underscored. Two highly original forms of Judaism were locked in battle because one was the Judaism of Islam, the other the Judaism of Christian-feudal Europe. Each was so distinctively the creation of interaction with its non-Jewish world that they confronted each other as enemies. Physical violence was restrained, but only because the non-Jewish ruling authorities refused to relinquish their monopoly on its use. The wish to root out heresy was expressed with venom, however, and such coercive weapons as excommunication were widely utilized. It is no exaggeration to affirm that the anti-Maimonidean Solomon of Montpellier (c. 1230) had much more in common with contemporary inquisitors than with such a philosophically minded Jew as David Kimhi (d. 1235), even though each dipped into the same reservoir of sacred texts to expose the heresy of the other.

The struggle was long and bitter. When it was over, though neither side could claim total victory, the self-governing type of Jewish community of the Christian-feudal world took over, along with the independent, dialectically oriented scholar class. Once power had been effectively transferred, the intensity of the struggle against the Maimonidean heresy subsided, and even a degree of freedom to dabble in philosophy was sanctioned.

The Zohar

 है The transformation of the ideological climate can be seen in the spreading popularity of an esoteric work, the *Zohar*, "Brilliance," published in Spain in the middle of the thirteenth century. The *Zohar* ascribes itself to the great tannaitic sage, Simeon bar Yohai. Moses de Leon, who circulated the work, denied that he had written it; it was, he claimed, a commentary that reached back to the tannaitic period. The book was written in Aramaic, not Hebrew. Its concern was the elucidation of the secret mysteries that God had hidden away in the naive wording of the Pentateuch. The mystical structure of reality is unfolded as emanations and gradations of Godliness, luring the mystically bent to spiral upward, by a process of refinement of the soul, to the highest of the spheres.

The *Zohar* was a unique response to the shattering by Christian feudalism of the rational and structured world of Muslim Spain. Disorder was more real than order; irrationality more permeating than rationality; the individual soul more dependent on communing with God than on understanding Him.

The intellectual world of Maimonides and Aristotle was out of joint and irrelevant. *The Guide to the Perplexed* was no guide at all. The secrets that Moses had sought to reveal were not, as alleged by Maimonides, the metaphysical truths of Aristotle, but the mystical truths of the *Zohar.* God was no Unmoved Mover, bereft of emotion and feeling. Rather, God was the lure of emotion, the source of compassion and love.

The *Zohar* broke with Maimonides' metaphysics, but not with his appeal to the intellectual elite. The *Zohar* was no more a book for the masses than was the *Guide*. In some ways it was even more difficult, for Aramaic could be understood only by the very learned. Moreover, its ideas presuppose minds trained to handle complex ideas. Like so many anti-philosophic works, it reached out to disillusioned and discontented philosophers who found their ideas bankrupt but their minds still sharp and active. The *Zohar* offered a mysticism for the intellectuals, a mystic experience which opened to those who can grasp intellectually that salvation lies in the abandonment of the intellect. Far from undermining an elite, it sustained and nurtured one.

Had the *Zohar* simply served as a solution for a disillusioned and disheartened intellectual elite, it would scarcely have justified mention here. But the *Zohar* became the cornerstone of the so-called Cabala, the mystical tradition that developed into a legitimate and authoritative rendition of Judaism. Though the *Zohar* was stocked with novelty, and though it was not, as claimed by its author, the repository of teachings from the tannaitic age, it enjoyed such a warm reception from the intellectual classes that it achieved almost canonical status. A potential source of heresy and disruption, the *Zohar* got a hearing largely because the Jewish scholar class of the Christian-feudal world had become habituated to the commentative mode of expression, which, by its very nature, proliferated a variety of ideas. So long as the commentator seemed to be reaffirming that the sacred text was the sole source of his exegesis, and so long as he refrained from divided loyalties (i.e., did not accord Aristotle or Plato equivalent authority), his novel opinions were taken as evidence of the endless store of teaching locked in the divine word. With the *Zohar* cast as the lost esoteric commentary of the sainted Simeon bar Yohai, its radically new ideas could be welcomed by true believers.

Lurianic Cabala and Shabbetai Zevi

ટ⬧ The *Zohar*, garlanded with esteem and sanctity, thus became a generating source for esoteric teachings that were to launch tumultuous mass movements. In the sixteenth century, in the city of Safed, a mystical movement associated with a cabalist, Isaac Luria, spread concepts which nearly turned the Jewish world upside down. These concepts—*gilgul*, "the transmigration of the soul"; *zimzum*, "the voluntary shrinking of God to make place for the world"; *shebirath ha-kelim*, "the shattering of the bowls containing the divine light"; *tikkun*, "the process of restoring these bowls by the collection of the lost divine sparks"—were taught by Isaac Luria and his followers and spread among the masses. They were no longer the esoteric doctrines of a mystical elite. The person of Isaac Luria became the focus, not a book. His teachings were transmitted orally, and when they began to circulate in writing they were made inseparable from his activity. His life became a paradigm for both the learned and the unlearned.

The volcanic possibilities inherent in the Lurianic type of Cabala—in contrast to the abstruse mysticism of the *Zohar*—erupted in the only messianic movement in Jewish history, which reached out to every part of the Diaspora. Shabbetai Zevi (1626-76), a disturbed but highly gifted and sensitive cabalist, hypnotized the masses, especially within the decaying Ottoman Empire. Even the learned could believe in him, because his doctrines were saturated with the teachings of the prestige-laden Cabala. Everything he said was as believable as *gilgul*, and as possible as the miraculous events in the life of Isaac Luria. The loyalty he stirred was so tumultuous that it seemed at one point to be on the very verge of exploding as a violent revolution against the Ottoman regime. His arrest and subsequent conversion to Islam shocked the multitude out of their frenzy, and the hysteria subsided.

Hasidism and the Baal Shem Tov

ба The power of cabalistic teachings to stir the masses did not die with Shabbetai however. About a century later, in Podolia and Volhynia, a saintly teacher and miracle-worker, the Baal Shem Tov (1700-60), won the hearts of the poor, semiliterate, and despairing village Jews and launched a movement of tremendous appeal and power, *Hasidism*. His teachings, though highly original, resonated with cabalistic motifs. Although he made no messianic claims, his faith in the Messiah's ultimate coming was sure and comforting. He became the prototype of a new leadership elite. The charismatic person, not the text, once again became the source of authority, for the Baal Shem Tov, like Jesus and Isaac Luria, was a teacher who did not write down his teachings. Concern with dialectical mastery of the Talmud and the legal literature was replaced by a concern with the untutored masses who loved to hear the tales of the wonder-working Baal Shem Tov. They enjoyed the homilies that intermingled the world of demons, the evil eye, and miraculous doings on earth and in heaven with the shimmering promise of the world to come with its gay feasting on the flesh of leviathan and its merry, but pious, drinking. They were transported as their *zaddik* – the "righteous leader," the title adopted by the new Hasidic elite – spun from the biblical verses worlds of fantasy without end – terrifying and reassuring, sad and joyous, threatening and promising. One did not have to know the Bible or Talmud, or *Zohar*. One simply had to listen and allow one's imagination to play. If a person could feel, could dream, and could put simple trust in the *zaddik*, his or her salvation was more certain than that of the most learned dialectician whose heart was cold and whose dreams were sober.

The Ebb and Flow of Influences

ફ્ફ્ The migration of the Jews from Christian-feudal France into Spain thus set in motion a process of exquisite complexity. The two Jewish worlds — the one imprinted with Islam and the other with feudal Christendom — clashed and pried loose elements in each that clustered into configurations, which were neither totally the one nor the other. In this way, the self-governing structure of northern Europe shaped the Spanish Jewish communities, yet the centralizing principle of the Islamic Jewries was not totally eradicated. Commentaries and responsa proliferated, even as preeminent dialecticians tried their hand at code making. Jacob ben Asher's compendium, the *Tur*, followed in the Maimonidean tradition at the same time that it sought to reinforce the basic independent approach to legal sources characteristic of Rashi and the Tosaphists. So, too, the more sophisticated urban society of Christian Spain created an intellectual elite whose interests were not confined to legalia, and whose thoughts could not be hemmed in by naive, traditional beliefs.

It was this amalgam that was exported from Spain following on the expulsion in 1492. Most of the refugees found their way to the Ottoman realms. They thus shifted from a Christian society that had overwhelmed a Muslim society to a vast empire ruled by Muslims and inhabited by Muslims, Christians, and Jews. Large numbers settled in Salonica, which had previously been under Christian hegemony. Others settled in Constantinople. Still others pioneered the growth of Safed from a small town into a thriving industrial and commercial center.

Wherever they settled, the Spanish Jews constituted themselves into communities modeled after the self-governing *aljamas* of Spain. They cultivated the responsa form so assiduously and brilliantly that such collections as that of the Rambam (Maimonides) became classical examples of the creative balance between traditional and innovating authority. One of them, Joseph Caro (1488-1575), not only was a great responsist, but wrote a commentary to Jacob ben Asher's *Tur*, called the *Beth Yoseph*, which brought to bear on the codified law the entire responsa literature then extant. Yet his dialectical interests did not deter him from compiling a code of his own, the *Shulhan Arukh*, which came to be recognized as the code par excellence — a code which itself spawned a new wave of dialectical comment.

The European Situation

&. I have traced the intermeshing of Christian-feudal Jewish forms and Islamic Jewish forms in Spain and their extension and reshaping in the Ottoman Empire. Now I shall go on to sketch the process by which the Jewries of France, England and Germany intertwined with the Jewries of Italy and Poland. The Italian Diaspora stretches far back to the period of the Roman Republic. Its history is not a simple one. So long as Abbasids maintained control of the Mediterranean, Jewish communities thrived in the southern Italian ports of Bari and Otranto. The decline of the Abbasids and of Bari and Otranto went hand in hand with the aggressive growth of the North Italian cities. Excluded from these new centers of trade and commerce, not so much for being Jews but as alien merchants, Jews settled in the new towns emerging in northern Europe. When, however, the Jews were expelled from France and emigrated in large numbers from the increasingly hostile environment of Germany, many found their way to such cities as Florence, which were now open to them. The opening was largely the consequence of the need for loan bankers to lend money on pawn to the lower classes, at a manageable rate of interest. By undertaking this function Jewish loan bankers mitigated some of the social hostility generated by the periodic economic crises that plagued the Italian city-states.

Jews and the Renaissance

&æ Since the settlement of the Jews in the North Italian cities coincided with the Renaissance, the Italian Jews did not simply reproduce the Judaism that they had brought with them. Although the communal structure of France and Germany was transferred, and although the scholar class cultivated the dialectical and responsa method — some of the most respected collections of responsa are by Italian rabbis — the cultured elite developed a Renaissance Judaism. Like the Italian humanists, Jewish intellectuals became enamored of grammar and philology, and saw in the Bible remarkable examples of the art of rhetoric. Such Jewish intellectuals as Johanan Alemanno (his name, Alemanno, reveals that his family had come from Germany) could not restrain their enthusiasm for the brilliance with which the prophets communicated their "divine madness" in superb models of rhetorical style. For the first time since Josephus, a Jewish thinker, Salomone Rossi (c. 1565-c. 1628) took historical factuality seriously and sought to examine with a critical eye the sources for the history of the Jews during the Second Commonwealth. He did not shrink from rejecting evidence from the Talmud when it conflicted with seemingly more reliable evidence from Greco-Roman sources. Like his Italian neighbors he turned his thought to Greco-Roman civilization. He dared to call attention to the Letter of Aristeas, though it was a non-sacred book written in Hellenistic Alexandria, and to admire Philo and his teachings.

Poetry flourished along with philosophy. Immanuel of Rome, who wrote at the time of Dante, may have been the first and foremost of the Italian-Jewish poets, but he was by no means the last. Leo Ebreo (c. 1480-c. 1540) was as dazzled by Plato as was Pico della Mirandola, and his *Dialoghi di amore* simply takes for granted that Moses was a Neoplatonist. Even music was cultivated. Salomone Rossi's *Ha-Shirim asher le-Shelomoh* applied the most advanced musical forms of the day to traditional liturgical pieces. Nor should the sermon be overlooked. Not only was a distinctly Italian Jewish sermon form developed by such gifted preachers as Judah Moscato (died c. 1594), but it served as the medium by which humanistic ideas and motifs were braided with biblical and rabbinic texts. Even the pagan deities served symbolically to teach monotheistic truths.

By the sixteenth century, Renaissance Jews were as distinctive as Renaissance Christians. Their prototypes could be found among no other Jewry; their model was the Christian humanist, not Rashi. They were not what their forebears had been in France and Germany, nor were they identical with any of their contemporaries, even in Turkey. Educated in the classical texts of Judaism, they mastered secular studies and, as befitted would-be gentlemen, were bred to music, dancing, and *belles lettres*. And though the Italian Jewish grandees did not enjoy social equality, they moved with more freedom among the wellborn than is generally imagined.

The decline of the Italian city-states and the Counter Reformation that accompanied it made short shrift of the Jews. Herded into ghettos, they were degraded and disfigured; and except for a brief golden glow in the seventeenth century the Renaissance Jew dissolved with the Renaissance. Once again, the difference which had made little difference now seemed to make all the difference. The Renaissance had placed its stamp on a distinctive type of Jew, and a distinctive type of Judaism, whose creative originals still recall an age when diverse glimpses of divinity brought the divine into clearer perspective.

Polish Jewry

❧ Still another distinctive type of Jewry and Judaism radiated out of the disintegration of the Jewish communal structures of Central Europe. Pressed by the steady deterioration of their status and prodded by the steady foreshortening of economic opportunity, large numbers of German Jews, particularly in the fourteenth and fifteenth centuries, threaded their way eastward to Poland. Here an emergent and consolidating feudal type of society desperately needed the very talents that the disintegrating feudal order of Central Europe could no longer integrate. The Polish monarchy, nobility, and even the Church needed able managers for landed estates, competent financiers to handle fiscal affairs, ready merchants who could stimulate commerce, and experienced burghers to sustain a vigorous town economy. Tutored in all these functions by centuries of Western feudalism, Jews found that neither their Jewishness nor their Judaism bothered the ruling elites of Poland. Not only were they permitted to settle freely, but their communities were granted charters, endowed with privileges which afforded them special protection from such charges as that of ritual murder, which so endangered their lives in Central Europe. The relationship between the Jewish townsmen and German Christian burghers in the Polish cities was not always smooth, and though the clergy was a frequent source of irritation, Jews enjoyed until 1648 the favor and protection of king and noble, and sustained dozens of prosperous and vital communities.

The German Jewish settlers brought with them the self-governing independent community structure, the dialectically oriented scholar class, and the feudal-Christian form of Judaism that they had developed in Germany. But in transferring these from Germany to Poland, the Jews transformed them radically; for whereas in Germany feudalism had become a disintegrative force, in Poland it was playing an integrative role. Hence, the Jewish self-governing community, which had been deteriorating in Germany, demonstrated a capacity for renewed growth; the scholar class, whose skills had been atrophying in the stagnant communities of Germany, now sharpened their dialectical tools to forge novel designs from traditional sources; the feudal-Christian form of Judaism, which had been on the point of withering away, now blossomed forth.

The Polish "Golden Age"

༔ For approximately two centuries Polish Jewry glowed with creative life. Its *yeshivoth*, "academies," equaled, if they did not surpass, those of its predecessors. Its scholar class developed a nobility of learning that is still held up as the model for aspiring young scholars in contemporary orthodox *yeshivoth*.

The communal pattern of Polish Jewry displayed a harmonious balance between centralization and decentralization. Although each community enjoyed a wide degree of autonomy, some sovereignty was assigned to regional groupings, which in turn granted to the *Vaad Arba Aratzoth*, the "Council of Four Lands," some degree of authority to legislate in the common interest for all communities.

Polish Jewry thus can be viewed as the ultimate creative achievement of that form of Christian-feudal Judaism that was launched by Rashi and the Tosaphists. In Poland, it was given a range and scope and style that permitted every aspect of its potential to be pushed to fulfillment. The edges of the form were stretched to its outermost limits, as the individual scholar pursued the freedom to develop the twofold Law system to its farthest reaches.

This achievement had been possible only because a withering form had been transplanted from an area of stagnant feudalism to an area of developing feudalism. Its waxing and waning was not controlled by some immanent principle, but by the interaction of Judaism with the external world. And the proof is tragically evident in the collapse and disintegration of this Christian-feudal form of Judaism after 1648, when Polish

Jewry disintegrated as a result of the breakdown of Polish society. Anti-Semitism, unleashed by the Chelmenitzki massacres, was used to justify the bludgeoning of proud Jewries; it dazed, humiliated, and impoverished Polish Jews. The dismemberment of Poland divided their agony among three rival states: Russia, Prussia, and Austria.

Examining the Pattern of Creativity and Disintegration

𝒆𝓪 The tragedy of Polish Jewry was no anomaly. It was simply another variation of a pattern we have witnessed again and again in the course of medieval Jewish history. Simply put, in the Sassanian, Muslim, and Christian worlds, Jews experienced phases—some long, some short—of positive and creative interaction with the dominant society, only to be followed by phases of disintegration and breakdown, accompanied to a greater or lesser degree by destructive hostility. The repetitive nature of this pattern is especially striking because it occurred in response to structures that were radically different from each other.

The problem is seen as all the more intriguing when we scrutinize carefully the subsystems of both the Muslim and Christian worlds. Here we discover that the positive and the negative frequently operated simultaneously in two different subsystems of Islam or Christendom. Thus, in the tenth century, the Jews in the Islamic east were undergoing a disintegrative experience at the very moment when Jews living under Islamic auspices in Andalusia were on the threshold of a golden age. Similarly, when Andalusian Jewry was compelled by the Almohades to accept Islam or leave, Maimonides found a ready welcome in Egypt.

The Christian-feudal world reveals the same story. From the eighth to the thirteenth century, the Jews in France and Germany had been granted charters of privilege encouraging the growth and spread of Jewish communities. Even the pogroms that accompanied the First Crusade did not for long disturb this development. In the thirteenth century both the papacy and the secular powers supported policies of degrading, pauperizing, and expelling the Jews. Yet at the very moment when these destructive operations were being initiated in the north, Jews were being welcomed and offered charters of privilege in Spain, Italy, and Poland. Pariahs in France, England, and Germany, accused of responsibility for the crucifixion, they enjoyed the special protection of Christian princes in other lands—even in Spain, which had been redeemed from Islam by crusading Christian zeal.

In each of these havens of refuge, Jews were to undergo agonizing reversals of policy. In Christian Spain, where in the thirteenth century Jews had become influential members of the courtier class and where the Jewish communities had boasted charters of privilege, pogroms in 1391 made a shambles of Jewry. The legislation of 1412-15 pressed the Jews into impoverishment, and the expulsion of 1492 erased the last hope of rehabilitation. A similar fate, falling short of total expulsion however, befell the Jews in Italy and Poland.

Is this repetitive patterning coincidental or does it reveal the operation of some basic principle? Clearly the explanation is not to be found in the Jews' difference per se—for difference, though always present, was surmounted again and again. No hostile sacred text proved so immutable that it was permitted to stand in the way of creative interaction. Again and again, the white heat of the Passion narrative was dampened as Jews, now in one Christian society, now in another, were accorded privileges that elevated their status above that of the Christian masses.

At times of negative interaction the sacred texts regained their power to generate intense hostility and were called upon to justify pogroms, the dismantling of privileged status, the confiscation of wealth. There was nothing, so it was alleged, which Christ-killers were not capable of doing in order to destroy Christians. The Jews, it was charged, poisoned wells, killed Christian children to make wine and matzah for Passover, spread the plague to wipe out Christians, consorted with Satan and his hosts, and pierced the body of Christ by desecrating the Host.

The Logic Behind the Pattern

&❧ The answer to the riddle is relatively simple. Societies undergoing economic growth and expansion are little troubled by ideological differences. Contrariwise, societies experiencing economic, social, and political crisis or breakdown exploit ideological differences to stave off disaster. Because the Jews preserved their difference in viable forms and institutions, they were especially vulnerable when breakdown set in. The umbilical link to both Islam and Christianity exposed them to reactive hostility whenever economic, social, and political systems sustained by Islamic and Christian teaching were subjected to crises.

Every phase of interaction underwrites this generalization. When the Abbasid Empire suffered disintegration and shrinkage, the Exilarchate dissolved into a shadow of its former splendor and the glory of the Gaonate was dimmed. Every phase of Islamic growth was accompanied by a positive and creative reaction among Jews. Every phase of Muslim breakdown was accompanied by a disintegration: a golden age when Spain's wealth grew; humiliation and exile when it dwindled. When the feudal system was emerging and consolidating itself in the Christian world — along with the growth of agricultural surpluses and a town-and-money economy — a way was found to accommodate Jews. When the system began to break down, Jews were the first to be sacrificed. When the conquest of Spain by Christians brought with it undreamed of wealth, Jews were given incentives to settle in the cities and towns. When in the course of time economic growth could not be sustained, the ruling groups ushered in an age of terror for the Jews. So long as the Italian city-states flourished, Jews lived in luxurious *palazzi* and indulged in sensuous delights. With the decay of Italy's economic and political power, Jews were locked into ghettos and reduced to become the dregs of society. During the years of the expansion and consolidation of Polish feudalism, Jews were accepted, and the kings put into Jewish charters of privilege special clauses protecting their lives and property from Christian fanaticism. When economic growth was followed by social and political decay all this proved to be of no avail.

Though we, with our analytical techniques, can discern this remarkable process, the participants had little or no awareness of how they were shaping and being shaped. And what they understood least of all—Sassanians, Muslims, Christians and Jews—was that ideological, formal, and verbal differences were mental responses to the pressure of economic growth and decay. They could not discern the powerful economic forces that made great empires possible, or rendered them impotent. So long as economic growth could not be infinitely sustained, neither mind nor creative imagination nor dogged obstinacy could keep a society from foundering. The medieval experience of the Jews illustrates this again and again. Economic growth: positive integration; economic breakdown: reactive hostility. And, throughout, the Unity Principle proved its resilience.

VI
The Rise of
Capitalism

The Marranos

&❧ Capitalist development overthrew the medieval world and shaped the modern world. Entrepreneurism undermined venerable institutions, corroded sacrosanct values, shattered the Pharisaic threefold belief system, and separated the individual from the security of revealed religion. The cutting edge of the capitalist spirit carved out niches of freedom for the individual and established beachheads for the overthrow of the old regimes. The capitalist revolution emancipated the Jews, liberated Judaism, and opened up the possibility of vanquishing the most stubborn obstacle to the individual's humanity: the inadequacy of economic systems to produce and distribute enough goods and services to nurture the physical well-being of every individual and to sustain the individual's right to pursue a freely chosen life style. However unclear this may have been at the outset, the fate of the Jew and of Judaism came to hinge on the triumph of the capitalist revolution and on its success in shaping a form of society that reliably augmented wealth, profitably liquidated poverty, and by the demands of its very nature educated the individual for freedom.

Jews and the Rise of Capitalism

🙂 The vital relationship of Jews and Judaism to the rise and expansion of capitalism is paradoxical and ironic. Jews were *not* the first great entrepreneurs, and Judaism was *not* the breeding ground of the capitalist spirit. The great proto-capitalists were proud Florentine and Venetian merchants and bankers who excluded Jews from participating in international trade or finance during the heyday of their economic growth, tolerating them only as moneylenders to the lower classes. The Peruzzi and the Medici were not Jews; neither were the great entrepreneurs of Antwerp. The notion that Jews let loose capitalism is one of those persistent myths that seems to flourish with exposure. Every major capitalistic center during the sixteenth century was in a territory where Jews had been forbidden to live for several centuries, or where they were restricted to economic activities that did not lend themselves to rapid capital accumulation. Furthermore, the areas of densest Jewish settlement, Central and Eastern Europe, were the parts of Europe that were drawn into the capitalist orbit only in the eighteenth and nineteenth centuries. Where Jews were most numerous and Judaism most flourishing, the capitalist spirit was weakest. Where Jews were absent and Judaism unrepresented, the capitalist spirit was being nourished for its revolutionary transformation of Europe and the world.

The Marranos

🙂 Though Jews did not pioneer capitalism, some "Jews" were among its early practitioners. These first Jewish entrepreneurs were not Jews at all, but professing Christians, who could become entrepreneurs only because they were *not* Jews, but so-called *Marranos*.

Who were the Marranos? They were either Jews who had converted to Christianity or the descendants of these converts. They had first appeared in Spain when large numbers of Jews converted to Christianity following the pogroms of 1391 and the restrictive economic legislation of 1412-15. Until 1449, the "Conversos," or New Christians, were deemed to be faithful Christians; they freely intermarried with the nobility, occupied high and respected positions in the state, and even found their way to the upper reaches of the ecclesiastical hierarchy. During those years they were rarely, if ever, called by the opprobrious epithet *Marrano* (literally, "pig"). After 1449, however, their decline was so precipitous that by 1480 the Inquisition was brought in to regularize and legalize their exclusion from positions of leadership and to confiscate their property. The justification for these steps was the charge that, though professing Christians, the Conversos were crypto-Jews. The term *Marrano* was meant to convey this infidelity. So long as the New Christians had enjoyed a respected status, they were not identified with the Jews; indeed, they hated the Jews, and the Jews hated them. Once the Inquisition branded them as secret Jews, however, they became identifiable with Jews and Judaism, even when the charges may have been unfounded. The Marranos were forced into this identification, not by choice, but by Inquisitional fiat. A Converso might be loyal to Christianity, but as far as the Christian world was concerned, he or she was a secret Jew.

The Marranos were thus marked off as a religious body. The Spanish Marranos were not confined to a single class. They had been engaged in a variety of occupations and differed radically from one another in wealth and culture. They were not an entrepreneurial class, but rather a congeries of diverse classes welded together under a single name because of their Jewish origins.

The Marranos in Portugal

&✿ The welding of the Marranos into an entrepreneurial class first took place in Portugal. This was not the intent either of the Portuguese king, who in 1497 compelled the Jews to convert, or of the Jews who now found themselves to be Christians. The motives prompting King Dom Manuel were political and religious, and devoid of any long-range economic goal. As for the newly created Marranos, they had only the Spanish experience available to them, and this contained no intimation that before them stretched undreamed-of opportunities for profits and power. Yet a conjunction of circumstances pressed these Portuguese Marranos into economic activities that transformed them.

Portugal's circumstance was unique. The discovery of the ocean route to India, followed by the seizure of the spice trade, opened up for Portugal, as for the Western world, a new economic era. The Portuguese gained control of a trade that could be translated into fabulous wealth, provided that translators could be found. Though Portugal had taken the lead in discovering the ocean route, it was ill-prepared for fully exploiting its economic potential, for it had not kept pace with such centers of economic innovation as Florence, Venice, and the Low Countries. Lisbon was not favorably situated for the distribution and marketing of commodities, nor was Portugal a center of the European money market. Portugal did not have an entrepreneurial class that had mastered the most advanced economic techniques, yet such a class was vital for reaping the profits from her heavy investment in exploration and in maintaining posts overseas. Portugal needed a class with some accumulated capital and a special incentive for risk taking that could be counted upon to master quickly new economic techniques and take the initiative in financing and marketing. As though created to meet these needs, the Marranos of Portugal were available, as soon as the enabling legislation was forthcoming.

A royal decree of 1507 launched the Portuguese Marranos as entrepreneurs. Its intent is clear, for it sought to encourage the very activity that the decree of 1499 had forbidden. The 1499 legislation had sought to prevent Marranos from leaving the country: it forbade the sale to New Christians of bills of exchange for money or merchandise and prohibited buying land from New Christians without royal permission; it deprived New Christians of the right to emigrate without royal consent. The decree of 1507, on the other hand, was a veritable magna carta for the Marranos: it granted them full permission to leave the country permanently or temporarily, and the right to trade on land and sea and sell property and freely export money or merchandise, so long as it went to Christian countries in Portuguese ships. It promised never to promulgate exceptional laws for New Christians living in Portugal; granted émigrés the right to return without fear of punishment; canceled the sureties New Christians had advanced to guarantee that other New Christians would not flee Portugal; made common law in its entirety applicable to New Christians; and renewed protection for twenty years from any inquiry into the New Christian's religious practices.

The result of this sweeping decree was a release of New Christian energies. Free to move and seek profit, and free of persecution, the Marranos took full advantage of the flood of opportunities unleashed by the Portuguese discoveries. They welcomed the decree of 1507, not as an opportunity for leaving Portugal to embrace Judaism in the Ottoman realms, but as a sign of the monarch's trust in the permanence and sincerity of their Christian affiliation. For approximately three decades (1507-36), the Marranos confined their economic activities almost exclusively to Christian lands. They sought out Antwerp, not Constantinople; Lyons, not Salonica; Lisbon, not Alexandria. So long as the Portuguese state was guided by the decree of 1507, and so long as the Marranos could move freely, traffic freely, and accumulate capital freely, they never betrayed the trust reposed in them.

The House of Mendes

๙ The House of Mendes was the most illustrious exemplar of this mutuality. Francesco Mendes operated the banking house in Lisbon as a good Catholic till his death in 1536; his brother Diego directed the family interests as a Christian in Antwerp from 1512 till his death in 1542 or 1543; Dona Gracia Mendes took up residence as a Christian in Antwerp after her husband's death. Joao Migues (subsequently Don Joseph Nasi), the nephew and heir of Francesco and Diego, sought profits, as a Christian, in Antwerp and Lyons. Only after the Inquisition was introduced in Portugal in 1536, and only after it became clear in 1542 that it was to have the power of the Spanish Inquisition to torture, kill, and confiscate without the safeguards of the common law, did the Marrano entrepreneurs flirt with a change of religious identity.

Before 1536 the Mendeses and their fellow Marranos had not sought their profits in the Mediterranean area. Their wealth had grown from the Portuguese usurpation of the spice trade previously held by the Levantine and Italian merchants, and by the development of a new system of commercial relationships that accompanied the distribution of spices out of Antwerp. Their financial dealings were exclusively with the royal houses of Portugal, France, England, and the Holy Roman Empire, and their associations were confined to the merchants absorbed in the trade centering in Antwerp. Marrano contact with Italy had been an extension of commercial interests from Antwerp and not a consequence of direct involvement in Mediterranean and Levantine trade. To all intents and purposes the Mediterranean had been for them a sea that was losing its commercial primacy.

New Opportunities in the Ottoman Empire

ɞ The emergence of the new trading complex in the west may very well have blurred the evidence of a resurgence of commerce and industry in the Mediterranean, the Levant, and in the Balkans, a resurgence that was largely independent of the fate of the spice trade. It had been set off by the brilliant victories of Selim I (1512-20) and Suleiman the Magnificent (1520-66), which brought under a single absolute monarch a vast Turkish empire uniting Anatolia, Syria, Palestine, Egypt, Mesopotamia, the Balkans, and Hungary. This process of unification virtually compelled new economic and commercial ties. The potential clearly existed for an industrial commercial complex sustained by the unity of the Ottoman Empire. The spice trade might well be lost to the west, but economic growth and prosperity could be sustained independently of this trade, or for that matter of any trade with Western Europe. A self-sufficient realm might well be supported by the interchange of raw materials available in one part of the empire for the manufactured goods produced in another. Such self-sufficiency underwritten by political absolutism and by military and naval power could be used as a powerful weapon for wresting economic concessions from the west.

While Selim and Suleiman were hammering out a unified empire, the economic opportunities unleashed were being exploited along traditional lines. Trade and commerce were carried on by individual merchants, and manufacture by individual craftsmen. Although some merchants may have engaged in trade on a rather large scale, it could not compare in scope or sophistication with that of their western counterparts. The equivalent of the guild system that had been successfully utilized in such cities as Florence and Bruges for quantity production of cloth or of the putting-out system had not evolved. Western-style banking and accounting had not developed, and the bill of exchange was not used extensively.

The Ottoman Empire thus enclosed an area tremendous in size, rich in resources, highly urbanized, and vast in population, but lacking the advanced forms of economic organization that had recently developed in the west. The Ottoman Empire had an empire, a smoothly functioning absolutism, rich resources of raw materials, manpower, and refined skills; all that it lacked for a mercantilistic system was western entrepreneurship. And what the Ottoman Empire needed, the Marranos possessed. In the years of Selim's and Suleiman's empire-building, the Marranos of Portugal had been mastering the entrepreneurial art.

The *Marranos*, be it noted, not the *Jews*. The two are not identical even though they are connected. The Jews who had come to the Ottoman Empire after the expulsion from Spain in 1492 had found ample economic opportunities there. They settled in such cities as Salonica and Constantinople, engaging, for the most part, in trade and commerce, along lines they had been accustomed to in Spain. Basically, they had a narrow and limited grasp of economic possibilities — thinking in terms of inter-urban trade, of shopkeeping, of limited markets. They lacked a global orientation, for their experience had been limited to Spain — a Spain that until only a few years before the expulsion had been, in fact, two separate principalities, Aragon and Castile. Indeed, their range of experience had actually narrowed in the fifteenth century following the restrictive economic decrees of 1412-15. The professing Jews, therefore, who sought out the cities of the Ottoman Empire might very well stoke an economic resurgence of the Mediterranean and the Levant, but they could not achieve a major economic transformation by themselves.

The Role of the Portuguese Marranos

₨ The Portuguese Marranos, on the other hand, had been tutored by the commercial revolution. Their economic success had followed on their mastery of the most advanced entrepreneurial practices in vogue. They had attained skills in distributing, marketing, and finance and had become adept in calculating and discounting risks. They had found means of effective cooperation for economic and political ends. But, above all, they had confronted and solved economic problems, with all the multiple variables that a worldwide trading complex involved. As a class, they had gained these skills *after* their forced conversion and *because* of their conversion. Professing Jews could not gain this experience, even had they desired it, because the education was available only for Christians. *Professing Jews were excluded totally from settling in the areas of commercial, financial, and industrial innovation.* They thus had no opportunity to learn, for the Ottoman realms to which they fled were in need of this knowledge, not a school for learning it.

The Marranos eventually shifted their economic activity to the Ottoman Empire, but they would never have sought out the empire merely because possibilities for profit were there. They would have continued their profit-seeking efforts in the economic matrix that had proved so rewarding. Their decision to shift their major interests to Salonica and Constantinople was dictated by political and religious factors. The introduction of the Inquisition in 1536 was the first spur. The failure to limit its powers, despite costly diplomatic and political machinations between 1536 and 1542, was the second. Third was the mounting evidence that Antwerp, though not under Portuguese control, was not a secure city for directing their economic affairs. Clear signals that the Holy Roman Emperor had his eye on the Mendes fortune and that the French king was eager to renege on repayment of his loan to the

Mendeses was the fourth. Compelled by factors such as these to seek radical solutions to their problems, the Marranos gradually became aware of the Ottoman Empire, not only as a haven from the Inquisition and not only as an area offering many economic possibilities, but as a vast secure enclosure of resources, skills, and markets which might yield, if skillfully exploited, profits yet undreamed of. If an Antwerp could become an entrepôt for much of Europe, why could not Salonica and Constantinople become the same for the extensive Ottoman domains? If Florence and Venice could supply international markets with cloth, why should not Ottoman cities serve distant markets? If banking could finance trade, commerce, and industry in the west, why should it fail to stimulate in the east? If profits were generated by the widening of the markets in one part of the world, why should the same effect not follow on the same cause in another?

Not only did the allure of profits accompany this assessment but the assurance that the profits themselves would be secure. The sultans wielded an absolutism that had as yet no counterpart in Europe. Neither Selim I nor Suleiman was plagued with refractory nobles or financial penury. Their empire was not rent by war or torn by religious and civil strife. Religious diversity was respected and the fruits of trade, commerce, and industry were taxed but not expropriated. A vizier may not have been safe, but a merchant was. The Ottoman record over many decades was free of significant instances of arbitrary interference with the economic activities of its subjects or with their religious preferences. The mantle of absolutism enveloped with protective security the vast reaches of the empire and offered the prospect of a common market. The opportunity and the challenge afforded by the Ottoman Empire were variables that the Mendes family and their Marrano associates could calculate as highly conducive to profits. The decision could scarcely have been other than it was: without abandoning Europe, the vital center of Marrano entrepreneurship was shifted to the Ottoman Empire.

Tracing the Marrano Network

&. The drift toward a more Mediterranean and Ottoman-oriented policy was initiated after Diego Mendes was arrested in 1532 on Judaizing charges. Although cleared, Diego recognized the potential dangers in Antwerp, and directed Marranos leaving Portugal to settle in Italy — especially in Milan, Ferrara, Ancona, and Venice — or in Turkey. The network of Marrano agents was gradually extended in the 1530's and 40's, and new commercial links were forged between key Italian cities and such centers as Ragusa, Brusa, Salonica, and Constantinople. Thus, long before the final decision was made by Dona Gracia and Joao Migues Mendes to establish their residence in Turkey, the economic foundation for the transfer had been worked out.

Indeed, the actual movement of the Mendeses was from Antwerp, to Venice, to Ferrara, to Ragusa, to Salonica, and to Constantinople. The final decision, however, awaited the outcome of the large-scale Marrano efforts to thwart the Inquisition, efforts which collapsed by 1542. And it was in 1542 that Dona Gracia settled in Venice. The years intervening, between 1542 and 1555, when Dona Gracia arrived in Constantinople, were dedicated to the implementation of the decision: securing new connections, liquidating and transferring as much of the family holdings as possible, and providing for the continuity of a Marrano network within Christendom.

For the Marranos, the Ottoman Empire was a political unity with unpatterned and unstructured economic relations. Trade, commerce, industry, and banking had a random and haphazard character, and lacked a unifying direction, a direction the Mendeses and their associates could offer. They could visualize an economic structure parallel to the political structure. They represented a westernizing complex that could transform the Ottoman realms into an area of economic innovation. In a word, they could visualize the triumph of western entrepreneurship through an alliance with eastern absolutism. For Suleiman the Magnificent, the Mendeses and their fellow Marranos were welcome for this very reason. The Portuguese usurpation of the spice trade and its economic consequences had not escaped his notice. The wealth that accompanied the distribution of spices throughout Europe was envied; the power that made the usurpation possible was appreciated; and the role of the Mendeses and the Marranos in this economic-political complex was known. Just as Suleiman had used an army to extend his empire on land and a navy to extend it on sea, he was ready to use the Marranos to exploit its wealth.

Christian or Jewish?

છ⁀ The consummation of an alliance between the Marranos and the Sultan was dependent on a decision fraught with consequences. The Mendes-Marrano entrepreneurial system could take advantage of the Ottoman offer only if it were willing to adopt Judaism as its religion in the Turkish realms. As Christians, the Marranos were unwanted by Suleiman, and, as Christians, they would be unable to utilize a major resource of the Ottoman Empire: the Jews already living, trading, and producing there. Suleiman had no intention of entering an alliance that could easily be broken by a decision of the Mendeses and their associates to abandon Turkey for Europe. Such a move would be impossible once they had adopted Judaism, for in publicly renouncing their Christianity they were sentencing themselves to death in Christian Europe. Suleiman therefore demanded Judaism as a guarantee of loyalty. He did not insist that the Marrano system in Europe be dismantled, but he did insist that those who, like the Mendeses, controlled it must take up residence in Turkey and openly embrace Judaism.

The decision was not casually made. After 1536, to be sure, the Mendeses had begun to build bridges to Turkey when they settled Marranos in Ferrara, Ancona, Venice, Milan, Ragusa, Salonica, and Constantinople. Yet for a time (1536-53), the Italian cities seemed often a viable alternative to Turkey; for neither the Mendeses nor their Marrano associates were too eager to abandon Christian Europe, and they glimpsed the possibility of using such cities as Venice, Ferrara, and Ancona as bases for the exploitation of the Levantine trade by a link to a system of European distribution out of Antwerp, Lyons, and so on. This was evident when Dona Gracia chose Venice rather than Salonica or Constantinople on leaving Antwerp in 1544.

The failure to restrict the powers of the Portuguese Inquisition; the efforts made, especially by Marie of Austria, to declare Dona Gracia Mendes a Judaizer and confiscate her fortune; the threat of confiscation of Mendes holdings in France; the expulsion of the Marranos from Venice in 1550; the persistent dangling by Suleiman of a Mendes-Ottoman alliance with its offer of direct intervention with Venice on behalf of the Mendeses; the precariousness of Marrano status in any Christian country — all conspired to compel the Mendeses to risk the collapse of their European system by forming an alliance with Suleiman and openly embracing Judaism.

The decision to throw off Christianity and adopt Judaism was thus primarily an entrepreneurial one. Religion for the Mendeses and the Marranos generally had become an entrepreneurial variable. It had to be taken into account because it affected business decisions. Freedom of religious choice would have accorded best with the economic outlook, for there is no necessary connection between entrepreneurial functions and religious systems. At the moment, however, if one were not a professing Catholic, then one could not pursue profits in Catholic countries. Religion was not necessary for their functional role, but without proper religious affiliation the Mendeses could not function.

Marrano Motives

ह्ष्ठ्ल The structure of the action reveals the overriding motive. From 1507 till 1536, the Mendeses and their Marrano associates were free to emigrate to Turkey and embrace Judaism. *This neither the Mendeses nor a majority of the Marranos had done.* From 1536 till 1554, ample opportunities existed for the Mendeses to settle in Turkey and adopt Judaism, but they had refused to take them. The decision for the Ottoman Empire and Judaism was delayed until there seemed to be no viable alternative, and even then every precaution was taken to leave behind an elaborate network of Marrano agents and factors, even though this carried with it the necessity of a Christian identity. Judaism, like Christianity, was basically an irritating limitation on economic freedom, to be reckoned with by entrepreneurs in the same fashion as the erratic policies of monarchs and the hazards of the seas. The anomalies of their class status forced them to separate religion from economic function, to recognize it as a non-economic variable with economic consequences, and enabled them to make a choice of a religion that seemed most likely to support the economic function.

But there was yet another entrepreneurial element in their decision to return to Judaism, one equally as important as the alliance with Suleiman. To tap the economic resources of the Ottoman Empire, it was essential that the professing Jews already living there—Jews who had never been Marranos but had come directly from Spain and Portugal—be drawn upon for their skills as merchants, shopkeepers, and artisans. Though these Jews may have carried on their economic activities along traditional lines, and may have been comparatively small-scale merchants with limited capital and markets, and although they may have been independent artisans and petty shopkeepers, they were nonetheless an economic resource of inestimable value for the more sophisticated Marrano entrepreneurs. They were predominantly city-dwellers whose skills were already developed. They were, thus, readily employable for more complex economic ends. In addition, they represented a vast segment of the total internal market of the Ottoman Empire, for Jews formed a majority of the population of Salonica and a considerable portion of the population of Constantinople, Adrianople, Brusa, and other centers. Indeed, the cities of the Ottoman Empire offered a potential market far greater than that offered by the cities and towns of Europe. The Marranos, in choosing Judaism, were thus identifying themselves with more than a million individuals, concentrated almost exclusively in cities, a significant percentage of whom were economically prosperous and possessed highly developed skills and talents. This identification also linked them to a scholar class of rare brilliance, whose prowess had fashioned Jewish law into an instrument sensitive to innovation. So long as, therefore, an entrepreneur in Turkey, as in Europe, had to have a religious identification, he could have chosen none better fitted for attaining his economic goals than that of Jew. For the Marranos, donning the new identification was facilitated by their origin as Jews and by the Inquisition's insistence that they had been Jews all along.

The Results of Choosing Judaism

   The implementation of the alliance and the utilization of the resources followed swiftly on the heels of the decision. Dona Gracia Mendes was ushered into the Ottoman realms in 1554 with all the pomp of royalty, and with open promulgation of her adherence to Judaism. A year later, Don Joseph Nasi, the co-administrator of the Mendes fortune, took up residence in Constantinople and publicly embraced Judaism. Suleiman made clear his personal interest in the alliance by according Don Joseph direct access to his person, granting him the city of Tiberias (1561), allocating to him the farming of taxes and custom dues, bestowing monopolistic privileges on him, affording him the opportunity for establishing preferential economic relations with Moldavia and Poland, utilizing his services in the conduct of foreign affairs, underwriting his financial claims against France, and throwing his full support behind Don Joseph's efforts to secure the throne for Suleiman's son Selim.

The economic activities of the Mendeses and their associates kept pace with their political privileges. They engaged in large-scale trading operations in cloth, textiles, grain, pepper, wool, etc., that knit together Poland, Hungary, the Balkans, the Levant, and Italy. Their interests included shipping, finance, and industry. Don Joseph turned the village of Tiberias into a center for silk production and cloth manufacture, seeking out Jewish artisans, especially from Italy. Indeed, no branch of commerce, industry, or banking was left untried by the Mendeses and their Marrano associates.

The Ancona Boycott

𝄞 The sophistication of the Mendes-Marrano complex is perhaps best illustrated by the Ancona boycott (1556-57). Neither the Mendeses nor the Sultan wished to see disturbed the system of Marrano agents and factors that had been built up in Christian Europe, for it offered an efficient and reliable link to the European markets and commodities. When a group of these Marranos was arrested in Ancona and when several were burned at an auto da fé, Don Joseph secured rabbinical sanction for a boycott against the city. All Jewish merchants were to refrain from trading at Ancona, and were to transfer their business to Pesaro.

Although the boycott could not be sustained for more than a year—the Jewish merchants who were independent of the Mendes-Marrano system withdrew—it did wreak havoc with Anconese trade and did demonstrate the ability of Don Joseph and Dona Gracia to mount a complex cooperative venture to attain entrepreneurial goals. The scope of the undertaking is particularly impressive in view of the fact that it was launched scarcely two years after their arrival in Turkey.

The organization of the boycott likewise reveals the astute utilization by the Mendeses of the legal system of Judaism. Jews living in the Ottoman Empire fell under the jurisdiction of Jewish law in all matters that affected their relationship to each other. This jurisdiction extended to the economic sphere. Cognizant of the need for a secure legal base for their operations, the Mendeses established academies of law and jurisprudence and provided subsidies for eminent legal authorities. They were most fortunate in their choice of Samuel de Medinah to head the Salonican academy, for he proved to be one of the most brilliant legal minds in a century that was to become illustrious for its legal giants; he had a remarkable gift for transmuting seemingly immutable laws into fresh legal insights, and in finding solutions for highly complex entrepreneurial problems. Although appointed and sustained by the Mendeses, Samuel de Medinah was an independent thinker whose legal principles far transcended the specific cases to which they applied. His decisions were a response to the challenge of economic innovations that the Mendeses had let loose in the Ottoman world, rather than to the specific interests of the Mendeses themselves; for many of the decisions did not involve the Mendes family directly.

The Mendeses were fully cognizant of the need for brilliant legal talent and were careful to cultivate it. The Ancona boycott was thus promulgated by some of the greatest legal scholars of the day, and for this reason its support was unanimous at first. Of even greater significance than the impressive legal support for the boycott was the epoch-making decision to assure all former Marranos that their property was secure. Here, too, Samuel de Medinah took the lead. In dealing with the issue of Dona Gracia's legal right to the fortune bequeathed her by Francesco, de Medinah affirmed that the right to Marrano property, legally acquired in accordance with the laws prevailing in Christian countries, could not be challenged by an appeal to Jewish law. Thus Dona Gracia was entitled to half her husband's estate in conformity with Portuguese law, even though she would have been entitled only to her dowry according to Jewish law. Thus, as long as they were Marranos they were not deemed subject to Jewish law, even though it was assumed that all Marranos were intent on an ultimate return to Judaism. The intent made it unnecessary for them to undergo conversion, but it did not affect wealth accumulated in Christian garb.

Reaching the Heights

໓ The Mendes-Marrano shift from Christian Europe to the Ottoman Empire was carried out with a smoothness and an efficiency that excites admiration. A political alliance on the highest level was accompanied by an upsurge of economic activity as the Marranos became Jews and, in partnership with the most illustrious legal authorities of the day, grasped the reins of leadership in the Jewish community from Jews who had never been Christians.

The apex of Marrano power and wealth was achieved during the reign of Selim II (1566-74), when Don Joseph Nasi was virtually co-vizier. Selim's successful bid for the throne was due in no small measure to the financial support of Don Joseph, and he lost no time in showing his appreciation. He made Don Joseph Duke of Naxos, bestowed upon him the title of *muteferik,* granted him a monopoly of the wine trade, allocated to him the farming of taxes and customs dues, and sought his counsel on matters of state. It was in this latter capacity that Don Joseph gained Selim's support for a bold mercantilistic policy.

The Ottomans were dynasts, not entrepreneurs. They were absolute monarchs dedicated to strengthening their power and extending their domains. They appreciated wealth, even if they did not create it. Their recognition of the role that trade, commerce, and industry could play in their own enrichment was evident in their relationships with Venice and France, and in their desire for an alliance with the Mendeses. The Ottomans had to determine whether their dynastic aggrandizement could be best achieved by further extension of territory in Europe, or by a more intense exploitation of the economic resources of their empire consolidated and freed of foreign interlopers.

Don Joseph Nasi was the great champion of the latter course. Already in Suleiman's day the first steps had been taken in this direction, when the Sultan put forward a claim to Cyprus, and when he demanded that the King of France pay back his debt to Don Joseph. The Cyprus claim was a declaration of intent to destroy Venetian power in the Mediterranean; the demand on France, a warning that the Franco-Turkish treaty might not be renewed. It is significant that Don Joseph was prominently involved in both issues.

Selim took more vigorous action. In 1568 he ordered that all French ships in the harbor of Alexandria be seized and their goods confiscated for the money owed Don Joseph. It seemed that a complete rupture with France was being contemplated, a rupture that would deprive French merchants of access to the Levant. Although Selim retreated from this strong position and renewed his treaty with France, the move against French merchants indicates that the possibility of eliminating French commerce from the Mediterranean was being seriously considered.

The Cyprus War (1570-73) was a strong bid by Selim for a monopoly of the Mediterranean. Had the Turks been successful, Venice's economic power would have been shattered. The Mediterranean would have been the economic preserve of the Ottomans, and a single self-sustaining economic region would have emerged — an area vast in size and population, rich in raw materials and skills, joined together in a great common market, protected by Ottoman absolutism and enriched by the entrepreneurship of the erstwhile Marranos.

This was Don Joseph's dream. And Selim sought to have it realized. He sought to pursue a mercantilistic policy that would have favored the Marrano interests by excluding foreign merchants; encouraging industrial self-sufficiency; stimulating the interchange of agricultural commodities and raw materials for finished goods, especially textiles, in the trading area; and offering powerful diplomatic support for access to European markets. Under the nudging of Don Joseph, Selim was even contemplating support for the Calvinists in the Low Countries, with all the rich possibilities a Calvinist victory would have for a direct link with the Marrano system still flourishing there as well as the Protestant entrepreneurs who found Catholicism an impediment to profit-making.

A Failure of Will

ᢓᢧ᠆ The dream began to evaporate when the treaty with France was renewed; it dissolved completely in 1572 when the Turks were defeated at Lepanto. Don Joseph's mercantilistic policy had never garnered unanimous support. The vizier Sokolli favored the traditional aims and goals of the sultans and was opposed from the outset to Don Joseph's radical schemes. The audacious attempt at a complete break with France was viewed as too hazardous, and Selim acquiesced in the renewal of the treaty. But this would have been a minor setback. The Battle of Lepanto, however, indicated that the Ottomans might not have the strength to carry through Don Joseph's policies. Even a rebuilt navy would be no guarantee of victory. Selim thus acquiesced in the abandonment of mercantilistic goals. Venice was to be conciliated, not destroyed; the Mediterranean and the Levant were to be open, under appropriate treaties, to the merchants of all nations; the Ottoman emperors were to resume traditional dynastic goals; and the Mendes-Marrano entrepreneurs were to continue to enjoy the right to pursue profits, but without full Ottoman power sustaining them in their efforts.

The collapse of the Ottoman trading area was not precipitous, but it was steady. Don Joseph's fall from power set into motion centrifugal tendencies. The unifying force was spent, once the state retreated from active support of the new entrepreneurship. Economic ties were no longer knit together into an elaborate and complex pattern, but into simpler relationships. For several decades heightened economic activity continued and merchants and entrepreneurs flourished. But by the beginning of the seventeenth century it was very evident that a permanent decline had set in. The entrepreneurial impetus that had, with state support, stirred the Ottoman realms with an economic quickening never before felt and never again to be restored, was blunted. The three or four decades of its trajectory were marked by a surge of trade and industry that was phenomenal, however neglected by economic historians. Evidence of its existence has, nonetheless, caught the eye of sensitive historians who have recently called attention to a revival of Mediterranean trade in the mid-sixteenth century. The extent and intensity of this revival, as well as the reasons for its short duration, have not been appreciated because the economic and political significance of the Mendes-Ottoman alliance was obscure.

The Ottomans' withdrawal from mercantilism was fraught with significance. It doomed Turkey to a dynastic history, and precluded the triumph of entrepreneurialism. Before the Battle of Lepanto, Turkey was about to become the first truly mercantilistic state, and the Mendes-Marrano entrepreneurs were about to become privileged capitalist innovators. The victory of Venice was thus a defeat of the new economic order in the Mediterranean. It shattered the dream of a great common market, secured by absolutism and enlivened by capitalism.

The Marranos and the Unity Principle

ह As for the erstwhile Marranos, many continued, as Jews, to exploit the economic possibilities still available in the Ottoman Empire. Their leadership, however, collapsed with their leader. The brilliant concept of an international trading system with Jewish entrepreneurs in Turkey linked to Marrano entrepreneurs throughout Europe was dependent for its realization on the Mendes-Ottoman alliance. With its dissolution, the European Marranos preferred to align themselves with the more enduring economic patterns of the west. With the emergence of the new great centers of entrepreneurship in Amsterdam, Hamburg, and London they could once again freely make the same entrepreneurial decision that the Mendeses had previously made in Antwerp. They could choose the identity that was most compatible with maintaining the widest range of economic connections. In choosing to become Jews they could maintain their ties with those who were still Marranos even as they gained access to Jews wherever they might be: in Germany, Italy, Turkey, Poland, or North Africa.

They could thus construct trading patterns of considerable complexity.

Don Joseph Nasi was the prototype of the ideal entrepreneur, for his identity was rooted in his economic function. And though not every Jewish entrepreneur of the seventeenth century was an embodiment of this ideal, there was not one who did not approximate it.

Such an approximation was unavoidable. To the extent that these Jews were entrepreneurs, they were engaged in functional operations of an economic character. As such, they reckoned with political, religious, and national factors, but were not motivated by them. They were co-members of a class incorporating all entrepreneurs similarly motivated, irrespective of political, religious, or national differences. Exemplars of the entrepreneurial function are to be found among Jews, Protestants, Catholics, and pagans, as well as among Englishmen, Dutchmen, Italians, and Japanese. For the true entrepreneur, as it was for Don Joseph Nasi, the goal is profit, and the means, calculation of all known variables. The Marrano capitalists of the sixteenth century, in their struggle to master the complex problems confronting them, exploited the Unity Principle to find viable solutions in the forging of an entrepreneurial identity.

VII
The Grand
Universals

The Emancipation of the Jews

&❧ The rise of capitalism and the new entrepreneurial spirit reshaped the direction and history of mankind. Wherever capitalism emerged, crystallized, and consolidated itself the status of the Jews underwent a radical transformation. Where Jews had been forbidden to live for centuries, as in Holland, England, and France, they were permitted to resettle; where Jews had been subject to discrimination or treated like pariahs, as in Germany, they were liberated and emancipated; where Jews participated in the creation of a capitalist society, as in the American colonies, they enjoyed a high degree of equality from the outset. Wherever capitalism failed to gain a secure foothold, however, as in Spain, Portugal, and Eastern Europe, Jews were either expelled or subjected to discriminatory treatment and persecution.

Capitalism and capitalism alone emancipated the Jews. This proposition can be simply tested. Although the ideas of individual freedom and equality spread *as ideas* throughout Europe from the very moment they were born in the great capitalist revolutions of the seventeenth and eighteenth centuries, they had concrete liberating effects only after the penetration of capitalism. The Jews were not emancipated in Germany until the latter part of the nineteenth century. The *idea* of emancipation was around, but the power to concretize it could not be marshaled effectively until capitalistic development had reached a stage where further development was possible only if the country were modernized. Where capitalism triumphed, Jews received emancipation with little or no prodding from themselves; but where capitalism made little headway, no amount of appeal to the ideal realm yielded results. This crucial role of capitalism has been obscured because, in the minds of Jews and non-Jews alike, the connection between the liberating ideas and the new economic system was not obvious. The ideas were couched in transcendental and universal language; they laid claim to be evaluated simply as ideas, free of entanglement with economic affairs. The truth or falsity of a proposition was stressed, not the concrete consequences that would follow its acceptance or rejection.

The pattern of Jewish emancipation reveals, as does no other, that *developing* capitalism generates individual freedom, so that the entrepreneurs will be free to test ideas for making profit. Neither the entrepreneur nor anyone else can be certain in advance that a particular idea will reap a profit; but there must be a climate that will be supportive to innovating notions. Such a climate cannot be turned on and off arbitrarily. It must be built into the structure, institutions, and laws of society. Inevitably, the freedom to pursue profit necessitates the generation of freedom for the individual. The realm of ideas is thrown open for free exploration by those who seek truth and knowledge rather than profit. Thus capitalism bred free thinkers. In exploiting the freedom capitalism opened up for the individual mind, these thinkers subjected capitalism to harsh criticism, denying that it was the source of free entrepreneurship in the realm of the mind and spirit. Yet the history of the Jews in the modern world makes explicit the connection between individual freedom and developing capitalism.

Developing Capitalism as a Force

è❧ Developing capitalism — not just any kind of capitalism. For we shall have occasion to see that stagnant, disintegrating capitalism was devastating to freedom. Here, too, the historical experience of the Jews between World War I and World War II exposes the connection between stagnant capitalism and the lack of individual freedom.

Let us first turn our attention to testing the proposition that developing capitalism is the prime factor in the liberation and emancipation of the Jews. When modern capitalism emerged in the sixteenth century, Jews were to be found scattered throughout Europe. They were found in Germany, Italy, Eastern Europe, and in the Ottoman Empire. They were not, however, living as Jews in Spain, Portugal, the Netherlands, England, and France, having been expelled from these territories sometime before the sixteenth century. Furthermore, Jews were *not* modern capitalist entrepreneurs, though they may have been engaged in trade, commerce, and money lending, and were, for the most part, settled in towns. Though they might be described as proto- or potential capitalists, they were not, unambiguously, of the new breed of entrepreneurs. Their economic activities functioned within a pre-capitalist society, constrained by medieval assumptions, which subordinated economic activity to salvation-seeking. The Jews' involvement in money lending and shop keeping was natural outgrowth of a town economy in a feudal structure, not of an entrepreneurial, profit-centered, and competitive economy.

The process attending the birth of modern capitalism was complex, but it is clear that the kind of business enterprise that manifested itself in Antwerp at the beginning of the sixteenth century and in Holland by the end of the century was capitalistic. The sixteenth-century revolt of the Netherlands against Spain, which pushed Holland to the fore, was the first of the revolutions that the dynamic entrepreneurial system carried out against a restrictive dynastic absolutism. No sooner did this dynamic capitalist enclave in the northern Netherlands emerge than Jews, entrepreneurs themselves, secured the right to settle and to engage freely in the entrepreneurial sector of the economy. Jews—who had no coercive or political power—did not extricate these rights; the rights were extended to them by a society of professing Christians who were not bound in any way to allow Jews to resettle in a territory from which they had been excluded for centuries. The impulse to extend these rights can be traced to no other source than to the drive inherent within capitalism to elevate the principle of individual freedom to pursue profit above the principle of divine revelation. Restrictions against Jews continued to operate in the non-entrepreneurial sectors of the economy, in retail trade and guild-structured industry, for example, and in politics. Virtually no constraint was set upon freedom of thought, so long as it did not spill over into action. The first openly professing Jews in Amsterdam had been professing Christians who were given the option of becoming Jews openly or being expelled because they were the wrong kind of Christians—Catholics. A similar situation emerged in England.

A New Ideology

ε**ω** As capitalism spread from its first centers in Holland, England, and France, it was accompanied not only by an opening up of economic freedom for the Jews, but also by the extension to Jews of ever wider degrees of political equality. In each instance, the initiative and pressure for such emancipation was not undertaken by the Jews themselves. Jews may have participated in the process, but the main impetus came from spokesmen for the new ideological climate that capitalism needed, as an economic system, to underwrite the individual's pursuit of freedom. Since, as already pointed out, this climate was, perforce, a universal one, it cultivated freedom in general, not freedom solely for those who were capitalist entrepreneurs. Each major revolution against the old, pre-capitalist order and its intellectual world—a world that maintained a concept of external authority unchallengeable by reason—justified itself by an appeal to a transcendental realm open to all rational minds.

Thus John Locke, defending the Glorious Revolution of 1688, looked back to a time preceding the first divine revelation at Sinai, when the individual was not yet subject to any authority whatsoever. When, under these circumstances, the mind sought to discover what an individual's natural rights were, it seemed evident they were those that gave the person sovereignty over *personal* life, liberty, and property. In order to protect these inalienable rights, the individual might enter into a compact with other like-minded individuals to form a state in which sovereignty might be transferred, with the proviso that the contract be inviolable, that the state never arrogate to itself the right to exercise sovereignty on its own behalf or in the interest of some non-natural right or principle. Sovereignty, as such, inhered in natural rights and natural rights alone, and these rights were conceived to be those that granted the individual as large a measure of individual liberty as was compatible with the preservation of the rights of all the individuals involved in the contract. The individual was to be restrained only when one individual intruded on another individual's right to life, liberty, and property. Such restraints as existed were to be determined by the enactment of laws rationally related to preserving basic natural rights; laws should never legislate these rights away.

Locke formulated a concept of sovereignty that the development of capitalism made necessary. Capitalism emerged into a world it had not made, within societies that operated with principles that were alien to the competitive pursuit of profit as an end in itself. Absolute monarchs may have encouraged the first entrepreneurs, through mercantilistic policies, enabling them to enrich themselves as they enriched the king; the kings' aim was to forge a despotism at the expense of the feudal nobility and the Church. Nonetheless, these kings were not amenable to capitalism, for they did not wish to exchange their divine right to rule for a sovereignty that was contingent on the preservation of their subjects' inalienable rights.

The challenge to divine-right monarchy in England was launched under religious auspices, with an appeal made to Holy Scriptures to justify, first, opposition to the king and, second, regicide. But because Scriptures sustained many interpretations and supported all the forms of Protestantism that proliferated during the Puritan Revolution, basing sovereignty on them was begging for anarchy.

Locke's appeal to a state of nature and to the inalienable rights of the individual solved this dilemma. Since natural rights and the formation of the state antedated revelation, and since these natural rights did not include a specific religion, free choice of religion did not conflict with the principles of state sovereignty. So long as a religion did not subvert the principle of natural right by insisting that state sovereignty be grounded in revelation, it was regarded as benign.

Universal Ideas and
Spiritual Entrepreneurship

 Thus, out of the struggle with the old order, emerging capitalism not only made room for its own expansion but opened up a limitless realm for the mind and spirit far beyond the realm of economics. Those in power were freed from the necessity of buttressing their thoughts with biblical proof texts; minds were released for free mental and spiritual exercise. Philosophical speculation was let loose from its ties to religion, scientific experimentation released from the clutch of authority, and religion unshackled for spiritual innovation. The new economic system forged a system of ideas that was universal and open to mental and spiritual entrepreneurship.

The emancipation of the Jews was an inevitable result, then, not only of the development of capitalism, but of the new order of freedom that capitalism generated and sustained. In Holland and in England the extension of wider opportunity to Jews was equivalent to extending it to Jewish capitalists.

In France, however, it was a different story. There, on the eve of the French Revolution, there existed both entrepreneurial Jews in such great trading centers as Bordeaux and many pre-capitalist Jews in such cities as Strasbourg. Radical spokesmen for the French Revolution insisted that all Jews, irrespective of the kind of Jew they were, be emancipated and given the full rights of Frenchmen. This was demanded by non-Jews; Bordeaux's great entrepreneurial Jewish families of Sephardic Iberian descent opposed lumping together Jews of every economic and social status. But all Jews were emancipated as a result of the ideas created by capitalist development, under the hegemony of universal reason. The blueprint for the new capitalist order called for an individual-centered society with religion an individual choice. All individuals were entitled to natural rights, even Jews.

In Central Europe

The link between developing capitalism and the liberation and emancipation of the Jews can also be discerned in Central Europe. In the seventeenth century, capitalism began to reach into Germany. A small but hardy group of German-Jewish entrepreneurs emerged as factors and suppliers of the many courts and principalities of Germany. The seventeenth century witnessed the rise of the court Jew who provisioned armies, managed the finances, and supplied the courts with jewels and fineries. In the course of their operations, they were drawn to the great capitalist centers of Amsterdam and London. By the beginning of the eighteenth century, these court Jews had become a privileged class freed from many of the onerous restrictions on movement and settlement that held most German Jews in thrall. A community of some size flourished in Berlin during the reign of Frederick the Great, and could show off a Moses Mendelssohn as a polished son of the Enlightenment.

But it was only *after* capitalism had made considerable headway in the eighteenth century that voices began to call for the eradication of irrational discrimination against Jews. The most persuasive of these was that of the Gentile Christian Wilhelm Dohm. In *On the Civil Emancipation of the Jews,* he claims that Jews are entitled to emancipation by natural right because they are human beings. He makes short shrift of arguments that prove Jews congenitally incapable of westernizing themselves. If they are disfigured, he reasoned, their disfigurement was a consequence of the harsh legislation they were subject to. Remove these restrictions and Jews, like other human beings, will demonstrate their capacity for civilized living.

Almost a century was to pass before the Jews of Germany were to gain emancipation, but it is significant that as soon as capitalism secured a beachhead in Germany the concepts that went along with it — concepts that applied to all individuals, regardless of race, nationality, or religion — gained a foothold too.

The link between developing capitalism and Jewish emancipation in Europe is frequently obscured because powerful pre-capitalist forms and institutions obstructed capitalist development. It was one thing to challenge and weaken the old order. It was quite another matter to utterly demolish it and create a model capitalist economic system and the institutions congenial to its development. Everywhere in Europe the capitalist revolution had to compromise with the possible. All kinds of irrationalities had to be accommodated. Kings might be stripped of all effective power, and yet monarchy usually remained. Religious freedom was attained, but not without major concessions to established churches. Even the nobility could not be totally eradicated, and a considerable degree of political power remained in their hands.

Yet the augmentation of capital between, say, 1750 and 1914 leaves little room for doubt that the old order underwent radical transformation. Ultimately, developing capitalism was able to secure the right kind of state and climate for capitalist growth, but only after waging a long, and at times indecisive, battle against the old regime. This made Jews particularly vulnerable, for their *total* emancipation was dependent on a virtually *total* triumph of capitalism—a triumph that never quite came off. The liberation of the Jews was an archetypal symbol: for the *ancien regime,* it symbolized defeat; for the new capitalist order, total victory.

The ebb and flow of capitalism's assault on traditional societies accounts for the fact that at any given time the status of the Jews was not simply a reflection of the degree of capitalist development, but rather a reflection of the degree to which economic development effectively restructured the society's political life and ideas.

The United States

&& Fortunately, the link between developing capitalism and Jewish emancipation can be observed relatively un-obscured in the one area of the world that was the creation of developing capitalism — the United States, which was founded and settled by the drive of the capitalist spirit. Here, the novel economic form penetrated an area virtually unobstructed by pre-capitalistic forms and institutions. The Indian natives were considered so primitive in economic, social, and political de-velopment that they could be *totally* eliminated as claimants to power. No compromise was necessary with them. There was no other pre-capitalist system of any significance to con-tend with, no powerful guilds to set limits on commercial and industrial experimentation, and (this in many ways proved decisive) no long-established peasantry with ties to an agri-cultural system reaching back to the dawn of the Middle Ages — a peasantry whose relationship to the land might vary from region to region and whose attachment to traditional ideas was intense. The painful, tortuous process by which de-veloping capitalism had to overcome the medievally struc-tured agricultural system of Europe was bypassed here. An enterprising farmer class, strongly motivated by the capitalist spirit, laid the foundations of American agriculture. To be sure, a system of imported slave labor developed in the South under capitalist auspices and proved a formidable obstacle to capitalist development in the nineteenth century. But this ob-stacle was a creation of capitalism itself. The problem slavery posed for capitalism was part of the internal development of the capitalist system itself, whose growth again and again was impeded by earlier obsolescent forms of capitalism. The slavery system in the South was introduced by profit-oriented planters committed to the operation of a market economy and was defended, until its eradication, as a legitimate utilization of labor to pursue profit.

Unhampered by vested pre-capitalist forms and their ideological concomitants, the colonists justified their struggle for independence from England on the grounds that their natural and inalienable rights had been violated, and gave assent to a constitution that based their new nation on concepts of sovereignty that were universal. All individuals could lay equal claim to sovereignty. The new state did not exercise sovereignty because of a *national* right, but because of a *natural*, hence universal, right. Had the British crown fulfilled its mandate to preserve the individual's rights to life, liberty, and property, the colonists would not have been justified in seeking independence on the grounds that their right to *nationhood* had been violated. The term "people" is found in the Declaration of Independence and the Constitution, but the term "nation" does not occur. The term "people" meant individuals forming a compact to protect their natural rights more securely than each individual could, doing again what it was believed individuals had done at the very dawn of civilization. Thus, unobstructed capitalism reveals that the kind of state most congenial to it is one grounded in the natural rights of the individual.

Such a state rests on universal rather than particularistic, traditional, or national grounds, and legitimizes a climate of freedom in the realm of ideas. This climate is essential for developing capitalism, for it allows entrepreneurial individuals freedom to innovate. Constraints imposed by systems whose essence is stability, order, and repetition obstruct capitalistic development. To develop the capitalist spirit of enterprise, a climate of total individual freedom must be created, even for those who do not choose to be entrepreneurs. Since entrepreneurial talent is not necessarily inherited, the ideal capitalist society must foster fresh entrepreneurial talent. To allow freedom to some and not to others threatens to choke off the very breath of capitalism—entrepreneurship. The Founding

Fathers of this country, not a few of whom were successful entrepreneurs themselves, recognized this by building into the constitution a system of checks and balances that gave support to competition and conflict of interest.

The Place of the Jew

ɛ̃ɬ The Jews were among the most notable beneficiaries. The new state did not emancipate the Jews; it simply assumed that they had as much claim to rights as any other individual. Jews had already enjoyed a free status in the colonial period; indeed, the British crown had accorded Jews a freedom in the colonies that was not enjoyed in England. In the years preceding independence, Jewish entrepreneurs had made their mark and earned the respect of their fellow entrepreneurs. It therefore never occurred to the Founding Fathers that the Jews were somehow analogous to slaves rather than to free men. There was no need for the federal state to notice Jews at all.

The Jews of the United States did not gain equality by recourse to any coercive power, for they had none. They were few in number and lacked any kind of effective organization. They were no power bloc or pressure group. They were simply free individuals, most of whom were either capitalist entrepreneurs or linked in some way with capitalist enterprise. Jews not only were accorded equality by the Constitution, but this equality was never rescinded. From time to time, it was brought into question, but in each instance the source of the questioning can be traced to the stresses attendant on capitalism's inner dynamic—the operation of the business cycle and the struggle between the growing, innovating sectors of the economy and the obsolescent sectors. So long as capitalism succeeded in developing and growing, opportunities widened for the Jews. This is perhaps most tellingly illustrated by the fact that the rampant industrial capitalism of the post-Civil War period opened the gates wide to Jewish immigration — despite the fact that anti-Semitism had won considerable support among the farming class and the rentier capitalists, such as the Boston Brahmins, who had accumulated their capital in an earlier phase of capitalist development.

A Reshaping of the European Mind

ะ๛ The generalization from American development is confirmed, though not so clearly, by the European experience. Although the process was rugged and jagged, emancipation and a tendency toward equality always went hand in hand with new outbursts of capitalistic energy. More astonishing than the fact that anti-Semitism was still virulent in Europe in the latter part of the nineteenth century and, in France, particularly frightening at the time of the Dreyfus case, is the fact that Jews did gain emancipation in every advanced capitalist country. When one considers the vast reservoir of hostility that had been built up over the centuries, especially in Germany, toward the Jews, it is remarkable that any concrete legislation removed discriminatory restrictions and proclaimed equality before the law. The reshaping of the European mind so as to countenance the Jew was the outcome of capitalist development, which unleashed the critical powers of the mind to challenge traditional assumptions. Anti-Jewish attitudes serve as a barometer indicating the degree to which capitalism successfully overcomes the obstacles in its path.

The Viability of the Unity Principle

ะ๛ It seems that we have come a long way from our leitmotif, the Unity Principle. But not really; for the development of capitalism set up crucial problems that the Unity Principle needed to solve to prove viable in the modern age. The dynamic thrust of capitalism encouraged the development of an open-minded approach, challenged all external authority, and granted sovereignty to the mind, abandoning the notion that truth was revealed by a deity and hence was immutable. Now, truth was something one aspired to and discovered; seeking it was an adventure, full of excitement and hazards. Truth, like profit, beckoned with no guarantee that it would be attained. As capitalistic ideology gained ascendancy, even the most sacred texts were subjected to critical scrutiny. It is no accident that it was in Amsterdam, the first great entrepôt of modern capitalism, that two thinkers of Marrano descent, Uriel da Costa (c. 1585-1640) and Benedict Spinoza (1632-77), directly challenged the dogma of a revelation given by God. Uriel da Costa proclaimed that God's revelation and God's law could be found only in the natural order that the human mind reveals. Spinoza articulated the same idea in more sophisticated and reasoned philosophical form. In addition, he turned to Holy Scripture and subjected it to a rational analysis that undercut the prevailing notions of a personal, revealing God. Spinoza also pointed out that it was in the state's interest to distinguish between thought and action and permit the individual to think freely. Religion, he argued, should be in the private, not the public, domain.

As it set free forces that emancipated the Jew, developing capitalism threatened the viability of Judaism. Up to now the Unity Principle had been drawn upon to solve a series of intricate problems, but never before had its devotees been confronted with problems such as those that now arose, when a new world view questioned whether a deity even existed. And this challenge was being articulated by the very minds who were exposing the irrationalities of the old regime's treatment of the Jews.

The challenge could not be met simply by creating another form of Pharisaic Judaism, touched up with modernity. The new order and new thinking raised fundamental questions about the core principle of Pharisaic Judaism: a single

Father God who, motivated by love, revealed the divine will to humanity in order that the individual might enjoy eternal life. The Unity Principle would either have to mutate or become obsolescent, and function only for those sectors of society nourished by pre-capitalist economics, institutions, and ideas.

In response, the Unity Principle mutated once again. Jewish intellectual and spiritual leaders, excited by the new liberal capitalist order, the lure of free thought, and the unshackling of the individual from irrational constraints, fashioned radically new forms of Judaism and novel concepts of Jewishness. It was a mutation that altered the core idea of Pharisaism without severing the historical connection to it. Judaism was reshaped and Jewish identity reconfirmed, although the new identity would not have been acknowledged as authentic by any form of Judaism that existed earlier. As before, the new forms and identity were deemed to express commitment to the Unity Principle.

A Multiplicity of Jewish Responses

૨ટ To trace this mutation process is not easy, for the Jews were not subject to modernization as a unit. The emergence of capitalism affected the Dutch and English in the sixteenth and seventeenth centuries; the French in the seventeenth and eighteenth; the Germans in the eighteenth and nineteenth; and Eastern Europe and the Balkans in the nineteenth and twentieth. Each national grouping had a unified experience. This was not the case with the Jews, who were not concentrated in a single territory. Each Jewry differed structurally from the others. The first professing Jews in Holland, England, and southern France were capitalist entrepreneurs when they entered the country; in other regions, Jews were drawn into entrepreneurship only as capitalism began to arrive. In the west, including the United States, Jews were few, whereas in Germany and Eastern Europe they were numerous. In the western communities, a majority of the Jews could actually be capitalist entrepreneurs, which was an impossibility in Germany and Eastern Europe.

Jews had multiple reactions to capitalism, which went hand in hand with the reaction of the host society. Thus, at the very moment when Macaulay in England was calling for the seating of a Rothschild in Parliament, the Jews of Eastern Europe were reeling under the harsh blows of a tsar committed to halting the westernizing process. In England, Jews had become a rallying symbol for developmental capitalism against the powerful vestiges of the old regime; in Eastern Europe, they remained the victim of pre-capitalism's tendency to saddle them with responsibility for the myriad ills of a collapsing society.

The Jewish entrepreneurs of Holland and England, who already shared the capitalist mentality, did not need to reorient Judaism. The pursuit of profit was not a spiritual concern; they simply took for granted that Judaism gave sanction to their economic activities. They did not have to struggle for emancipation. There was thus very little impetus for them to alter their Judaism, which was largely patterned after that of the Iberian Jews. The radical challenge to Judaism (and, for that matter, Christianity too) voiced by Uriel da Costa and Spinoza was violently rejected. Both were excommunicated by the Dutch Jewish community as threats to its security. The emergence of intellectual freedom for the individual, transcending economics and religious differences, did not mean that *all* entrepreneurs at any given time supported intellectual freedom. Nor does it mean that entrepreneurs were not sincerely committed to their religion. Nor does it mean that all entrepreneurs were innovators and hostile to traditional forms. The daring innovators of one generation become the conservatives of the next.

Moses Mendelssohn

ᐛ Dutch Jewry then reveals little mutation in religion. But when we turn to the community of the privileged Jews of Berlin, those who had gained wealth and status by entrepreneurial talents, we find a different story in Moses Mendelssohn (1729–86), who set the groundwork for new forms of Judaism. Nurtured in Pharisaic Judaism, Mendelssohn became thoroughly committed to the underlying presuppositions of the Age of Reason, which saw medieval Christianity and medieval Judaism as monstrous anachronisms. Mendelssohn westernized Judaism by making a sharp distinction between Jewish principles, which were universal and attainable by all rational minds, and those laws that were binding only upon Jews. Since God, by definition, must be rational, God could not possibly have proclaimed irrational doctrines. God could not compel belief, and therefore Judaism could not be dogmatic, precisely because it was of divine origin. Laws, however, belonged to quite a different realm. They related to the organization of a society and had to do with preserving a people. The original Moses had been portrayed as simultaneously a teacher-philosopher and lawgiver-statesman, with an uncanny resemblance to the model enlightened despot so dear to eighteenth-century thinkers. Committed to the eternal and universal truths of Reason, Moses could nevertheless legislate specific laws applicable only to the Jews, just as each enlightened despot, committed to Reason in general, would promulgate laws particularly suited to his own people.

Mendelssohn thus reshaped Judaism, erasing all those medieval aspects incompatible with the Enlightenment. His surgery primarily centered on removing irrational beliefs about God that marked the Jew as out of line with Enlightenment ideas. He wished to stamp out as un-Jewish and superstitious elements, such as dress, conduct, and language, that typed the Jews as belonging to another, pre-enlightened age. He wanted the Jew to be stamped by Reason's hallmark, so that one would not be distinguishable as a Jew, and would share the same world of universals as the philosophies of the Enlightenment. Stripped of medieval teachings, Judaism's laws compared favorably with the laws of the most enlightened states in Europe.

Mendelssohn called for a Judaism that could be viable in the new kind of society that capitalism had already created in Holland and England (in Mendelssohn's *Jerusalem* these two countries are held up as models for Prussia). Mendelssohn affirmed that Judaism could be a westernized religion, because, in principle, it had been a westernized religion from its inception. Historical vicissitudes had obscured its eternal essence, which was nothing other than the basic teachings of the Enlightenment. Westernization thus afforded Judaism the opportunity to become itself again.

Although Mendelssohn did not, like Uriel da Costa and Spinoza, directly challenge the concept of divine revelation, he reformulated it in such a way that it no longer conflicted with ideas of Reason. In effect, he proved it possible to reformulate Judaism not only to survive but even to welcome westernization.

The Haskalah

ح‍ا Mendelssohn's radical redefinition of Judaism resonated wherever circles of enlightenment were to be found. Indeed, the movement he initiated was called the *Haskalah,* the Enlightenment, and those who were its spokesmen came to be known as *Maskilim* ("enlighteners," proponents of Haskalah). They were, to be sure, primarily intellectuals, who made their appearance and gained recognition in great centers of capitalist advance, as in Germany and Galicia. Like their non-Jewish counterparts, they were entrepreneurs in the realm of ideas who undermined the spiritual and intellectual bastions of the old order as the capitalist entrepreneurs undermined the economic structure. The two movements went hand in hand. The Maskilim appear in Berlin, Brody, and Tarnopol, where capitalist enterprise had made its mark by the end of the eighteenth and the beginning of the nineteenth century. They do not appear until decades later elsewhere in Eastern Europe, and then only after capitalism had begun its penetration. The kind of society and the kind of Jewish identity that the Maskilim sought could emerge only out of triumphant capitalism. Without it, their ideas had no prospect for realization.

The Haskalah movement can be called the ideological program of those Jews saying yes to developing capitalism. Its opponents were spokesmen for continuing a pre-capitalist Jewish identity. To trace the evolution and development of the Haskalah — under which I include both intellectual and religious reformulations of Judaism and Jewish identity — is to trace the evolution and development of capitalism. The way for both was rough and jagged. Capitalism's march was not greeted simply with hurrahs. Wherever it established a beachhead it disrupted the patterns of pre-capitalist agriculture, trade, industry, and finance. The process was not always marked by violent struggle, but the buildup of capitalist forces persistently pressed for a reshaping of society. Its progress was jagged not only because of pre-capitalist resistance, but because a developing new form of capitalism, industrialism, challenged the predominance of the earlier, commercial form. Industrial capitalism emerged as the developing sector of the economy, the cutting edge of capitalism, the generator of radical critical thinking. It created a proletariat that was to pose problems as serious as those posed by pre-capitalism, and far more serious than the problems posed by the earlier form of capitalism.

Nationalism

❧   As capitalism developed and its problems became more complex, the ideas developing along with it became more complex too. In the seventeenth century its progress, in the Puritan Revolution, had been accompanied by an appeal to sacred texts, and in the eighteenth century its progress had been supported by the idea of Reason. In the nineteenth century, however, as more and more groups and classes were drawn into capitalism's processes, a bewildering array of intellectual options came to hand. Among the most powerful and enduring of these was the concept of nationalism, which became significant as the nineteenth century turned away from the Age of Reason.

Capitalism emerged in a Europe that was divided. These divisions had not arisen from any kind of rational decision, but had developed over centuries as a result of struggles among emperor, Church, kings, nobility, and virtually every other power originating from the feudal system. The lines of demarcation had little, if any, relationship to economic rationality; they had never been drawn with the maximization of profit in mind.

Capitalism was born with a global thrust. Its pursuit of profit recognized no geographical boundaries. Entrepreneurs risked their fortunes and lives to push to the outermost reaches of the known world. Entrepreneurs sought to transcend Europe's motley assemblage of territorial divisions. The Marranos were involved in trading relations that tied together Lisbon, Antwerp, Milan, Venice, Ragusa, Salonica, Constantinople, and points east. Don Joseph Nasi calculated global, not simply regional or national, variables. The only barriers to the global thrust of capitalism were pre-capitalist barriers, and the most resistant of these barriers proved to be the outmoded pre-capitalist system of Europe. Had capitalism burst forth simultaneously in every region of Europe, a continent-wide transformation might have occurred. But it established its first successful systems in only a very small area of Western Europe, and even here long and bloody struggles attended the formation of states that would secure the rights and protections essential for its development. The forging of a nation-state, under a benign government, that would protect the new economic mode at home and abroad from other nation-states and their entrepreneurs, was the only realistic goal that the new entrepreneurs could seek. The consequences were a Dutch nation- state, an English nation-state, an American nation-state, and, by the end of the nineteenth century, a German nation-state.

Within the territory of each nation-state, entrepreneurs not only competed with one another but also looked to the state to underpin the right of competition and to serve as an umpire between competing capitalists, restraining them from using too much force to resolve their conflicts of interest. The competitive spirit was tamed within the nation-state (though, even here, conflicts between new and old forms of capitalism could not always be resolved peacefully — witness the American Civil War); it could not be tamed outside, when capitalists sought competitive advantage at the expense of the entrepreneurs of a rival nation-state. The English and Dutch fought one another, as did the English and the Americans, the English and the French, the Prussians and the French — and so on. The pattern of warfare developed under pre-capitalist dynastic auspices was largely taken over and developed in the interests of the new entrepreneurial class.

This, then, is the grand paradox. The very same capitalist entrepreneurs who drew together to secure a state that would protect competition in the pursuit of profit encouraged their state to war against other entrepreneurs — only because they were not living within the same boundaries. The moment any group of capitalists was brought under the same flag, the competitive drive was to some degree sublimated by a willingness to abide by the laws setting the rules of the game. Had capitalism emerged in the sixteenth and seventeenth centuries throughout Europe, entrepreneurs could very well have marshaled their resources to create a single European nation-state.

Napoleon and the Jews

છ। This is demonstrated by Napoleon's drive to bring all of Europe under French hegemony. A single nation-state sought to reorganize Europe in such a way as to further the process of capitalist development at the expense of pre-capitalism. Napoleon certainly attempted to dismantle the old order in Germany, and this was symbolized most tellingly in his release of the Jews from the ghettos as soon as he marched in. For decades after his defeat Jews were, as a result, denied emancipation on the pretext that they were really French and not German.

The defeat of Napoleon's grand design for a continental system did not come from the forces of the old regime — though these were powerful indeed. The prime architect of his downfall was another capitalist nation-state, England, which, in the interests of a nation-state system of entrepreneurs, undermined the potential victory of the new economic system and of its ideology and institutions. England formed alliances with and gave crucial support to the dynastic pre-capitalistic nation-states. Thus the development of a capitalistic Europe was thwarted by the most advanced capitalistic state because historical conditions had confined capitalist development within old territorial boundaries

American Nationalism

More telling evidence of capitalism's refusal to recognize territorial limits comes from the American experience. Though there were on several occasions attempts to organize the United States into separate nation-states, these attempts failed. Indeed, when a powerful grouping of southern states sought to create an independent nation-state in order to preserve by violence an anomalous form of planter capitalism, it was beaten and deprived of its source of profit—slaves. The principle of a single nation-state was reaffirmed, a principle that recognized no limits on expansion and absorption other than those imposed by countervailing force or unmastered logistic and communication problems. Canada and Mexico remained independent nation-states only by fighting; they were able to withstand the force that was mounted against them. There was no inherent national quality that precluded their integration. The fact that both Alaska and Hawaii achieved equal status with the states of the continental United States demonstrates that a dynamic capitalism encourages integration; it seeks, so far as possible, to establish a state on universal, not national principles. It strives to integrate and accommodate differences and conflicting interests by acknowledging and legitimizing them within a flexible legal system. It does not consider difference as a justification for separation. Capitalism's inner dynamic seeks to break down artificial and irrational obstructions to the expansion of the market and the pursuit of profit. In Europe such an alternative was unavailable, and capitalism settled for nation-states.

If we press this thesis further, we note that not only was the American population in Colonial times drawn from all the nationalities of Europe, and not only was there a continuous influx of ethnic groups in the first half of the nineteenth century, but millions drawn later from those vast reservoirs of ethnic, national, linguistic, and cultural differences—Italy, the Balkans, Poland, and Russia—were integrated without overt and coercive destruction of their distinct identities. The immigrants organized themselves into ethnic communities, and even held on to the languages and mores of their ancestral home. But they did not form nation-states. And here, once again, the Jews refracted this process. The state did not coerce them into altering their identity or place any legal impediment to their efforts to persevere in their religious and ethnic loyalties. It simply left them alone to wrestle with the realities of American life, and allowed each person to opt for an individual kind of Jewish identity. Indeed, the individual was free to dispense with a Jewish identity entirely, even though others might refuse to acknowledge this choice. Those Jews whose highest loyalty was to a Jewish ethnic identification always had a platform to proclaim their ideas, and freely organized themselves to preach their cause more effectively. But they were not impelled to seek a separate nation-state or even, for that matter, the right of national self-determination.

Capitalism and the Nation-State

೫⊌ There is thus solid ground for affirming that the inner dynamic of capitalism—the pursuit of profit and the competitive principle—drives it to seek global bounds, and not a nation-state. Its growth is possible only to the extent that profit and competition are possible; any human-made or nature-made impediments that block the way threaten its development and must be removed. Failure to overcome blocks to development sets the system reeling and plunges it toward disintegration. Infinite growth, infinite markets, and infinite innovation are the prerequisites for its continuation.

The nation-state can temporarily augment capital by creating a national rather than a provincial market, but this very augmentation and the vigorous growth that it lets loose, sooner or later, saturates even the widest of national markets.

The nation-state can also generate resources to protect the national market internally and externally and can even, through coercion, expand that market at the expense of other nation-states or pre-capitalist societies. But so long as no single nation-state has the economic and coercive might to fashion a global capitalistic society, i.e., to organize the world as though it were a single nation-state, the global drive of capitalism as an economic form is blocked by the nation-state system. The nation-state that in one stage of capitalist development encourages development threatens, in another phase, to strangle it.

The history of capitalism in the United States reveals clearly what its history in Europe reveals only obscurely: capitalistic development, when unobstructed, creates a state form based on abstract universal principles, on inalienable rights bestowed by nature, not by the nation-state, on every individual. The only reason why the United States did not encompass under this single state form the entire continent and indeed the entire world was that it did not have the power. And because it did not have the power, it too ultimately had to settle for nation-state status, and it too was drawn into the intricacies, subtleties, and coercive solutions of the European state system — that amalgam of capitalist and pre-capitalist forms that bred ever more violent wars to keep an irrational system in balance. Hemmed in by the nation-state system, even so vast an internal market as the United States was ultimately saturated, and capitalism, its global inner dynamic blocked, was emasculated and writhed in desperation. To be sure, since this did not occur until the Great Depression, it falls outside of the period that is our immediate concern. Nevertheless, it was the outcome of a process that was moving inevitably to a denouement as capitalism, a universal economic mode with an infinite reach, was forcefully blocked by the system of nation-states that were proving finite in resources and power.

VIII
The Triumph of Nationalism

The Entrapment of Capitalism within the Nation-State

ᴈ⃛ Once again, it may seem that I have lost sight of Jews, Judaism, and the Unity Principle, but this is by no means so. The basic dilemma that was to confront Jews in the nineteenth and twentieth centuries was posed by the entrapment of capitalism within a nation-state form. The nineteenth century spun off ever more intense rivalry between the national enclaves of capitalism. Such rivalries, in the seventeenth and eighteenth centuries, were resolved by force that was limited and that did not directly affect the entire population. The French Revolution and the Napoleonic wars changed this. Revolutionary France's draft call, the *levee en masse*, demanded an emotional commitment from every individual. The relentless drive of Napoleon was sustained as much by the intangible magic of *la patrie* as by strategy and tactics. To counteract this kind of selfless dedication, Napoleon's enemies had to evoke equivalent emotions. They responded in kind, basing their patriotism not only on national feelings but on a whole set of ideas connected with romanticism. Traditional forms and institutions were cherished. The pre-capitalist medieval world was venerated. Differences between peoples were hailed as essential and ineradicable. Individuals were no longer variations of the concept *Human,* but stubbornly separate. A German and a Frenchman could not be blended or assimilated, because each was stamped with an ineradicable national spirit. And the Jews remained bound to their essential differences, whether they willed it or not.

Romanticism and the Jews

≥❧ The triumph of romanticism, particularly in Germany, had devastating consequences for the Jews. They no longer could appeal to transcendent Reason to justify erasing discriminatory legislation. Being a "human being" was no longer one's crucial identity. Instead, identity depended on what kind of "human being" one was. One could not simply slough off one's eternal essence and don someone else's. To proclaim that one was being victimized on irrational grounds was, in Germany, to brand oneself as having succumbed to the alien doctrines of France. Indeed, these very doctrines were now alleged to be Jewish and hence harmful for every other nation. That the Jews had an essential identity all their own and that this identity was provocative and threatening was driven home forcefully to the German Jews when Jews were beaten and subjected to pogroms during the *"Hep! Hep!"* riots of 1819. The fact that Jews had laid down their lives to drive Napoleon out of Germany weighed very little when compared to their alien, anti-German, pro-French essence. The rational arguments of Christian Wilhelm Dohm; the proclamation by Lessing of a universal realm where Jew, Christian, and Muslim shared a common identity; the faith of a Mendelssohn that a rational Judaism would earn for Jews appreciation and respect — these had become irrelevant.

Enlightened westernized Jews could no longer react with the intellectual tools of yesteryear. As customary, Jews adapted to the social and intellectual environment. If romanticism in the larger society insisted that Jews had an eternal essence, then clearly such an essence must be there. But this essence need not be debilitating or threatening to the host nations. It could be different, but not competitively national. Might not the Jews be a historical people, the bearers of the idea of the one and ethical God, who long before had foresworn land and political independence to spread this idea among the nations of the world? Nationhood would destroy the essence of such a people, not preserve it. Jews, the argument went, were thus most loyal to their identity when they adhered to their universal spiritual mission. Indeed, their spiritual mission demanded of them undivided loyalty to each and every nation within whose jurisdiction they lived.

Haskalah as a Jewish Response

و‎ Jewish history had been unique — a history of steadfastness to spiritual values and belief in monotheism. Despite harassment and persecution, Jews, their representatives maintained, had kept alive through the ages the eternal spiritual truths which humankind needs and which only now were beginning to be recognized by the truly enlightened philosophers of Western civilization. The Jews should be appreciated for their heroism, not attacked for the scars and blemishes acquired in centuries of valiant struggle. And their religion, which under stress had formed protective rough husks around the precious kernel, could now be exposed in its essential beauty, grandeur, and nobility.

This was the message of the Haskalah in the first decades of the nineteenth century. It was historically oriented. It recognized that Judaism was an outcome of process, its inner essence being not the immutability of Law but the power to develop and change. The narrow notion of a single revelation by an external deity was transformed to a concept of revelation as immanent, as the awareness of God by human beings in different times and under different circumstances, the unfolding of an ancient idea. Even the laws could lay no claim to bind eternally. The history of Judaism revealed that the laws had never been absolutely sacrosanct. The Pharisees and the rabbis following them had never held back from discarding the outmoded for the efficacious. And now that a modern world had rendered possible a Judaism that could be true to its essence—the spiritual teaching of ethical monotheism—without the protection of the Law, there were adequate historical grounds for abrogating its binding authority. Indeed, it was maintained, the outmoded Law might even endanger the essence of Judaism.

Romanticism had been born as an intellectual and spiritual assault against developing capitalism and had shored up the eroding pre-capitalist order, but it was double edged. The idea of distinct national essences, of the uniqueness of age-old institutions, of the precious weight of traditional motifs could support progress too, particularly if the development carried with it the recognition that the *essence* of reality was historical: ideas develop, institutions change, the traditional does not simply renew itself. Romanticism could justify a new stage in working out an old idea.

Romantic Ideology, Capitalist Economy, and the Nation-State

ৡ   This happened with intense, emotional nationalism. Romantic ideology undergirded the new idea of the nation state as an end in itself, grounding the nations' claims in the romantic principle of national differentiation. The state was considered an instrument for preserving a largely indefinable essence, a national spirit, an elusive quality, though none the less real. The nation-state might accord the equivalent of inalienable rights to its citizens, but it was not bound to do so. It might be done if they happened to be rights that made the nation more potent, but they flowed from the genius of the national spirit and not from a universal ideal beyond it. This heightened sense of national feeling did yeoman service for developing capitalism in Germany and Italy.

In allying itself with the nation-state, capitalism had to embrace and cultivate nationalism as the prime spiritual and emotional resource for protecting its market against the encroachment of rival states and for securing expanding markets. This dependence on a basically irrational ideology, with its need to cultivate the most primitive and elemental urges, was in conflict with the inherent principle of capitalism — capital augmentation as an end in itself. The division of Europe into rival capitalist nation-states was detrimental to the free operation of this principle. It was not profitable to call upon millions of young soldiers to lay down their lives for an emotion — which, though real enough, was ephemeral, being attached to separate territories that under other historical circumstances might never have been separate at all. Once again, the American experience is illustrative. The South, which had for decades displayed strong national feelings and until the very last moment would have preferred to continue to attach these feelings to a single nation, almost fashioned a separate nation-state. When it set out on this course there was little difficulty in arousing emotion to such a high pitch that thousands willingly laid down their lives. When disaster ensued, the strong feelings did not immediately evaporate. But there finally came a time when the South once again could muster such strong feeling for the nation as a whole that thousands more would die for it in World War I and World War II.

The irrationality of a territorial system based on the nation-states is seen in the unification of Germany. Austria was excluded not because it was un-German but because Bismarck realized that he did not have sufficient power to incorporate it into the Reich. A strong German nation that treated Austria as another power to be evaluated pragmatically, rather than an essential ingredient of the German national genius, was built.

The nation-state blunted capitalism's revolutionary thrust. Capitalists had to compromise with pre-capitalist elements to gain the basic freedoms that capitalism needs and settle for less than total control for the security of their interests. They especially needed the officer class, in which, for the most part, remained largely the prerogative of the old pre-capitalistic nobility. And they were tied to the ideologues of nationalism, philosophers and politicians who usually were committed to traditional values and institutions. It was thus impossible to fashion an ideal capitalist state. Capitalists had to settle for a state in which the classes of the old regime continued to exercise considerable economic and political power.

Imperialism and the Proliferation of Conflict

୫ But there were other dilemmas posed for capitalistic development in the triumph of the national idea. Whereas developing capitalism had let loose integrative forces in the West, it had a reverse effect in the East, where the intellectual vanguard of progress and westernization was committed to nationalism for its own sake. The national idea took tenacious hold in the dynastic empires of Austria-Hungary, Russia, and Turkey. Here, no segment was too small to claim, if not sovereign nationhood, then at least national self-determination. Economic viability was sacrificed for ideological fervor, and the new nations that sprang up were almost as hostile to each other as they were to the dynastic states that oppressed them. Nationhood everywhere now spelled out conflict and rivalry.

The fragmentation of the national idea thus created insuperable problems for capitalism. More and more it came to be constrained by the limits the nation-state placed on economic growth. More and more, national enclaves of capitalists were pitted in destructive rivalries against one another. More and more, capitalism was compelled to work out compromises with pre-capitalist forms and institutions. More and more it was constrained to blunt its thrust.

Caught in a *cul de sac,* nation-state capitalism embarked on a potential solution — imperialism. The nation-state, which limited capitalist expansion in Europe, need not have limited it in the pre-capitalist societies of Asia and Africa. But in reaching out for this solution, the nation-states of Europe did not seek to destroy these pre- capitalist societies in order to rebuild them as capitalist nation-states; rather they intended to retain their pre-capitalist structures and yoke them to the capitalistic nation-states of Europe. The entrepreneurs of the West looked upon the underdeveloped lands as a source of profit precisely because they were non-capitalistic. Just like the slave-owning entrepreneurs in the American South, they sought a pre-capitalist supply of cheap labor to produce primary products. England, France, Belgium, Holland, and Germany all entered into arrangements toward this end with the traditional rulers in underdeveloped areas, sustaining them so long as the traditional rulers were willing and able to cooperate.

But European nation-state rivalries were intensified rather than allayed as a result of this turn to imperialism. Nationalism became even more indispensable. To the degree that imperialism offered a way out for each nation, each nation desperately reached out for all it could grasp. There could be no joint approach to the underdeveloped areas. Africa and Asia got parceled out with little or no regard for economic rationality, with no consideration given to continents as a whole, because entrepreneurs were constrained to think in nation-state terms. And since each nation-state had its own concept of how underdeveloped areas should be exploited, nation-state differences were exported, with the result that adjoining underdeveloped areas were ruled in very different ways. Nation-state imperialism, operating on the principle of capitalism at home and pre-capitalism abroad, enveloped Africa and Asia in its rivalries. Thus nation-state imperialism made it even more difficult for capitalism to fashion a global capitalistic system.

Industrial Capitalism and Karl Marx

&. The dilemma of the capitalist classes is mirrored in their reaction to the rise of the industrial proletariat. This proletariat was the child of industrial capitalism. The antagonism between worker and industrialist, rooted in the drive of the capitalist for profit and the worker for subsistence, led to bitter and intense conflict, and to exploitation. The conflict was heightened by the prevailing assumption that industrial capitalism offered no secure promise of a rising standard of living for the working classes. Indeed, this particular form of capitalism pressed profits out of the hides of workers in mine and factory. Karl Marx (1818-83) translated this fact into an ideational system of seductive brilliance and impassioned righteousness. Recognizing that capitalism had bred revolutionary transformations, he assumed that it had exhausted its dynamic potential when it created the industrial proletariat, and had reached the end of the road. According to Marx's theory of surplus value, capitalism must be self-destructive because profits depended on exploitation of the worker, since there was bound to be a differential between what the worker produced and what he could buy back. This differential doomed capitalism to ever-worsening crises that gave the proletariat opportunities for supplanting capitalism with socialism. Henceforth, in advanced countries, capitalism would play a reactionary role; Marx delighted in exposing its links to remnants of the Old Regime. Among these was capitalism's commitment to the nation-state. Now, global vision was the dream of the proletariat. "Workers of the World Unite" was the slogan that fit so well with the workers' situation as cogs in machines that were everywhere the same—whether in England, France, or Germany. The worker had no fatherland, for the worker's plight was universal, and in breaking free the worker would free the world.

Marx had a discerning eye and a mind of rare brilliance. He did indeed see what was there and he did indeed extrapolate from what he saw. But he failed to carry his premises through to their dialectical conclusions. If capitalism had already shown itself to have been both developmental and revolutionary, and if industrial capitalism was its outcome, what precluded capitalism from changing? Why should not industrial capitalism be simply a preparatory phase for a higher form of capitalism? Perhaps the increasing tempo of capital augmentation would create a pool of capital available for profitable investment in less developed areas, such as the United States, that could mitigate the problems associated with the industrial phase. At the time Marx wrote, this capital transfer was already occurring in Germany, with the export of capital throughout Central and Eastern Europe and the Balkans, laying the groundwork for a spinoff into economic growth there. Raising the productivity of labor through the exploitation of capital might reduce the profitability of brawn and raise the profitability of brain, with all the upgrading in worker quality that such a substitution would necessitate. What a tour de force—capitalists driven by the profit motive to elevate humanity rather than degrade it. Greed gives birth to altruism; selfishness to sharing; scarcity to abundance; constraints to freedom! Exploitation becomes profitless, while human enrichment becomes the mother lode of capital accumulation.

Marx did not foresee such possibilities in the immanent dynamic of capitalism largely because the capitalism he saw was brutal. Furthermore, the most advanced European capitalistic country of his day was England and not as yet Germany. For Marx, England was the archetype of a capitalist society. However, the anguish of primitive accumulation was the fate of the pioneer and forerunner, not the inevitable destiny of those who followed in its wake.

The Truly Destructive Rivalries

&. What blunted Marx's dialectical acumen most effectively, however, was the evolution of capitalism *within* the nation-state system of Europe. He analyzed capitalistic dynamics as though they were a universal, but he did not follow through to the logical conclusion that the nation-state must be a more basic obstacle to capitalistic development than the industrial proletariat was, for by blocking off expansion, it doomed capitalism to ever-widening economic crises, with all the dangers to the system that bitter and hungry workers represented.

This hypothesis can be tested simply. The most destructive rivalries since 1860 in the advanced capitalistic countries have not been between capital and labor but between capital and capital: the American Civil War (industrial and free-farming capitalism vs. planter capitalism); the Franco-Prussian War (Prussian capitalism vs. French capitalism); World War I (English, French, and American capitalism vs. German capitalism). Is there any capital-labor struggle that is comparable? The suppression of the workers in the revolutions of 1848? The Paris Commune? The Pullman strike? In each of these major wars, workers proved that they were more committed to their nation than to their class. Not only were they willing to lay down their lives or work long hours to produce weapons for war, but they were also ready, in Germany, to support the suppression by force of their fellow workers who had rallied around Rosa Luxemburg and Karl Liebknecht. Furthermore, when the chips were down the most distinguished Marxist scholars and most respected Marxist politicians proclaimed that they had more in common with capitalist class enemies in their own countries than with alien working-class comrades. Workers of Germany unite, lest French workers overrun your land! Workers of France unite, lest the Huns sweep civilization away! The nation-state in 1914 triumphed over capitalist and worker alike. The carnage at Verdun exposed capitalists and workers as victims of the nation-state.

Marxism thus misread a phase of capitalism for capitalism's inner dynamic, mistook capitalism's nation-state entrapment for its fulfillment, and misjudged the fundamental antagonisms by giving precedence to capitalist-labor conflict rather than to those among capitalists. It also failed to see that *developmental* capitalism must generate radical and revolutionary thought because of its built-in dynamic — the spur of profit — predisposing it to innovation and self-renovation, whereas there is no such built-in bias in Marxism. In Marxism the economic factor is displaced. Marxists are not entrepreneurs. They do not pursue economic power for its own sake, and there are no built-in features, such as profitability, within the system to measure efficiency. The measure of effectiveness seems rather to be the ability to maintain power. In advanced capitalist countries Socialist spokesmen pressed for an accommodation with capitalism, i.e., they became advocates of developmental or progressive capitalism — capitalism that could ultimately sustain *both* high wages *and* high profits, *both* a rising standard of living *and* a rising quality of life. In underdeveloped countries, such as Russia, Marxism proved highly effective in corralling desperate workers, land-hungry peasants, and war-weary people to create surplus value for the Bolshevik elite and withhold it from capitalists and landowners. Workers now toiled in mine and factory and peasants plowed and seeded and harvested for Marxists in return for subsistence wages sweetened by verbal reassurance that exploitation had withered away with the transfer of title from private to proletarian-peasant ownership.

The Problem of Marxism

ᕤ Marxism was thus not a solution but a problem. It proved as opportunistic and pragmatic as any of the ideologies that it disparaged. Its verbal principles gave little inkling of what to anticipate from it in action. A vote for a Marxist politician was as hazardous as a vote for a bourgeois one. Marxism revealed itself to be bound by a law more potent than its own verbal fulminations, a law that has proved highly tenacious throughout history. It can be simply phrased: *Ideational and verbal systems fashioned in response to the sufferings of the poor and the dispossessed lend themselves to the exploitation of the poor and the dispossessed by elites who are richly endowed with verbal and idea-fashioning talents.* The downtrodden trade off trust for the psychic reassurance of ideas saturated with fantasies of ultimate liberation. So it was with Christianity, again and again. So it was with Judaism, again and again. And so it has been with Marxism, again and again. So long as there is a gap between the imagined and the possible, between wealth dreamed of and the wealth at hand, the plight of the masses can only be overcome by psychic restructuring. In this restructuring only those who are gifted in shaping and reshaping symbols and articulating words, ideas, and mental images attain leadership.

The flourishing of Marxist opportunism from about 1900 through World War I is of more than fleeting interest for it confirms a basic thesis of this book. Ideological purity did not preclude political compromise when it became clear that capitalist development could generate both rising real wages and rising profits. Marxist politicians were as pragmatic as economic growth demanded. Everywhere they were ready to trade language for rising wages, ideology for seats in parliament, words for a ministerial post. Real Marxism became as different from ideal Marxism as the real Church had become different from the ideal Church. The concrete acts of the Marxist parties can thus underwrite the following generalizations: (1) to the degree that capitalism raises real wages, Marxist leaders become, as in Germany, France, and England, adherents of developing progressive capitalism, their radical Marxist criticism being reserved for pre-capitalist residual and outmoded forms of capitalism; (2) to the degree that capitalism collapses and either fascism or Marxist totalitarianism takes over, Marxism ceases to be radical; i.e., it is either annihilated by fascism or stripped of its revolutionary potential by Marxist totalitarianism. There is no free market in Marxism in any country where Marxists or fascists have come to power. There is a free market in all capitalistic countries experiencing economic growth. There is a fluctuating market when capitalist societies are in trouble. Historical experience would seem to indicate that Marxism can enjoy creative freedom *only* in developmental capitalist societies.

The Vulnerability of the Jews

৪৯ The process that entrapped capitalistic development within the nation-state form had momentous consequences for the Jews. Capitalism had emancipated Jews, but nationalism made them highly vulnerable. The Jews' claim to emancipation was now clouded by the elusive quality inherent in the definition of nationalism. Ideologues now determined whether Jewish differentiation was religious or national. Jews could be viewed either as sharing in the German or French national spirit or as a threat to it. They could be charged with being an international nation that seeks to rob other nations of nationhood, their role abetted by a religion that had allegedly crucified Jesus and had throughout the ages acquired a reputation of misanthropy.

We have already seen that the Jews attempted to ward off attack by insisting that they were a spiritual, not political, nation and that Judaism was a universal religion that taught Jews loyalty to the nation in which they lived. Jews were ready to lay down their lives for their country and felt no compunction in killing foreign Jews on the field of battle.

As a solution, German Jews developed what might be termed nation-state Judaism. Its most radical exponents, such as Abraham Geiger (1810-74) and Samuel Holdheim (1806-60), were the founders of a new form of Judaism, generally called "Reform" or "Liberal" Judaism, which urged westernization and the severance of links to the traditional Law. As German nationalists, they were willing to strip Judaism of all elements that might resemble Jewish nationalism. Even the liturgy was revised to remove any notion that Jews, even in prayer, looked forward to a time when they would no longer be Germans. Germany, not Palestine, was their Fatherland.

Not all westernizing Jews were willing to go quite so far as to break in principle with the Law or alter the liturgy, but they all affirmed that Judaism bound them to be loyal to the nation-state. When Samson Raphael Hirsch (1808-88) called for a rededication to all the minutiae of the Jewish law in his influential *Nineteen Letters of Ben Uziel,* he wrote his book in the popular romantic epistle form, composed it in German, and insisted that his neo-Orthodoxy was more committed to the German nation-state than Reform Judaism was. Affirming that the messianic age would be ushered in by a personal messiah, he condemned as heretical any human effort to return the Jews to Palestine.

For a time most Germans were convinced that the Jews could be loyal Germans. And Jews were convinced that in time no more questions would be raised. Their Judaism served, so they believed, as an ever-present witness of their religious obligation to give undivided loyalty to the nation.

Questions of Loyalty

ટ⯭ In the last decades of the nineteenth century, however, indications kept cropping up that the status of the Jews was not all that secure. In France and Germany every crisis was pounced upon as evidence that sinister forces were destroying the nation. And since many of these crises were attributed to the capitalist system, conservative forces exploited them to expose the crass, crude, and materialistic values of capitalism, in contrast to the pure, spiritual, and uplifting values of the old regime. The Jews were held up as both the source and embodiment of all that was evil in capitalism and in society. They were attacked for money-grubbing greed and for determination to crush other nations in the pursuit of their international goals.

The Dreyfus case (1894), in which the assimilated French Jewish officer Alfred Dreyfus was accused of spying, shockingly revealed the destructive potential inherent in an alliance between nationalists and anti-Semites. To be for Dreyfus was to be against France. To challenge Dreyfus's enemies — the military establishment — was to leave France wide open to her enemies. To call for equity was to elevate the individual above the nation. Under the circumstances, how could even the capitalists take a decisive stand in favor of Dreyfus when to do so exposed them as enemies of France in her moment of danger?

Elsewhere in Europe and in America the spread of anti-Semitism in nationalist circles revealed that the Jews were especially attractive as symbols of internationalism and thus by definition as enemies of the nation-state. And because Jews were linked to capitalism, their emancipator, and because many Jews were city-dwellers and entrepreneurs, they could easily be made to appear as the source of capitalism's evils. Jewish vulnerability was made even greater by another and quite different source. Not only had Karl Marx been born a Jew, but sensitive Jews were drawn to the promise of liberation that Marxist doctrine held out for the working classes and for suffering humanity. Anti-Semitic ideologues therefore did not hesitate to attribute simultaneously both capitalism and Marxism to the Jews. The Jews' international goals, it was alleged, impelled them to use every instrument possible to destroy the nation. Then, too, many followers of Marx did not hesitate to peddle a socialist brand of anti-Semitism, drawing on Marx's own affirmation that the essence of Jews and Judaism was money and the spirit of capitalism. Jews and Judaism thus were dangling on the edge of a precipice. Nevertheless, the threat to their status did not materialize, even in France. Dreyfus was eventually exonerated, and a new phase of radical reform undercut the powers and prestige of the army and Church. The Jews, along with other French citizens, marched off with patriotic fervor to the carnage of the First World War.

Nationalism and Eastern European Jews

ఎ When the Jews of Eastern Europe were swept into the modernization process, ideologies of change were no longer those that had prevailed in the Age of Reason or in the Age of Romanticism. The nationalist idea was dominant. After a brief illusory period in Russia (from 1855-81) under Tsar Alexander II, during which it was supposed that Jewish emancipation might follow western models, the modernizing Jewish leadership abandoned the idea of integration in favor of nationalist goals. In their eyes the Jews were indeed a nation, seeking either a territory of their own, such as Palestine, or national self-determination in the countries in which they lived. Jewish essence for them was an indestructible national spirit that had always found embodiment in self-governing institutions, *even* in the Diaspora. Jews were not assimilable— anti-Semitism and discrimination proved this—and those Jews of the West who had thought otherwise were turncoats and traitors. The national idea, not Judaism, had kept the people alive. Judaism, to be sure, was the religion of the Jewish nation, but it was a creation of the national spirit, not the creator of the nation. A devout Jewish nationalist was far more Jewish than the religiously orthodox German patriot Samson Raphael Hirsch, who remained loyal to the Law but betrayed the Jewish nation. The modernizing Jewish intellectuals of Eastern Europe, like their non-Jewish counterparts, viewed religion as basically outmoded—to be tolerated only in the interests of national unity.

Jewish Nationalism as an Answer

&. Jewish nationalism was thus the major solution advocated by the Jewish Enlightenment movement of Eastern Europe. To adopt nationalism was to be in the avant-garde of modernization and revolutionary change. Developing capitalism, entrapped by the nation-state form, had opened up the sluice gates for nationalism in Eastern Europe. The implication for Jews was ominous; now capitalism deprived Jews of a universal claim to emancipation and equality. This was recognized by Theodor Herzl (1860-1904), who, though thoroughly westernized, was exposed in Vienna to the realities of burgeoning nationalism. He could see that the Austro-Hungarian Empire was being torn apart by national variations. Everywhere he saw differences as self-authenticating and self-justifying. What was real was that elusive quality that made one feel either that one belonged or did not. When, therefore, the Dreyfus affair encouraged intense anti-Semitism, Herzl attributed it to bedrock emotion—an intuitive rejection of the alien. Instead of railing against it, he maintained that Jews should cultivate their difference and preserve it through the creation of a nation-state. For Herzl, Judaism could not be the essence of Jewish identity, since he felt Jewishness but no attachment to Judaism. Conversely, Jews who concentrated on Judaism spurned a national identity.

Jewish nationalism thus took hold as a viable solution to the problem of westernization in Eastern Europe. But there was a need to clarify the kind of nation that was to be sought, and other ideologies also played a crucial role. Should Jewish nationalism advocate a return to Palestine or should it favor national self-determination with autonomous institutions wherever Jews happened to be? Should the nation be democratic or socialist? Should the national urge be channeled within a single class or be diffuse? Should the language be the language of the masses, Yiddish, or should Yiddish be scorned as a product of the Diaspora? Should the Diaspora be totally negated or assigned some national function? Should religiously oriented Jews denounce Jewish nationalism as ungodly, or should they win it over to God and Torah? The proliferating ideologies of the day gave the Jews numerous answers to these questions.

Since the rise of Jewish nationalism coincided with the spread of imperialism, opportunities for its realization appeared. The breakup of the Ottoman Empire was arousing interest on the part of the great powers, which were eager to seize its territories and, in so doing, outmaneuver each other. The emergence of Jewish nationalism, which was seeking to create a nation in Palestine, did not go unnoticed. Indeed, the new imperial powers looked on proliferating nationalisms as solvents to corrode rival empires; the resulting small nations could then be controlled with relative ease. Herzl recognized the potential inherent in imperial rivalries and sought to exploit them. Though nothing materialized in his lifetime, the Balfour Declaration of 1917 revealed that England, at least, was trying to utilize Jewish nationalism to further its interests in the Middle East.

Immigration as an Alternative

ૐ But the Jews of Eastern Europe had an alternative to nationalism. Expanding industrialism in the United States opened wide the door to immigrants from the territories that were undergoing the painful convulsions attendant on the modernization process. Millions of Jews came. In doing so, they did not leave their ideological baggage behind. A majority brought with them the traditional pre-capitalist religious identity. Others had already worked through to a combined religious and national identity. Still others were primarily oriented ethnically and nationally. And there were those who were radical socialists. In the United States each sought to preserve his specific variation of Jewish identity.

Each had left a society that was in a state of transition from pre-capitalism to capitalism, from traditionalism to modernity, and had come to the most advanced capitalist society in the world, a society where individuals could choose among a variety of identities. Here one could be an Orthodox Jew, a Reform Jew, an ethnic Jew, a secular Jew, or a non-Jew. When exposed to the freedom of choice that developing capitalism had made possible in the United States, most Jews perpetuated the identities they had brought with them. But, their wish to perpetuate these identities was balanced by an acculturation process that was forging a new American Jewish identity—an identity shaped in part by the fact that there were many options for Jews. These options could persist only so long as capitalist development was assured. A failure to maintain economic growth could set off severe crisis and, with it, a turn to anti-Semitism.

Jews came to the United States in successive waves, each stirred by the breakup of a European pre-capitalist society resulting from the penetration of capitalism. The first Jews had been representatives of that entrepreneurial vanguard that had taken up residence in Holland and England; they were simply an extension of these western Jewish communities. In the seventeenth and eighteenth centuries, the Jews living in the pre-capitalist societies of Central and Eastern Europe hardly budged, even though they were suffering under discriminatory laws and living a pariah-like existence. The handful of German Jews who did come were those who had been drawn to Amsterdam and London and were taken up by the capitalist spirit. When, however, in the first decades of the nineteenth century, the pre-capitalist structures of Central Europe were in the throes of disintegration, Jews emigrated to the United States in large numbers—not because of intensified persecution, but because of the snapping of the links connecting Jews to the old pre-capitalist agricultural system. These German Jews were unlike the Dutch and English Jews who had preceded them.

Then, during the last decades of the nineteenth century, the Jews of Eastern Europe poured into this country in hundreds of thousands. Though it is true that they were fleeing persecution, pogroms, and harsh discriminatory legislation, these were not the fundamental cause of their departure. In the 1820's and 30's East European Jews were ground down by far more draconian laws and suffered much more hardship than the Jews of Germany. But most of them stayed put. The basic cause of their departure subsequently must lie in an essential difference: whereas the discrimination of the first decades of the century occurred within a predominantly pre-capitalist Russia, the discrimination of the 1880's was a response to the revolutionary turmoil that accompanied the disintegration of the old order. This collapse wrenched the Jews loose from their pre-capitalist moorings and made emigration possible.

Industrialism and Urbanization

ੴ Thus, as a result of the process of capitalist development, three major waves of Jewish immigration were propelled to America, a land created by capitalism and continuously being reshaped by its innovating dynamic. The absorption of these waves was made possible only because capitalism had not achieved equilibrium. The mercantilist phase that had attracted Jewish entrepreneurs from England and Holland had been followed, in the first decades of the nineteenth century, by the rise of the factory system in the North, by a flourishing plantation economy in the South, and by the expansion of a free farming class into the West. These developments opened up opportunities for the German Jews. As a pre-capitalist urbanized class that had functioned as merchants, tradesmen, and moneylenders for the peasantry, they could with relative ease become capitalistically-oriented itinerant merchants, shopkeepers, and distributors, serving the former German peasant, now an American farmer. In the context of American capitalist society, a formerly hostile symbiosis was transformed into a mutually profitable partnership.

The rapid spread of industrialism and urbanization in the post-Civil War period offered the East European Jew an equivalent situation. The rise of a large industrial proletariat, concentrated in large metropolitan cities, opened up a need for the production and distribution of consumer goods and foodstuffs. The Jews of Eastern Europe were adapted for such functions, since they had been limited to urban occupations and had lived almost exclusively in villages, towns, and cities. When, therefore, the pre-capitalist symbiosis was broken up and Jews and non-Jews emigrated to the United States, most of the non-Jews found their way to mine and factory, while the Jews, whenever possible, turned to those functions that the burgeoning cities needed. Large numbers of Jews did become proletarians to be sure; but — and this should be stressed — when they did, it was rarely in heavy industry, and the process occurred for the most part in very large cities such as New York, Philadelphia, and Chicago, which offered to the alert and enterprising myriads of opportunities to pull themselves out of the proletariat. Particularly emancipating was the availability of free education. If it were latched onto, despite considerable economic hardship, in preference to an early entrance into the labor market, it could lead into law, medicine, and teaching, and into the widening fields of communication. These options were available to all immigrants, but Jews tended to exercise them more readily because they had not been peasants. Though they may have been degraded, the Jews of Eastern Europe were urbanized and placed a high value on learning. Their Judaism had encouraged this value system, for among the pre-capitalist Jews of Eastern Europe the scholar class had enjoyed high status. This value was severed from its traditional moorings and set free to attach itself to the intellectual options offered by American capitalism. And since capitalism was beginning to recognize the potential for profit-making inherent in intellectual productivity, placing a high value upon intellect proved to be a farsighted entrepreneurial decision.

The pattern of capitalist development in the United States was decisive for the Jews, for it drew to these shores all of the multiple Jewish identities fashioned in Europe and sustained their coexistence. It also gave all these multiple Jewish identities a security that could not be matched elsewhere. Although anti-Semitism did not totally disappear, it made little headway as an effective ideology. Its appeal was largely limited to those classes especially hard hit by rampant industrialization in the eighties and nineties. Vigorous economic growth soon relegated it to the outer fringes of the social order. The advancing capitalist sector refuted anti-Semitism year in and year out by pressuring for unlimited immigration, irrespective of ethnic origin or religious preference.

One Principle, but Multiple Judaisms

&⁊ On the eve of World War I, Jews and Judaism revealed that they had undergone a bewildering mutation, a mutation made necessary by capitalism's reshaping of the world. The Jewish mutation had been a painful, uncertain, and arduous process compounded in complexity by the Jews' dispersion, which had made them face the modernization process at different times, in different territories, and under different ideological conditions. This led to multiple Jewish identities, multiple Judaisms, and multiple ideologies. This mutation is of a very different order from Pharisaism, a single form emerging, which then created multiple forms out of itself. Here something quite different occurred — a mutation characterized by multiple independent forms. Reform Judaism did not generate Jewish nationalism, and Jewish nationalism did not generate Jewish socialism. The Unity Principle coped with the novel type of problem by affording all the various identities a justifiable claim to being Jewish. So long as there was a determination to solve the new problems by reaffirming a Jewish identity, there was a link to all prior phases of Jewish history and a link with all other contemporary Jewish identities. Reform Judaism may have broken with the Law, but it did not break historical ties to it. To explain its new identity, Reform had to trace its history back to the birth of the Unity Principle in the patriarchal period. Jewish nationalism may have subordinated Judaism to the national idea, but it justified that by appealing to the biblical record of the birth of a nation. The Unity Principle thus met the modernization process through a mutation that, even as it fragmented identities, bound all these fragments together by recalling their shared history. Every Jewish identity was a public avowal of a link to Abraham, Moses, and the Pharisees.

Particularly worthy of notice is the fact that by the end of the nineteenth century a Jewish identity had emerged that did not necessarily include a commitment to Judaism. Such a phenomenon had never previously appeared in the thousands of years of Jewish experience. Yet not only did such an identity emerge in the form of Jewish nationalism and Jewish socialism, but, by 1914, it was well on its way, even in the United States, to becoming the most acceptable identity, even for Jews who had strong attachments to Judaism. A Jewish ethnic identity could incorporate within itself religion—a nation-state could accord its nationals religious freedom—whereas Judaism by itself could not command the undiluted loyalty of secular nationalists.

Invoking the Past

ᡃᢙ Every one of the new identities insisted on labeling itself Jewish, claiming not the forging of a new identity but a rediscovery of a discarded though essential one. Mendelssohn really believed that Moses in remote antiquity had been a spokesman for the Age of Reason and that the Pentateuch revealed eternal universal truths side by side with particularistic laws. German-Jewish spokespersons of the nineteenth century—Geiger, Krochmal, Holdheim, and Samson Raphael Hirsch—really believed that the Jews had always been destined to be a light to the nations, a landless spiritual people free of any ambition to have a state of their own and utterly devoted to the nation-state that accepted them as citizens. Nationalists—Herzl, Pinsker, and Dubnow—were absolutely convinced that the Jews had always been a nation, even in the

Diaspora, and ought to preserve their nationhood, either in Palestine or in the Diaspora, or in both. Even Jewish socialists sought to adjust their Marxian internationalism to their urge for an ethnic social-democratic party, rallying the Jewish working class against its Jewish and non-Jewish exploiters.

Each identity insisted on reconstructing and reshaping the total Jewish past to legitimize its radical alterations. The Bible, the Talmud, medieval literature — all were ransacked for proof that what the Jews now considered themselves to be was what they had, in essence, always been. For the Jews of the Age of Reason, the great Jewish philosophers, Philo, Maimonides, and Crescas, proved that Judaism had always been rational in essence. Romanticists found ample evidence to proclaim that Judaism had never ceased being creative, even in the Diaspora, and that it had always adjusted the Law to life without compromising its commitment to God. Nationalists had a field day digging up all the evidence that proved not only that the Jews had once been a nation in its own land, but that they had displayed sheer genius in fashioning a wide variety of self-governing institutions in the Diaspora. And as for the Jewish socialists, Judaism's leitmotif of social justice and the struggle of the lower classes for communal rights in the medieval Jewish communities convinced them that they could make fair claim to a Jewish identity.

Historical experience thus proved the underlying source for a Jewish identity. If asked what made one Jewish, the individual would sooner or later have to begin to trace Jewish identity back step by step to the beginning, seeing each previous Jewish identity as the creation of a historical, dynamic, and developmental Unity Principle. Though each identity might quarrel about the one God it worshiped, it could not deny that it was the outcome of a history that had, in its beginnings, affirmed that its God was one, not many, or that the earliest recorded history of the Jews is attributed to the agency of this one God. Without that historical foundation in unity, there would have been no Jewish identity at all.

The Unity Principle and Variations of Identity

࿇ The new mutation thus consisted of a shift from the conception that the Unity Principle was identical with an immutable single God to the notion that it was rather a principle, an immanent principle revealing itself in historical process. The nationalists presupposed this. They never wearied of proclaiming the intangible operation of the national spirit. The Unity Principle thus coped with the problems of capitalism and westernization by explaining fragmentation as a legitimate response to the novel problems set for Jews by westernization.

Every variation of Jewish identity that emerged in the modern period rested on historical foundations. Every variation recognized that the Diaspora created anomalous problems for the Jews in a society of nation-states espousing nationalism. But it should be noted that these problems would scarcely have been distressful if developing capitalism had shaped a single European state founded on inalienable rights and exercising sovereignty over all the ethnic and religious groups from the Atlantic to the Urals. The Jewish difference then would have been one among many. European identity would, by definition, have been an identity of differences, even as American identity came to be.

Jews and Judaism were thus entrapped by the triumph of the nation-state and nationalism in much the same way as capitalism was. Only with the greatest of difficulty could the Jews constrict their identities and religion within the boundaries of nation-states. Judaism as a universal religion was caught up in a flagrant contradiction between the continued affirmation that God was the God of all humankind and that

Jews were a spiritual people teaching this truth among the nations, and the equally strong affirmation that this God commanded absolute loyalty to the nation-state. The most universalist, modernized Jews were the most vociferous in trumpeting their loyalty to the nation in which they lived. Jewish nationalists, in turn, were constrained to cut the Jews down to nation-state size. The unique world history of the Jews was for them to reach its apogee as another Italy, or Greece, or Poland — even the wildest dreams of Herzl never dared to fantasy an England or a France, or a United States. But, as a nation-state, could the Jews escape inexorable involvement in nation-state wars, wars so devastating as to threaten western civilization itself? Compelled to preserve its own nation-state existence, could it refrain from whipping up nationalist emotion of hatred for the enemy of the moment and love for the ally of the hour? The triumph of the nation-state thus threatened to strip Jews and Judaism of their unique role in history: the working out, in and through history, of the Unity Principle as the ultimate ground of reality.

IX
The Road to
Auschwitz

The Disintegration of Nation-State Capitalism

&⬧ World War I was a great watershed. Until it broke out in all its destructiveness, the illusion could be maintained that the nation-state system would somehow devise means short of war to resolve conflicting interests. But the war exposed this as an illusion. The nation-state constrained capitalist development. Once the domestic market had been saturated, further growth was impeded by the unavailability of expanding markets. Each enclave of nation-state capitalists held on dearly to its protected markets and sought to gain exclusive rights to colonial and semi-colonial areas. Conflicts of interest between entrepreneurs, peacefully resolved within the nation-state, occasioned violence when rival nations competed for new markets and sources of raw materials. The disintegrating dynastic states of Austria-Hungary, Russia, and Turkey were looked on as opportunities for expanding not *capitalism*, but nation-state *capitalists*. The mushrooming nationalisms throughout these territories were fostered by capitalists for their disintegrative tendencies and for the exploitative potential inherent in the replacement of an empire by weak nation-states. The nation-state dams up the drive of capitalism for profits. Unless barriers to further growth are broken down, the system stagnates, disintegrates, and collapses. But breaking down the barriers of a complex system of nation-states is not easy. It can be effectuated only by power of awesome magnitude. By setting itself limited goals, Prussia was able to win a quick victory over France in the Franco-Prussian War, annexing Alsace-Lorraine and pocketing indemnities as her rewards. But the Germany of 1914 could not settle for such meager pickings. She was now a mighty capitalist power with Europe's most advanced and efficient banking and industrial system. She faced imperative pressure to break through her boundaries or face the prospect of suffocation. In launching World War I, Germany hoped that a lightning victory would bring France to her knees, keep England isolated, and afford Germany the opportunity to restructure Western Europe along more rational economic lines, establish a powerful capitalist beachhead in Eastern Europe, and stake out imperial claims comporting with her economic prowess.

When England decisively intervened, Germany soon learned that lightning-like coercive solutions were no longer possible. Indeed, both sides learned quickly that nation-state warfare had unleashed a new level of violence, and that humankind had reached the threshold of self-destruction. The development of military technology, combined with mass armies motivated by intense national feelings, brought death to millions and destructiveness of a new order. Though each side marshaled all its resources in repeated efforts to push through to victory, a decision was unattainable. Had not the United States thrown its forces behind the Allies' cause, a stalemate would have been the likely outcome — unless internal revolution and mutinies would have tipped the scales.

The Treaty of Versailles

ે♪   The tragic outcome of the nation-state carnage was the Treaty of Versailles. It unabashedly revealed what triumphant nation-states demand of their beaten rivals. Germany was plundered in the interests of the now distrustful Allies, virtually stripped of the economic prerequisites for nation-state existence. Her potential for economic growth and development was emasculated. Since German capitalism had attempted to solve its problems at the expense of French and English capitalists, it was now the latter's turn latter to wreak vengeance by putting German capitalism in an even tighter straitjacket than it had been in before. But since capitalism cannot survive without profits, the German nation-state had little alternative but to try once again to break out of its bounds, or capitalism would have to give way to some other economic form. By perpetuating the nation-state system, the Treaty of Versailles not only set the stage for a second, more devastating round of destructiveness, but undermined capitalism as a viable economic form, even in the victorious nation-states, by again restricting economic growth to nation-state limits.

A grand reversal followed World War I. Until 1914, the development of capitalism had gone hand in hand with certain universal ideas, even during the heyday of nationalist fervor. Whenever a new capitalist nation-state emerged, representative institutions were established, voting rights extended, equality before the law instituted, freedom of religion bestowed, and the mind freed to explore physical and metaphysical reality uncoerced. Although these principles were endangered by nationalism, they were, until World War I, deemed among the valuable rewards that true nationhood could bestow. World War I and the Treaty of Versailles reversed these trends, unleashing in their stead a drift toward totalitarianism, seemingly the only political system that by instituting rigorous controls over both capital and labor, could keep capitalism from *utter* collapse in a world of antagonistic states—capitalist and, now for the first time, anti-capitalist.

The Bolshevik Revolution

&❧ This grand reversal was abetted, even before World War I had come to an end, by the Bolshevik Revolution. The significance of the Bolshevik Revolution lay in the fact that, for the first time since the birth of capitalism, modernization was being championed by an oppressive and uncompromising anti- capitalist leadership. For the first time the drive toward modernization passed into anti-capitalist hands.

The Bolsheviks' usurpation of revolutionary leadership posed dilemmas that left capitalists bewildered. For capitalism to grow it must innovate, but innovation involves refashioning, breaking down, discarding. To justify innovation, radical, even revolutionary, criticism is essential. If capitalism is to develop, it must dismantle traditional systems, challenge old ruling classes, and foment and sustain revolutionary onslaughts against the old regime. Developing capitalism generates permanent revolution, and up to now had done just that. Faced by an uncompromising Bolshevik anti-capitalism, sowing revolution against *both* the old traditional order *and* capitalism, how could capitalists foster a revolutionary economic system? The ideology of revolution became the monopoly of anti-capitalists. This dilemma was compounded by the limitations set on capitalist growth by the nation-state system at Versailles. To be for capitalism was to be for nationalism, and for the conflict-ridden nation-state system. The vision of a global order became exclusively a Bolshevik ideal. This global ideal could be used by the Bolsheviks with devastating effect to arouse the colonial and semi-colonial peoples against the imperialist nation-states;

for here nation-state capitalism was especially vulnerable, having exploited the traditional pre-capitalist societies of Asia and Africa instead of restructuring them, thus turning its back on underdeveloped societies' aspirations to become capitalist nation-states. European capitalism viewed nascent capitalism in the colonies as a threat to nation-state imperialist capitalism, rather than as a prerequisite for a global capitalist order. Thus the Bolsheviks fell heir to the principle of innovation, change, and development.

Not being rooted in universals that proclaimed inalienable rights for the individual, the Bolshevik revolution was grounded in principles that bore little resemblance to those that had gone hand in hand with the development of capitalism and opened up reality to free intellectual and spiritual entrepreneurship. The Marxist state did not offer a wide range of opportunity for individuals, irrespective of class, to fulfill their varied aspirations. Its essential metaphysic was class oriented. No status transcending class interests or class needs was accorded to the individual. There was no recognition of the freedom to explore reality without any precommitment as to what one would find. Reality for the Marxists was known once and for all, and all statements about it, in any field, could be scrutinized by the Bolshevik elite and rejected on class grounds. Similarly, individual variation and difference were highly suspect, for they threatened to break through class boundaries. Artistic and religious interpretations of reality were also fraught with danger, for they threatened to reveal dimensions hitherto unsuspected and unknown. The core principle of Marxism was authority rooted in the writings and ultimately the persons of Marx and Engels. Scholastic exegesis displaced free critical thought. Sophisticated interpretation was called upon to tone down glaring totalitarianism. Equally frightening was the proliferation in the United States of anti-Semitic ideologues who could no longer be simply shrugged off as a lunatic fringe. Hitler's secure control of the German state was a daily reminder that the lunatic of today might very well be the faultless hero of tomorrow. The totalitarian principle was everywhere proving its allure, either as fascism or as Marxism.

The Jewish Predicament

ह৶ The Jews were especially vulnerable, for their anomalous history exposed them to the danger of extinction from the triumph of the totalitarian principle, whether Left or Right. Any Jewish identity could be made suspect because it was rooted in a history which preceded and transcended both the nation-state and the modern social-class structure. Jews everywhere were threatened by what happened to Jews anywhere in the world. For the Nazis and Fascists, Jews were the demonic symbol of imperialism: a supranational capitalist-Marxist secret predatory "superstate"; for the Bolshevik Marxists, they were—as Marx himself had declared—the embodiment of the capitalist spirit; even Jewish proletarians could not totally escape the mark of Rothschild.

The Jews were trapped in a very special way by the disintegration of nation-state capitalism and by the evaporation of those values that before World War I had allowed them to be both different and free. The Jews, whether they liked it or not, were assigned a universal, international, global status by the triumph of totalitarianism, and were compelled to play a global role in the ideologically based economic theories of totalitarianism. Since the totalitarian systems did not permit Jews to participate, there was seemingly no escape for a Jew, whatever his class or personal sympathies. This casting of the Jews in an international mold is tellingly illustrated by the emergence in the 1930's of anti-Semitism in Japan, a nation-state harboring no Jews and free of any tradition of Christian anti-Semitism. Yet the very fact that Jews were *not* there was, for the Japanese anti-Semites, powerful proof of international Jewry's shrewd machinations behind the scenes to destroy the Japanese empire.

These anti-Semitic charges were, to be sure, monstrous fabrications, but the success attending their dissemination attests to their believability. They took hold because Jews were indeed an anomalous phenomenon. Their history was *not* the history of a nation-state, but a history that had deposited them in every nation and territory of Europe, every nation and territory of North and South America, the Middle East, Australia, New Zealand, Africa, and even parts of the Far East. Though in every area Jewish identity was different, and in many countries, including the United States, multiple Jewish identities existed side by side, Jews were all Jews because of shared historical origins. Furthermore, Jews were not confined to a single economic or social class. There were Jews who were world-renowned capitalist bankers, like the Rothschilds; there were Jews who were world-renowned writers, artists, journalists, and scientists; there were Jews who had made their mark as distinguished adherents of Marxism and other forms of socialism; there were Jews who held positions of responsibility and trust in a variety of nation-states; there were Jews who were ardent proponents of Zionism; and there were Jews who rejected uncompromisingly all forms of Jewish nationalism—all of them were linked, through history, to the birth of Christianity and the trial and crucifixion of Jesus.

The Eventual Outcome of Totalitarianism

ᓚᕠᗢ These facts served as the foundation on which malicious and brutal fabrications were built, for they lent credence to an amalgam of contradictions. The championing of the racist form of anti-Semitism by the most powerful totalitarian state, Germany, made Jewish survival hinge on the outcome of Hitler's drive to reorganize Europe on totalitarian, racist principles, giving his state the right to dispose of human surpluses—a cancerous problem for stagnating and restrictive capitalism—so long as they were labeled non-Aryan. How long the United States could have resisted these fascist principles is fortunately not known, but in view of the rising tide of anti-Semitism and the sympathy of a considerable portion of the American people with Hitler's goals, it is by no means inconceivable that a Nazi victory would have increased the pressures for totalitarianism here. Confronted with economic breakdown and stagnation, the American people would be ultimately driven to make the same desperate, disastrous choice: annulment of the grand universals underwriting the individual's inalienable right to personal life and liberty. The extermination of the Jews by Hitler symbolized the ultimate fate of every human being, stripped of every claim to an inalienable right to live.

X
The Road from Auschwitz

The Emergence of Global Capitalism

ðŸ•Š The Holocaust is the ghastly monument to the triumph of the nation-state. It symbolizes, as does nothing else, that there is no limit to the savage impulses of frightened humankind. Rage fed by terror and violence fed by rage transform ordinary human beings into thinking savages and rational beasts. Deep within the labyrinth of the mind, they find a cornucopia of righteous reasons for every murderous assault upon the autonomy of other human beings. This propensity is writ large on the historical record. Its indulgence is the mark of Cain that every race, people, and nation has imprinted indelibly upon its history.

"Root out the Amalekites, leave nary a one alive," was attributed in Moses' name directly to God, and the failure to heed this command when voiced by Samuel in Yahweh's name lost Saul his kingdom. "Tear Melos to the ground, put its menfolk to death, make off with the women and children," so the wise leaders of Athens counseled when Melos stubbornly insisted on the right to be neutral. "Kill the killers of Christ, and Christ will make you free," chanted faceless mobs, fresh from communion and in fervid religious heat, as they ventured forth to rob, pillage, and murder the stiff-necked descendants of the Israel of the flesh, so that the Israel of the spirit might go from strength to strength. "Kill the body to save the soul," cried out generations of inquisitors, meticulously chosen for their pious strength so that they might withstand the agonizing, heartbreaking pleas of wretched sinners, and with serene joy serve as humble instruments of Christ's all-embracing love. "Thou hast betrayed Marx; thou hast blasphemed Lenin; thou hast opened the gates to the counterrevolutionary enemy; thou hast sinned, thou hast transgressed, thou hast done abominably; thou hast sinned overtly and thou hast sinned covertly; thou hast sinned by commission and by omission; thou hast sinned in word and thou hast sinned in thought. Repent, seek forgiveness, make atonement, for who knows, perhaps mercy will soften justice, and cries of a contrite heart may turn away his wrath," chanted Stalin's cohorts as they cajoled and threatened revolutionary heroes.

The record is clear, grim, and decisive: humanity has always found a way to embroider its destructiveness with symbolic grandeur and impeccable logic. But I doubt whether in all of human history anything so innovatingly destructive as the Holocaust has been devised. There are other instances that beg for consideration, but they all somehow pale before this ghastly wonder. Such a plan to exterminate — so efficiently and cool-headedly — millions of human beings because they had been labeled "Jews" is hard to come by in all of the blood-drenched annals of humanity's blind stumbling toward humaneness. For the Holocaust was no simple extension of war; the Jews had no army, no navy, no air force, not even a land to call their own. Dispersed throughout the world, they could not marshal their forces and stand against their enemies in the noble tradition of nation-state wars. Yet they were exterminated because they were alleged to be the most dangerous enemy of them all, more threatening, so the Germans were told, than the millions of tons of bombs that pulverized the German cities and cremated their inhabitants. The real war was the war against Jewry, which had called up its minions from the four corners of the earth — England, the Soviet Union, and the United States — to effect the final solution of the Aryan problem. How necessary then to exterminate the disease at the root!

Accounting for the Holocaust

‽ Why the Holocaust? And why the Germans and not the French, English, or Americans? If there is no answer, then there is no hope; for if there is no discernible cause, there can be no way of offsetting the effect. But if the Holocaust can be explained — if this evil, like other evils, can be accounted for, then there may indeed be hope.

I have set forth above a credible explanation. The Holocaust is the final solution for an entrapped nation-state, reeling from economic breakdown and seeking to delay its own plunge to oblivion. The Holocaust is the nation-state tragedy writ large. The extermination of the Jews refracts the agony of Russian peasants starved to death by Stalin in his determination to carry through forced collectivization; the dazed suffering of uprooted minorities callously transferred to distant and alien lands; the humiliation of groveling souls seeking forgiveness for uncommitted crimes and doing penance for unthinkable thoughts; the cremating of suckling infant and aged graybeard in once-proud cities set to flames by endless waves of bombers with an endless supply of ever more potent bombs; the human debris scattered in the wake of determined and irresistible armies; the awesome new mushroom clouds signaling the tidings of sacrifices of young and old, innocent and guilty—a whole burnt offering—humble artisan and respected nobleman, fledgling poet and illiterate workman, pious priest and rugged skeptic, lover of peace and worshiper of war, to hasten the day when unconditional surrender would permit humanity once again to choose. All is there in the Holocaust: the nation-state versus the individual. Beyond the Holocaust there is nowhere for destructiveness, humiliation, degradation to go.

World War II, like World War I, was a great watershed. Fundamentally at issue was what kind of principles would shape the world. For most of the war, the choice seemed to be limited to some form of totalitarianism or restoration of the system of rival nation-states. The former clearly gave no option to Jews; but the latter was hardly more attractive, since it threatened to unleash again the economic stagnation and disintegration that had followed World War I. Its ominous features were clearly discernible, as World War II drew to an end, in the role that the Soviet Union was bound to play in the postwar settlement. There was precious little likelihood that the Jews in Eastern Europe could count on secure status within the Soviet orbit, and even the most sanguine recognized that there was no hope for a Soviet reappraisal of Judaism. The muted, though very real, Soviet anti-Semitism that had shown its destructive force even during the war could scarcely be expected to wither away so long as Stalinist totalitarianism went unchallenged.

A third choice emerged, however, as World War II was coming to an end, a choice made possible by a breakthrough in coercive power—the atom bomb. If this power were wisely and responsibly wielded, a global community might be fashioned that would render nation-state warfare obsolescent and dysfunctional and free the capitalist economic mode from artificial nation-state restraints. It opened up the opportunity to transmute the destructive rivalries of nation-state capitalists into vigorous but nonviolent competition. It would permit the reshaping of the globe as it might have been had developing capitalism had as free a hand throughout the world as it did in the United States. The American experience left little room for doubt that optimally capitalism flourishes best when there are no national or other irrational barriers to the pursuit of profit. It also demonstrated that ethnic, cultural, and regional variations can coexist under capitalism with tension but without recourse to large-scale bloody warfare.

Capitalism and the Pursuit of Profit

꿴 Capitalism is system in process. Its pursuit of profit has radically altered it. The historical record is clear: commercial capitalism bred industrial capitalism, industrial capitalism of small producers bred corporate capitalism, corporate capitalism concentrating on a single end product bred diversified corporate capitalism; this last, in turn, is now breeding such novel forms as conglomerates and multinational corporations. These developments can be made concrete by ticking off individuals illustrating each phase: Dona Gracia and Don Joseph Nasi (commercial); Carnegie and Ford (industrial); J. P. Morgan, Alfred P. Sloan (corporate); David Rockefeller, the Bronfmans (diversified). Each of these forms is capitalistic, since each was an outcome of the pursuit of profit and each is committed to capital augmentation through the profit motive. Furthermore, each is interlinked historically: the earlier form in some way generated the form that followed.

Though each form is interconnected and energized by the same profit motive and competition, each derives its profits from different sources. This means that these forms are antagonistic to each other and rivalrous. Their structural differences are so fundamental that some of the bitterest struggles since the sixteenth century have been between competing forms of capitalism. The bid of the industrialists in England in the first decades of the nineteenth century for adequate parliamentary representation was a rebellion against profit-seeking merchants and landowners. The Revolution of 1830 in France was an equivalent kind of conflict. But perhaps most enlightening is the American Civil War, for it took place within a constitutional framework that was designed to head off just this sort of conflict. In raw economic terms, it was a desperate effort on the part of planter capitalism to preserve itself in the face of developing industrial capitalism in the North and a proliferating free farming class in the West. I deliberately designate the economy of the South as "planter capitalism" since from the very beginning, the planter *capitalists* utilized slave labor because they reasoned that their special problems of recruiting a work force made slave labor more profitable than free. They were not committed to slavery for its own sake but for profit's sake. And so long as slavery proved profitable, they were more likely to reinvest in the plantation economy than in industry. The planters were dependent on capitalistic markets and concerned with the disposition of their profits; i.e., they calculated what percentage of their profits would be plowed back into production in relation to anticipated future profits or losses. Consequently, when a favorable political climate for a plantation economy was threatened by the rising industrialist and free farmer, the planters took up arms to protect their traditional source of profit: slave labor. The industrial capitalists and the free farmers for their part strove to remove the barriers blocking the extension of their mode of profit seeking. The result was a frightful civil war and, for the South, a century of underdevelopment.

The history of capitalism, especially in the United States, reveals that, with the exception of the struggle between planter capitalism and industrial and free-farming capitalism, the

transition from one capitalist form to another has been effectuated without resort to war. Thus, without a civil war the
older forms of mercantile capitalism in the United States gave
way to industrialism; laissez-faire industrialism gave way to
corporatism; the radical transformation of agriculture was
carried through; labor was unionized and the shift took place
from labor-intensive to capital-intensive production—all
without civil war. These transitions were not totally free of
conflict or violence, but they did not provoke civil wars. Since
1865, American capitalism has resorted to large-scale violence
only when imperialistic interests have been threatened (in
Central and South America and in the Middle East) and, most
massively, when nation-state conflict in Europe compelled intervention to preserve U.S. nation-state interests.

Pragmatism at Work

❧ Entrepreneurs seeking profits are pragmatists, not theo-
rists. They take into account the actual set of problems they
face and do their best to overcome them. We have already had
occasion to see this pragmatism at work when the Mendes
family left Antwerp to settle in the Ottoman Empire, trading a
Catholic for a Jewish identity. These early entrepreneurs simply used their ingenuity to overcome obstacles and limitations to attain what was attainable. They did not insist that an
ideal capitalistic world be shaped *before* they undertook an enterprise, but they contrived ways of working within existing
economic, political, and religious systems. Like the winds and
the tides, the existing structures were there to be reckoned
with.

This pragmatic bent of entrepreneurs accounts for modern imperialism, which was a solution to the problem of profit
making for nation-state capitalists with limited opportunities
for internal expansion. Imperialism was not necessitated by
the capitalist dynamic, though it is compatible with it. Imperi-

alism was a capitalistic response to the problem of the nation-state, not a response to the capitalist dynamic as such.

In the latter part of the nineteenth century English, French, Belgian, Dutch, and German entrepreneurs faced an industrial capitalism that had remarkably increased labor productivity and yielded an ever-growing abundance of commodities, which soon saturated the internal market. Thus Germany — a latecomer on the capitalist scene — sopped up its internal markets in a relatively short time. Where was this overflow to go? It had either to be diverted outward or dammed up. If outward, then imperialism was the most alluring option as markets in other nation-states became less available. If dammed up, then economic stagnation, breakdown, and ultimately civil war seemed inevitable.

When the European entrepreneurs opted for imperialism, what problems did they hope it would solve? First, markets for manufactured goods were needed. Second, outlets for capital had to be found. Third, cheap sources of raw material and food supplies were essential.

Asia represented highly developed civilizations, rooted in agricultural and urban systems that had proved relatively effective over millennia. Traditional ruling elites had proved their ability to run highly stratified societies with a minimum of internal disquiet. Peasants followed traditional modes of food raising without strong incentives to change; urban classes too tended to replicate rather than innovate. A balance between city and country and ruler and ruled was the norm. The term "underdevelopment" is therefore a misnomer for Asia. Pre-capitalism is a far more apt description. Africa's situation was much more complex, for it ran the gamut from highly developed traditional pre-capitalist to extremely primitive societies. Except for regional enclaves here and there, the sparsely settled and underdeveloped parts of Africa did not attract settlers from Europe. Capitalism was not extended via direct colonization. The less developed inland areas, therefore, were left to be exploited rather than developed.

The Profit Impetus

ও▶   This was the situation as it appeared to European entrepreneurs at the end of the nineteenth century. For them, profit making in the underdeveloped worlds seemed to be possible only if they exploited traditional pre-capitalist structures. The basic modes of wealth production had to be preserved, the traditional elites had to be utilized, and untapped labor resources had to be procured as cheaply as possible. Replication seemed far more profitable than innovation or renovation.

This exploitation of pre-capitalism in the interests of profit making was not new. The planter economy in the South had been dependent for its profits on slave labor. The highly profitable slave trade likewise testifies to the pragmatic bent of entrepreneurs. Indeed, imperialism proved so profitable that it undermined the development of capital-intensive investment at home. Tea, tin, rubber, oil, jute, produced by a pre-capitalist labor supply, offered richer returns than investment in the technologies of mass production. Thus England, France, and Germany failed to develop an automobile industry for the mass market because the internal market was limited, the productivity of workers was not sufficiently upgraded by continuous mechanization, and the return on capital in the underdeveloped countries was far higher than in capital-intensive industries in the highly developed countries.

There was little incentive to spread the capitalist revolution to the underdeveloped lands. It seemed more profitable to keep India yoked to traditional modes of production than to industrialize her. It seemed more profitable to utilize pre-capitalist labor systems to extract minerals and agricultural products in Asia and Africa than to diversify economies.

This decision by the European countries had far-reaching results. So long as the traditional modes of production were employed in the colonies, there could be no significant increase in productivity. This meant that the standard of living could not go up, and that the markets in the underdeveloped lands would be limited to a demand for cheap manufactured products, such as textiles. No pressure for upgrading the quality of manufactured goods thus emerged out of imperialism. On the demand side, colonies offered an outlet for commodities of limited range and quality; on the supply side, they offered primary, not manufactured, products.

The optimal solution would have been to restructure the underdeveloped world so as to spin off capitalistic development, extending the capitalist revolution. This would have required the overthrow of the traditional ruling elites in Asia and Africa and subsidizing the building of an economic infrastructure essential for capitalist development: transportation systems, energy resources, communications, agricultural renovation, and educational and health facilities. At the end of the nineteenth century no capitalist nation-state had enough capital resources for this. Nor could any nation afford the power or administrative talent to dispense with the native ruling elites.

Exploiting Capitalist Opportunities

&❧ The history of capitalistic development in the United States during the age of imperialism proves that when other alternatives are open, capitalism chooses developmental rather than predatory outlets. Thus, at the turn of the century, when English, French, and German capitalists were diverted to imperialism, American capitalists were drawn to exploiting the opportunities for profit, *within* the United States, of a continent-size nation-state. The potential for profit lay in the rich raw materials, a developmental and scientifically and technologically oriented agriculture, swelling reservoirs of immigrant labor, and a wildly growing urbanization. The sources of profit lay in skillful and effective utilization of factors conducive to economic growth. The market that lay before American capitalists was to be reckoned in the tens of millions, and its exploitation encouraged technologies of mass production. Efforts to broaden the market encouraged capital-intensive use of labor. Being capital-intensive in turn increased productivity. Productivity in turn permitted the rise in real wages. The rise in real wages widened the market. A spiral was set off that resulted in upgrading the quality of the labor force, elevating living standards, and opening up markets for a wider and more sophisticated range of products.

When the automobile industry began to produce cars for a broad mass market, a decisive structural breakthrough occurred for American capitalism. In developing its major industries for the unique American market, American capitalism cut off imperialism as a viable option for itself. Underdeveloped countries simply could not offer markets for such sophisticated and expensive products as automobiles, radios, refrigerators, and business machines. The standard of living of the masses had to be upgraded before they could enter the market for expensive commodities. English textile manufacturers could sell a dress or shirt to a native earning $60 a year; General Motors could not sell a car unless the buyer earned several thousand dollars a year. Imperialism may have been a way out for European capitalism. For the most advanced sectors of American capitalism, however, it was a *cul de sac*.

Other Defects of Imperialism

ﺦ On the supply side, too, imperialism proves unprofitable for the advanced economic sectors. At first glance it appears as if it could be a source of cheap raw materials for the capitalist and a cheap source of food for his workers and the population at large. But since profitability is enhanced with the shift from labor-intensive to capital-intensive input, there is more profit to be gained from the worker's brain than his muscle. There is more profit in automation than in unskilled labor. This is as true for the underdeveloped world as for the developed. Upgrading workers to operate machines in factories is more profitable than allowing labor resources to be wasted on agricultural and extractive industries. Industrialization of the underdeveloped areas opens up far more profitable opportunities for American capitalists than allowing them to lie fallow.

Nor is imperialism attractive for capital investment, for exploitation of traditional societies cannot satisfy the investment needs of American capital. How many billions can be invested in the production of tea, rice, tin, rubber, coffee, or even oil? There is a limit, and that limit would soon be reached. But this is not true of the expanding opportunities for investment spun off by a developing diversified economy where the dynamics of growth themselves renew and widen opportunities for investment. Imperialism may be a solution for replicating capitalism, but it would be a disaster for developmental capitalism.

The distinction between imperialist and developmental capitalism is structural, not national. Each represents a way of making profits. The test is not whether the enterprise is American or European or Asiatic, but how its profits are generated. Long before World War II there were many European firms that were capital-intensive and oriented toward upgrading mass markets, and there are any number of American businessmen and corporations whose profits derive from the utilization of cheap labor. These seek to perpetuate structures that are favorable to their interests. Such capitalists will, in principle, be nation-state imperialists, and they will strive to establish beachheads for their modes of profit making wherever possible. So long as there is profit in picking coffee or tea or grapes by exploiting underdeveloped, undernurtured, and underpaid unskilled labor, there will be entrepreneurs— American, English, Dutch, Japanese—taking advantage of the opportunity.

Global Capitalism

ટ⩗ The term global capitalism describes that economic mode whose profits are generated out of developed and developing labor, i.e., capital-intensive utilization of labor, and whose end products necessitate upgrading the quality of the markets. A capital-intensive enterprise in Germany, Japan, or Italy may be globalist, while a labor-intensive enterprise in the United States may be nation-state imperialist. However, the *dominant* sectors of capitalism within the United States are capital-intensive and oriented toward development, and, therefore, the executive power of the state is committed, regardless of the political affiliation of the incumbent President, to attaining, so far as it is possible, a national and world order supporting global capitalist goals. This despite the fact that any number of industries in the United States are rabidly protectionist or still utilize heavy inputs of brawn labor and that there are bitter struggles between these nation-state imperialist sectors of American capitalism and the most rapidly growing sectors.

A clear-cut illustration of the impact on foreign policy of these structural differences is England's initial rejection of a European common market, in contrast to the United States' vigorous support, and England's desperate efforts to keep her empire in contrast to the United States' support of decolonization. Britain was so concerned with the loss of imperial profits that she failed to take advantage of her pioneering breakthroughs in the new technology and press her potential for managerial development. The United States, on the other hand, calculated that widening and upgrading were precisely what the capital-intensive, mass-producing industries of the United States needed to enhance profitability, and so since the war the technological and managerial frontiers have been heavily subsidized by the state.

Global capitalism is thus a structural concept, not a national one. The leader in the drive for its realization happens to be the United States, only because the development of capitalism in this country generated this form, but it is a phenomenon that transcends nations. The multinational or supranational corporation — the "Cosmocorp" as former Undersecretary of State George Ball called it — in calculating profitability must prefer competence over nationality, and subordinate the nation to the region. For the Cosmocorp, capital flows to the areas of highest yield, not to the borders of a nation-state, encouraging the extension and upgrading of markets, and upgrading the labor supply wherever it is. Rice picking with its low productivity and low-paid labor force is not nearly as profitable as, for example, the manufacture of textiles, which requires the development of labor skills. Such upgraded labor is low cost by comparison with Western labor, and it effectively draws capital from the developed to the underdeveloped countries; but at the same time it represents an upgrading of native labor and the first spiral in elevating living standards.

Global developmental capitalism is thus driven by the profit motive to dissolve both nation-state imperialist capitalism and the sovereign nation-state. This includes the dissolution in the United States as well, of non-developmental capitalism, which, since the Civil War, has curbed development in the South and exploited blacks in both North and South as a semi-servile reservoir of unskilled, degraded, and replicating labor. To the degree, therefore, that American global capitalists control the state, underdevelopment is eliminated and the quality of labor upgraded. The global-capitalist state is driven to fashion a global community and ceases to serve narrow nation-state imperial interests at home or abroad. Instead of a Pax Americana where weaker peoples are made tributary, the developmental capitalists, in widening the opportunities for profit making, seek global development and a Pax Humana.

If the structural difference between non-developmental (nation-state imperialist) and developmental-global capitalism is understood, then much that is obscure about the history of the period since World War II will be made clear. By focusing on concrete economic interest, the fundamental economic and political forces that have shaped the world since World War II can be seen.

Restoring a Capitalist World

ᔧ When World War II drew to an end nothing could have been more frightening to American decision makers than the specter of a world plunged once again into chaos by economic collapse. The Depression in this country had not been resolved before the outbreak of the war, and there was no guarantee that capitalism could withstand the consequences of peace. Every contemplated solution to the problem had to reckon with the continuation of the nation-state system after hostilities ended and with its propensity to breed destructive rivalries. Statesmen could only guess the answers to such questions as: Would greater benefit and security be gained from a United States-Soviet understanding at Britain's expense, or an American-British alliance against the Soviet Union? Was a Germany stripped of industry and pauperized preferable to a rehabilitated Germany under strict controls? Was the Soviet Union amenable to economic arrangements that might prove profitable for American entrepreneurs, or was its fear of the consequences of such arrangements for the Stalinist system too overriding? And then there was the problem of the colonial and semi-colonial areas that the Dutch, Belgians, French, and English counted on for economic resuscitation after the war. Though one might brush aside the Dutch and the Belgians, one could not so easily dismiss the interests of a de Gaulle or the determination of Great Britain to hold on to its imperial system. The postwar possibilities for peace were thus threatened by the fact that so long as the nation-state system lacked a single nation-state with the coercive and economic resources to compel, if need be, all other nation-states to participate in a global community and surrender their sovereign rights in exchange for collaborative development, there would inevitably come a day when the limits of economic growth within nation-state borders would once again plunge the world into irretrievable disaster.

The atom bomb radically changed the calculus of possibilities. It made globalism a real option. If it were directed with constructive, liberating goals in mind, the atom bomb might never have to be used again.

The Cold War and Beyond

彩 What we have been witnessing since World War II is a revolutionary transition from the nation-state phase of capitalism to the global phase. Global capitalism is cutting down the traditional pre-capitalist societies (the underdeveloped societies) and penetrating the anti-capitalist societies through the experimental introduction of profit, interest, joint ventures, and the market mechanism. It is undermining and dismantling obsolescent, dysfunctional, and restrictive forms of capitalism (Dutch, Belgian, French, and British imperialism); cheap agrarian, uneducated, and low-productive labor in underdeveloped sections of the United States, especially the South; and inefficient high-cost industry habituated to high protective tariffs, a secure repetitive market, and a reservoir of cheap unskilled labor.

Developing capitalism has once again been unleashed, and the consequences are revolutionary. Innovation cannot but undermine inadequate, inefficient, and relatively unprofitable forms, irrespective of whether they are labeled pre-capitalist, capitalist, or socialist. Thus, a worldwide struggle is being waged between the revolutionary sectors of growing, developing, global capitalism and all less efficient systems. The extent of the violence that accompanies this struggle has varied and still varies from a mild case of civil strife, with the liberation of blacks and the eradication of poverty, illiteracy, and urban blight in the United States, through a bewildering mix of hostility and cooperation with the former states of the Soviet Union, to the agonizing upheavals of many centers of limited warfare.

Though the means used by the United States may at times be obscure, the end goal can scarcely be the preservation of obsolescent nineteenth-century and early twentieth-century forms of capitalism and imperialism—which represent a primitive phase of capital accumulation and are now obstacles to profit and economic growth. These are now as outmoded and obsolescent as is the personal ownership and management of multibillion-dollar firms. For the growth sectors of American capitalism, imperialism is a constraint, not an opportunity. Developing capitalism requires expanding markets, rising standards of living, and educated, healthy, and highly productive—hence non-exploited—workers, employed at expensive and efficient machines. It has to build viable free societies to maximize profits; cheap, servile, and hungry hands are as profitless for expanding capitalism as they are pitiable. The decision of Great Britain to move out of the regions east of Suez, for example, was tantamount to a far-reaching triumph of global capitalism over nation-state imperialism. All the years of French, Dutch, and British imperial sway produced not a single showcase of economic growth and development. The foreshadowing of what the future holds for Asia under global capitalism is revealed by the remarkable development of Japan since World War II. Japan was not exploited by the United States, but encouraged to compete with American capitalism, to expand economically throughout Asia, to innovate exciting new economic processes. The only freedom she lost was the freedom to use force to serve her economic ambitions.

When one looks back to the Cold War that followed so soon after World War II, one is struck that the surface of events in those days gave precious little indication that there would come a day when Germany and Japan would be models of economic growth and political stability, when the Soviet Union would cease to be exclusively an enemy, when the national rivalries of Europe would be sublimated in a common market, when virtually all colonial possessions would be well on the way to becoming independent nations. These developments cannot be attributed to accident, but are the outcome of deliberate and purposive leadership. The United States, as the instrumentality of developmental capitalism, has since World War II pursued, in its own self-interest, partnership, not imperialism, the ultimate goal being to widen the range of opportunity for capitalists of all nations that they would be persuaded that developmental global capitalism offers far more profit than nation-state imperialism, that there is more money in spinning off sustained economic growth in the underdeveloped parts of the world than in perpetuating semi-servile brawn labor.

A Growing Globalism

&. These developments in capitalism did not occur all at once, and their implications even now have not been fully appreciated. But their significance should not be overlooked. They mean nothing less than a resumption of the radical and revolutionary role that developing capitalism had played until World War I. The link to conservatism, traditionalism, totalitarianism, and chauvinistic nationalism has been severed. The growing sectors of capitalism are, with each passing day, becoming identified with globalism and the eradication of the festering vestiges of outmoded, obsolescent, and exploitative nation-state imperialism. These sectors in their pursuit of profit need a global community that gives the individual nurture and freedom. The new technologies cannot afford to lose the profit now going to waste in hungry, illiterate, and debilitated workers. The resurrection of the lost universals is now essential for the development of a global capitalist system, and *among these universals is the freedom of the mind and the spirit to explore reality uncoerced, opening realms that transcend the realm of economics.* But there is this difference: Whereas these universals in the early stages of capitalism could go hand in hand with a great deal of deprivation, suffering, and ugliness, now the augmentation of capital has reached such dimensions that poverty and exploitation become irrational anomalies more profitable to eradicate than to sustain.

The Jewish Stake in Globalism

ﱠ   Though we seem again to have wandered far away from Jews and Judaism, we have done so only so that the perspective will be unclouded by the eddy of day-to-day events and by the fears and tremors of each passing headline. For we are now poised to frame a sweeping generalization and prognosis: Since World War II Jews and Judaism have been liberated in every country and territory where capitalism has been restored to vigorous growth — and this includes Germany. By contrast, wherever anti-capitalism or pre- capitalism has prevailed the status of Jews and Judaism has either undergone deterioration or is highly precarious. Thus at this very moment, the country where developing global capitalism is most

advanced, the United States, accords Jews and Judaism a freedom that is known nowhere else in the world and was never
known in the past. It is a freedom unmatched even in Israel,
where only one form of Judaism — Orthodoxy — is truly free.
Jews in the United States are offered a remarkable range of
economic, political, intellectual, spiritual, and even social options. They are even free to slough off their Jewish identity
without converting to Christianity.

The phenomena thus sustain the conclusion: *To the degree
that capitalism is developmental, to that degree does it extend freedom of identity to Jews, and to Judaism freedom to develop and proclaim its teachings.*

The State of Israel

Israel was the first fruit of the anti-imperialist drive of
United States capitalism, the first successful intrusion into a
geographical area that had hitherto been sacrosanct. Palestine
was a strategic link in the imperial system, and had always
been treated as such by the British. In 1917, The Balfour Declaration had toyed with the possibility of channeling Jewish nationalist energies to serve British interests in the area. It had
also made more palatable to public opinion the exercise of
mandatory power. But it soon became evident that a westernizing intrusion in the Arab world was highly disruptive, for it
threatened to undermine the underdeveloped character of the
region. By the late 1930's, England had revealed its pro-Arab
orientation and had driven the *Yishuv* (the "settled" Jews of
Palestine) to the verge of desperation. Although World War II
mitigated the basic hostility, it broke out virulently again
when, at the close of the war, the British sought to cut off
immigration and supported a series of moves designed to
render the Jews helpless by disarming them. The Yishuv responded with a war of national liberation, and the United
States responded with overt and covert support.

The intervention of the United States could be justified because of the anomalous state of Palestine as a mandated area. Although the British looked upon the mandate as a facade for imperial interests, the United States looked upon it as legal justification for irritating and annoying the British. By insisting that the mandate was a trust, the United States could legitimately take the British to task for their moves against the Yishuv. Supported by a large, articulate, and politically powerful Jewish population, American politicians of both parties could capitalize on an issue that won them votes at the same time that it facilitated the basic foreign policy of the United States. There was no Arab constituency to consider, since the Middle East was basically British turf, and the Arab ruling groups were basically subservient to British interests. Thus, a pro-Jewish position would undercut the British, while a pro-Arab position would support them.

When, therefore, the British moved to turn over Palestine to the Arabs, the United States moved to support Jewish efforts to create the State of Israel. President Truman used every occasion to embarrass the British by calling for unrestricted immigration at the very moment when the British were clamping down forcefully on immigration. In a host of covert ways, the United States cooperated in the arming of the Jews. And, most significantly, Truman recognized the State of Israel only a few hours after it was declared.

This quick recognition of Israel was not politically motivated, though its political potential was thoroughly exploited. It was not simply a response to the powerful Jewish lobby. It was, rather, a logical and necessary consequence of the needs of the dominant forces of American capitalism. It was a wedge, a penetrative salient in an area hitherto blocked by British imperialism. The recognition of Israel was a dramatic commitment to the developmental principle. Unlike the

Arab world, the Yishuv had developed a diversified economy with a modern infrastructure.

Most striking was the advanced character of the agricultural sector. The peculiar problems of the Jews in Eastern Europe had channeled nationalist fervor into agriculture. The anomaly of the Jewish Diaspora, so the Zionist ideologues argued, lay in the distortion of the normal national profile. Jews had been forced off the soil. They had for centuries been denied peasant rights. They had been pushed into urban occupations that had tainted the psyche of the people. What was desperately needed was a renewal through land and soil. Palestine was to be the opportunity for this regeneration. There, enthusiastic Jewish nationalists could liberate themselves by reclaiming the land, dredging the swamps, and tilling the soil. Whereas the nationalist leaders of Central and Eastern Europe sought to free the peasant from the soil and release the worker for industry and urbanization, the Jewish nationalists called for liberation from urbanization and a return to the soil.

But the Jewish colonists were not peasants; they were urban dwellers turning to agriculture. This made all the difference. Precisely because they had been urbanized, and precisely because they had been westernized, they industrialized and westernized the soil, i.e., they applied to the land the most modern agricultural methods: fertilizers, machinery, pest control, and a productive orientation. Unlike the peasants, they had nothing to unlearn and were not warped by traditional practices. Since they were highly experimental in their attitudes and highly motivated by their nationalism, they voluntarily adopted cooperative forms of economic and social organization, which proved at first highly productive and emotionally satisfying. Thus, whereas the European peasant wished to be a free and independent farmer and looked upon collectives as enslavement, the Jewish colonizer saw enhanced individuality through cooperation and heightened productivity through collective effort. The development of an advanced agricultural sector had been inadvertently encouraged by British policies. Since imperial policy frowned on industrialization, there were no strong incentives for capital investment in industry, and no strong lure drawing human resources from the countryside.

Such concentration on agriculture proved most fortunate (though at the time counter to what was believed to be essential for modernization), because the highly developed agricultural sector contributed to an infrastructure that could enable the economy to spin off into sustained economic growth. The agricultural sector, having been modernized at the beginning, did not have to undergo radical restructuring when national liberation was achieved. Furthermore, the tillers of the soil did not have to be taught how to read and write or to engage in politics.

For British imperialism, the Yishuv was threatening; for American capitalism, it was promising. The British saw developmentalism as a threat to their interests. The United States looked upon the Yishuv as a prototype for the underdeveloped world. It was an alternative to imperialism, for it held out the prospect of reaping profits from sustained economic growth. Developmentalism was a process that could simultaneously enrich the investor *and* the nation in which investments were made.

American decision makers thus saw in the Yishuv's bid for independence a precious opportunity to establish a beachhead in the Middle East and, at the same time, offer an alternative to imperialism. Israel's successful bid for independence with the overt and covert support of the United States was the first war of national liberation. It was an antiimperialist uprising, for the Arabs at that time were the instruments of British imperialism, unleashed to crush the developmental principle. Had the Arabs been successful in crushing the Yishuv, the stagnation of underdevelopment would have been extended and England's imperial hegemony tightened.

The ideology denouncing Israel's right to nationhood, like any ideology, masks the real economic and political interests that prevail. The appeal to justice and righteousness by the Arab leaders at that time is to be taken as seriously as equivalent appeals of any ruling elite. Hitler and Stalin were never at a loss for noble words. The issue is not what was said but what the pattern of action reveals. Since the British did everything to halt immigration, to disarm the Yishuv, to give the Arabs every indication that the destruction of the Yishuv would be welcome, it is clear that they saw their imperial interests better served by the Arabs than by the Jews. And since the Arab ruling classes drew their wealth and power from underdevelopment, it is clear that the Yishuv was fighting a battle *against* imperialism and for developmentalism. Since the United States supported this war of national liberation, and rushed to grant recognition to Israel, such action must have served American interests. Whereas England supported the Arabs because they saw the Arabs as upholding imperialism, the United States supported Israel because it was potentially anti-imperialistic and developmental. The ideology used by the British, the Arabs, the United States, and the Jews was fashioned to attain ends that were not ideological at all. The conflict was between two forms of capitalism; it was made to appear as though it were a struggle between right and wrong, good and evil, justice and injustice. The real issue was the struggle between nation-state imperialism and developmental capitalism.

Although the United States and England clashed over Israel, the overriding need of joint action with England against the Soviet Union deterred the United States from pressing its long-range interests in restructuring the Middle East. It also inhibited the United States from establishing beachheads and salients of anti-imperialism in Asia, Africa, and South America. During the Cold War years, the principle was to avoid provoking the imperial allies of the United States. The United States did not embark on an aggressive anti-colonial policy, but she did take advantage of anti-imperial events to embarrass England, France, Belgium, and Holland. The United States thus recognized Israel, but had yet to follow through to alter decisively the balance of power in the Middle East.

Fortunately for the State of Israel, it came into existence at a time when the dissolution of the old nation-state system was the order of the day. Though its culmination is still many decades away and the transition is bound to be agonizing, the process is occurring. Israel's existence remained precarious only so long as nation-state imperialism remained potent and pre-capitalist traditional systems throttled economic regeneration in the Middle East. A favorable destiny for Israel would be dependent upon the removal of destructive nation-state rivalries in the Middle East and among the great powers. The hostility between Jew and Arab has no deeper roots than the mutual hostility that once existed between Americans and Japanese. Jewish history, as has been pointed out, is replete with evidence that Muslims and Jews lived in harmony under the Umayyads, the Abbasids, the Ottomans, and fructified each other in the past. There is no natural law that would preclude this as a possible future. The foundations of Israel's nationhood therefore would be sustained only if a developmental global society replaced the unrestricted sovereignty of the nation-state system.

Unprecedented Opportunities

8% Paradoxically, the rise of the State of Israel coincided with the blunting in the West of totalitarian tendencies and a regeneration of those concepts that had first brought emancipation to the Jews in Europe. The regeneration of capitalism in the United States after World War II was followed by a burst of opportunity and freedom for the Jew that had never previously been known, even in America. The artificial barriers that had been erected to protect an economy threatened by overproduction of commodities, labor, and talent collapsed one by one as evidence mounted that a new stage of capitalism had been attained with a potential of sustained economic growth. The Jews were among the very first beneficiaries of this breakthrough, for they had elevated themselves out of the proletariat during the last spasm of economic growth preceding the Great Depression. When, therefore, the new state of developmental capitalism was ushered in after World War II, Jews were, for the most part, concentrated in those sectors of the economy that were destined to grow — sectors dependent on brain power rather than brawn power, on capital-intensive rather than labor-intensive production. Jews found that their Jewish identity mattered less and less to society as it became more and more evident that capitalism was not headed for breakdown and disaster. The Jew came to be valued for competence; hence Jewish identity became a personal affair.

Perhaps nowhere was this evaluation more evident than in the highest government echelons, where Jews such as Lewis Strauss, David Lilienthal, Walt Rostow, and Henry Kissinger were called upon to serve in positions of high responsibility. Symbolically, the appointment of Arthur Goldberg as the spokesman for the United States to all nations in the United Nations was especially significant, since he represented the United States during the debate generated by the Six Day War; yet there was no cry of dual loyalty by the press. As a member of a developing capitalist society, Goldberg was chosen for his competence.

Following World War II and the regeneration of capitalism, Judaism was, for the first time, offered equal status with

Christianity. During the Cold War years, American civilization was popularly described as being the outcome of the
Judeo-Christian tradition. Church and synagogue were joined
together in the press, on the radio, and in political speeches as
sharing a common bond. The fact that Judaism differed did
not seem to be nearly as significant as the fact that they shared
a common God and the common spiritual values of universal
goodwill. There was an upsurge in the re-identification of
Jews with Judaism as religious affiliation came to be regarded
as an element basic to an American identity. Judaism was free
once again to develop as many variations as Jews would sustain.

The prognosis then is simple: the triumph of developmental global capitalism, affirming inalienable rights inherent in the individual, offers to the Jew and Judaism the
freedom to survive. Jews and Judaism must have a world
committed to unity, a unity that allows diversity.

The Meaning of Jewish Survival

ε❧ And indeed, is this not what Judaism's survival throughout the ages is all about? Judaism was born thousands of years
ago as a religion proclaiming that experience, no matter how
complex, bewildering, and fragmented, could be integrated
and unified. The Jews conceived of a single, cosmic God who
is omnipotent and who therefore must be the source of all variety and difference. And very early in their history, the Jews
canonized the Pentateuch and vowed to uphold it as God's
immutable revelation. This revelation did not simply tell of a
people and its God, but proclaimed in the very first verse that
God was the God of the entire universe, and in the very first
chapter that God had created one human being, an individual. From this one human being all the varieties of humanity,
so the Bible claimed, issued forth. The people Israel was chosen by this one God so that this teaching would not be lost and

this people might be a blessing among the nations. So long as the Jews acknowledged the Bible as the primordial source of their identity, they could not escape a global role, because they could not escape a global God.

And the historical experience of the Jews proved to be global. The Jews were not able to have an ordinary history. They were tossed about and dispersed throughout much of humankind. Wherever they found themselves they adapted creatively, shaping as many diverse forms of Judaism as there were diverse problems threatening their survival. But however the concept and the forms changed, the commitment to the Unity Principle was never abandoned. The one God was always conceptualized so that Yahweh's sovereignty over diversity was sustained and Yahweh's power to solve problems creatively reaffirmed through their solution. Jewish survival is proof that Jews have, thus far, been able to preserve their identity by periodically reshaping it.

Throughout the ages, then, Jews and Judaism have borne witness to a faith in the ultimate emergence of a global society where the One is recognized as the source and ground of the many. Adam, so the Bible taught, was created as a single individual, minted in God's image. Though it was not always phrased this way, the loyalty to the single God is the ultimate source of every Jewish identity, however secular or even atheistic it may be. The notions, then, of a global community, of a family of all humankind, of the transcendent worth of the individual in the scheme of things were first glimpsed by Judaism and subsequently refracted by Christianity and Islam. These concepts were not without impact on those germinal ideas of a single natural order, of universal inalienable rights inherent in every individual, and of a global society, where every individual of whatever race, nationality, class, or sex is deemed worthy of citizenship. The Jews proclaimed these concepts initially, and the Jews are still alive when they may be on the verge of fulfillment. On each and every form of Judaism is impressed some phase in the evolution of humankind to a global order, even as that global community will of necessity bear the indelible imprint of Judaism and the odyssey of the Jews.

The Unity Principle Now

ε♣ Jews and Judaism were not born with capitalism, but capitalism is crucial to them in our age because it is, thus far, the only economic system whose inner dynamic drives it to press for infinite economic growth; and without sustained economic growth there can be no social or political unity that still allows diverse groups to maintain themselves. This, Jewish historical experience points up again and again: creative energies were unleashed that brought Jews and non-Jews together in fruitful interaction; difference was cherished, not scorned. In each instance this occurred in societies strengthened by economic growth. When economic breakdown unleashed all that is destructive in humanity, the Jew suffered brutal hostility in the ancient, medieval, and modern worlds. The rise and fall of economic systems is thus the core problem that has prevented humankind hitherto from living in concord. Capitalism is a unique economic form. It has, unlike any other economic system, shown the capacity to create wealth and cherish individuation. Whenever it has developed it has opened up non-economic realms for free exploration. In no other system have the mind and the spirit been so free to venture forth unafraid.

But capitalism is liberating only so long as it develops. When its developmental drive is blocked, as it was blocked by nation-state entrapment, it is driven to destroy all the freedoms it generated as it agonizingly destroys itself in totalitarian fascism and in ever more destructive wars for survival. The Jews have known, as no other people, the ruthless disregard for human lives when, in desperation, frightened capitalists turn over power to a Hitler.

Fortunately, a new stage of developing capitalism has emerged, which in its drive for profits promises to spin off sustained economic growth that will eventually make possible the obliteration of hunger, poverty, illiteracy, disease, and war. The material base prerequisite for spiritual life lies in the awesome economic potential of compound interest, and in capital breeding capital. Religion will be free to concern itself with the individual as the jewel of creation, no longer embittered by hunger and envy to blot out those who differ. It will be, at long last, at liberty to help the individual master the transition to a higher order of being.

The role of Judaism and the Jews will on that day have attained fulfillment. The tenacious adherence by the Jewish religion and the Jewish people to the Unity Principle will have been redemptive for all humankind. The challenge throughout the ages has been the threat that human aspirations and hopes would be doomed by the fragmentation of reality; the response of the Jew has been that unity generates diversity. The one, so its history reveals, is the source of the many, not its negation. God—to paraphrase a vintage belief—so loved the human being that God made the human as an individual; so loved the world that God filled it with every manner of diversity; and so loved Israel that God destined her to an odyssey that could end only when every spot on earth was her cherished home and every individual a cherished variation of the divine image.

XI
Postlude

The Present and Beyond

In 1971, when *The Shaping of Jewish History* was published, the *cognoscenti* did not regard capitalism as the wave of the future. Marxist systems in the Soviet Union, China, and much of the Third World were believed to be flourishing; and the commitment to the welfare state in the capitalist countries seemed to be as unshakable as the linkage of capitalism to imperialism and exploitation seemed to be umbilical. Although in the *Shaping* I voiced the good news that global developmental capitalism would be the wave of the future — mine was a voice with few echoes.

Nor did the critics give my voice credence when I cast doubt on the assumption that the Soviet Union was a superpower, arguing that its infrastructure equipped it better to be a Third World country than a rival of the United States, Great Britain, France, Germany, or Japan. Indeed, I asserted at the time that the long-range goal of the United States was to actually integrate the Soviet Union into the West by encouraging the introduction of capitalism as the most efficient and least costly system for attaining economic growth and a rising standard of living. Once capitalist principles took hold, totalitarianism would wither away and the communist political elites would transform themselves into Western-style politicians.

These things have come to pass. Capitalism sailing behind its flagship "globalization" is now ruling the economic seas of the world, whether they are American, British, Russian, or Chinese. Ever since former British Prime Minister Margaret Thatcher called for a rebirth of free-market capitalism, the withering away of the welfare state, and the shaping of a world commonwealth of capitalist nation-states committed to freedom of the individual, the right to private property, and freedom of religion, each year has marked the triumph of capitalism over its communist and Marxist competitors for global supremacy. As Mrs. Thatcher crisply remarked at Aspen on August 5, 1990, "Communism is dead."

Also, in 1971, Great Britain was still not a member of the European community; the Vietnam War was still splitting the American people apart; the Yom Kippur War had yet to be fought; the Camp David Accords were as yet not even a glint in the statesman's eye; the Shah was securely seated on his Peacock Throne while the Ayatollah Khomeini was as yet a name no more fearsome than that of any other ayatollah; and the Cold War was still very much alive. It is not surprising, therefore, that my trumpeting of the coming triumph of global capitalism was dismissed as the blast of a trumpet off key. Yet it is now simply a matter of record that the Soviet colossus and its former satellites are riding the often turbulent waves of capitalism and that China is seeking to make itself shipshape for the tides of Hong Kong, which promises to lift China to the peak of capitalistic possibilities. Emerging economies of the former Third World, with Israel well in the van, are vying with one another to establish, however tempest-tossed the process, ever new miracles of economic growth; and vast regional free-trade communities, however fitfully, are opening up markets hitherto sealed off and securing hitherto closed areas for investment opportunities. "Globalization" is now as clearly one of the buzzwords of our day as "the

Cold War," "Iron Curtain," and "the welfare state" were the buzzwords of 1971. Globalization is the only real game on the global market today, and "globalization" is nothing other than "global developmental capitalism" reduced to a single word.

The voice of the last chapter of the *Shaping* in 1971 thus anticipated the working through of a transition from a struggle between free capitalism and state-controlled economic systems of bygone years to a struggle for a new world capitalist order of sovereign nation-states in the face of traditional hegemonic rivalries between Brito-Europe and the United States. It is the impact of this continued rivalry on the globalization process that is now beating the drum of destabilization. Since the end of the Cold War, the United States and Brito-Europe have not seen eye to eye on Bosnia, or on the new role for the Soviet Union, or on the expansion of NATO, or on China, or on Cuba, or on the direction of the United Nations, or on Africa, or on the Oslo Peace Accords. Yet what is at issue is not globalization *per se*, but rather what the design and structure of this globalization should be in the light of the "normal" and inevitable rivalries between capitalists, on the one hand, and the hegemonic ambitions of the superpower capitalist entities, on the other—ambitions that are bound to have a huge impact on the reaping of the harvest and the first fruits of globalization's augmentation of wealth. Whereas these hegemonic rivalries in the post-World War II period reflected, as I pointed out in the *Shaping*, a structural conflict between what I called global developmental capitalism, as championed by the United States, and nation-state imperialist capitalism, as championed by Great Britain, this structural difference scarcely exists today. Britain and Europe today are no less globalist than the United States. That earlier rivalry, a rivalry that had aborted whatever possibilities there may have been for a single global capitalist order either under a

United States hegemony or some form of interdependence and global partnership, no longer represents a structural constraint, for in the interim Britain and Europe have transformed themselves from a nation-state imperialist form of capitalism into a developmental globalist form. Britain may be said to be the "head" of this new European partnership. Since transforming its former empire into a new post-imperial commonwealth of fifty-four independent states recognizing the Queen—but not Parliament—as its head, Britain has become the very model of a developmental capitalist entity. Indeed, Mrs. Thatcher herself took the lead in bringing this transformation about and in drawing up a blueprint for a global capitalist society of sovereign independent states committed to a single world market and democratic governments with representative institutions. This blueprint, which Mrs. Thatcher unveiled on August 5, 1990, in Aspen was as sweeping as any global vision projected by the United States in the post-World War II period. Whereas its subsequent rejection by Presidents Bush and Clinton might have been explained in the past on structural grounds, it is now explicable only in the light of the hegemonic rivalry between the United States and Brito-Europe for global supremacy. Both the United States and Brito-Europe now share the same basic capitalist interests and drive toward a global capitalist world order. What sets their teeth on edge is the question of whether the President of the United States or the British Prime Minister on behalf of the European Union should be chairman of the board of a world commonwealth of free capitalist nation-states.

To sum up, the nations of the world are maneuvering through "straits of turbulence" as the inner forces of capitalism drive inexorably toward the logical outcome of capitalism's spirit and essence. The forces for globalization must contend, for the moment, with the rugged resistance of the two high towers of present-day capitalism, Brito-Europe and

the United States. Their ambitions and their rivalry for hege-
mony find expression in all the many flash points of the
world—in Europe (former Yugoslavia), in the former Soviet
Union, in Africa (south, central, and north—Algiers), in Asia
(China, India), in the Middle East (Iran, Iraq, Libya, Israel,
Palestine, Afghanistan), and in South and Central America
(Cuba). These rivalries account for the many unresolved eco-
nomic, social, and political issues of domestic concern as well.
It is these straits of turbulence that the Jewish people must
navigate, caught up as they are in the globalization process.

Jews must once again wrestle with issues of identity as
the powerful forces of globalization steadily erode all previous assumptions as to who is a Jew, as intermarriage continues apace, and as the essence of what Judaism is begs for
definition. Or, to state the question more pointedly: on the occasion of the republication of *The Shaping of Jewish History*
does the Unity Principle remain valid? Does the threefold dynamic (replication, variation, mutation) of Jewish peoplehood
and Judaism still operate? Is God-seeking still the imperative
that undergirds the legitimacy of even the most radical trans-
mutations of form and substance? And if so, how can the
Unity Principle help the Jewish people pilot its way through
the current straits of turbulence?

The answer to this question is, in my judgment, an un-
qualified "yes," *provided that we fully comprehend the unique role
that the Jews are playing in the globalization process itself.* Unlike
other peoples, the Jews are already a globalist people, sailing
ahead of globalism—whether in the United States, Brito-
Europe, Israel, Canada, Australia and New Zealand, Latin
America, or South Africa—and experiencing as they do in the
process all the pulls, tugs, and pressures that compel wrestling with the question not only of who is a Jew but why one
should remain a Jew at all in a world where historical identities and loyalties are eroding and new identities and loyalties

are beckoning—new loyalties spelling out self-determination, self-fulfillment, and self-expression. In short, in a world in which the individual is cherished as the highest resource and individual differences are viewed as the most precious of assets, does the Jewish people or Judaism have any relevance? The Unity Principle, its threefold dynamic, its God-seeking imperative, is in the process of shaping humankind in the image of Jewish peoplehood. This is the broad explication. What remains is to see how the "straits of turbulence" affect the process itself.

1
Jewish Security
and Intermarriage

&❧ As an outcome of its anomalous history, the Jewish people finds itself on the cutting edge of the globalization process—a process that is driven by the formation of knowledge, the processing of knowledge, the transmission of knowledge, and the dissemination of knowledge. Although knowledge has been with us since the beginning of time, and although knowledge has been linked with technology for almost as long, the nature of that knowledge and its relationship to technology underwent a quantum leap with the successful production of an atomic bomb by the Manhattan Project. Uniquely, the Manhattan Project began not with existent technology with the intent of extending it, but with an abstract formula, $e=mc^2$. The abstraction implied that technologies might be devised to produce a bomb of fantastic destructive power. The formula itself was the impelling force for finding and creating the technology. It was this success in translating

an abstract law of nature into technologies of the highest order that opened up a new era in the history of knowledge and
technology. Henceforth, the infinite laws of nature could be
tapped for ever more sophisticated technologies, and they
were. Human minds seemingly had access to the mind of
God, and there appeared to be no knowable limits. The results
were exponential, as the history of the computer makes so
clear and evident. Whereas before this translation process a
generation in technology was measured in years, since the
translation it is measured in shorter and shorter bits of time,
with no presumable end in sight. The practical outcome of
this new stage has been the opening up of a spiral of development for humankind that will enable it to overcome the constraints of scarcity with its perpetuation of poverty and other
attendant evils. Whereas in the past obsolescence of existing
technologies was a slow process, now technologies are driven
into functional obsolescence, swiftly opening the way to a spiral of development that has no foreseeable need to end. The
globalization process is thus one that generates infinite future
technological possibilities and wealth beyond limit.

The cutting edge of capital formation in our time is
knowledge—discovering it, creating it, processing it, trans-
mitting it, and disseminating it. Now what is beyond dispute
is that knowledge is universal. It is not racial, it is not national,
it is not ethnic, it is not class- or gender-based. More essen-
tially, it is also individual. Knowledge belongs to whoever
has it. Knowledge is a universal good. Its opposite is falsehood or error. To pursue knowledge is to pursue a universal
good. All those who pursue knowledge are thus linked together in a common bond that transcends whatever differences might otherwise divide them. To the degree that there is
division, it follows from the fact that knowledge is not self-revealing. It must be discovered, and in the course of seeking it
out falsehood and error always dog the pursuit. But so long as

the commitment is there, falsehood and error will be found out, admitted, and in time rectified. A truth seeker is thus an individual for whom truth is the overriding commitment and passion; and the essence of this new stage of capital formation is the acquisition of truth—the tapping ever more successfully of the mind of God.

So it is that in the United States, 90 percent or so of Jews of college age go to college. In Great Britain, the percentage is equivalently high, as it is in Canada, Australia, New Zealand, and South Africa. In Israel, even if the percentage is considerably lower for the nonce, the precocious development of the Israeli economy bespeaks of ever higher percentages in the future. In Latin American countries Jews with college-level education are increasing in numbers. Wherever one turns, Jews are either on the topmost rung on the ladder of educational opportunity or climbing rung by rung upward. Where Jews are less and less likely to be found is in the working class or in the permanent underclass. Thus, if one were to take the profile of the Jewish people worldwide and compare that profile with that of other peoples, one would have to conclude that the Jews have the most "globalizing" profile of any people in the world. Even when they are not as yet as extended on the globalizing frontier as they are in America, Jews everywhere are steadily moving toward it.

This remarkable fact flows directly from the anomalous features marking the history of the Jewish people in the European Diaspora from that of their host peoples—the very features that made the Jews an abnormal people. Although they enjoyed religious autonomy, the Jews were excluded from royalty, the nobility, the church, the fields, and the ranks of serfs and peasantry. They were an urban people who engaged in urban occupations. Since their autonomous rights made them dependent on their religious laws, the halakhah, those who were the recognized experts in this law— rabbis and scholars—became the most influential and respected class. Jews had no kings, no hereditary aristocracy, and no warrior class, and though the wealthy laity played a critical role in the governance of the community, they could not compete with the scholar class as role models. And since this scholar class spent day and night studying the folios of the Talmud, its commentaries, the codes, and the responsa literature, sacred knowledge defined the core identity of medieval and early modern Jewry. It was this knowledge that mapped out the road to eternal life for the soul and, in God's due time, the resurrection for the body.

So it was that when the Jews of Europe made their way to the United States, they came not as peasants looking for land or members of the proletariat seeking out mines and factories, but as city and village dwellers eager to find in American cities opportunities for bettering themselves; they came as people for whom sacral knowledge was the highest value and for whom the masters of this knowledge were heroes and role models. It is therefore not surprising that Jews took advantage of the opportunities the industrial phase of capitalism was opening up in the United States for the entrepreneurial-minded and those who availed themselves of free higher education leading to professional and academic careers. Even when no one anticipated that a time would come in which industrialization would have had its day and knowledge formation would become both the hallmark of capitalism and its most profitable sector, Jews, impelled by the centrality of knowledge in their scale of values, unknowingly pre-fitted themselves for the frontiers of globalization.

But such a time did come, and American Jews whose parents had gambled on knowledge as the highest value found themselves on the frontiers of globalization. As a consequence, American Jews are now structurally more secure than their non-Jewish peers, given that the future of American society is every day becoming more and more dependent on the triumph of globalization. In fact, the well-being and prosperity of the United States are assured only so long as the United States exploits its lead in knowledge formation, knowledge processing, and knowledge dissemination to the full — for only then will it be able to eliminate its annual deficits, cut down its dependence on foreign nations to fund these deficits, reduce the national debt, bring down the heavy interest burden that follows in its train, regain its status as the world's largest creditor nation, and build an infrastructure that renders a permanent underclass too costly to bear. For this reason, America's most fundamental interests require that those who people the knowledge and globalizing sectors be treated as assets nonpareil. The Jews, of necessity, have become the beneficiaries of this critical need. Whereas, in the past, the Jews could become hostages to societies in decline because their services could be dispensed with, now these services cannot be lost without threatening a devastating collapse of society as a whole, a collapse that would topple the elites who must either globalize or give up the ghost.

On the other hand, there is a lurking insecurity that cannot totally be discounted that ensues from the fact that the Jews as a people are concentrated on the frontiers of globalization. Should the globalization processes for whatever reason be fractured beyond repair, anti-Semitic demagogues, like Louis Farrakhan, could potentially exploit this in a devastating way. They could claim that the Jews were responsible for having rendered many jobless through the globalization process, in particular, those unfit for knowledge-based jobs. Because of their "overexposure" on the frontiers of globalization, Jews are an easy mark for Farrakhans who can blame the Jews for causing the real pain, the real suffering, and the real wretchedness of the victims of globalization, as though the Jews were the diabolical cause of a new stage of capitalist development rather than beneficiaries of a new stage of economic history. Intimations of such a possibility were to be seen in Farrakhan's "Million Man March" of 1995, accompanied as it was by a rise of respectable anti-Semitism, as displayed in the sympathetic remarks and gestures of Kemp and Buchanan in the 1996 election campaign. But such a possibility is remote so long as the globalization process becomes increasingly imperative for the survival of the United States and other advanced western economies and the more the abundance of wealth and opportunity it creates enables society to repair the systemic damage that it brings in its train, and so long as the permanent underclass incarcerated.

Be that as it may, American Jewry at this moment is better off than any other ethnic or religious grouping, or, for that matter, the rest of American society as a whole. As an entity, the Jews are the most advanced people of the world if being knowledge-equipped is the criterion of judgment. What is heartening is the fact that the globalization of the world economy, despite its jagged and rugged course, is proceeding apace, with the American, European, and Japanese economies well in the vanguard. The chances, therefore, of the American economy actually collapsing are remote. As long as Jews continue to be in the forefront of globalization, their overall security is likely to be as assured as any security can be assured. In this sense, the Jews may actually be the most secure people in the world, since the Jews in England, France, and Israel are likewise on the frontiers of globalization.

Yet the security Jews enjoy by virtue of their participating in the process of globalization intensifies their insecurity as a distinctive people. This is so because pioneers of globalization are also those most likely to intermarry. In the knowledge sectors, individuals tend to relate to one another as individuals — human beings who measure themselves and each other primarily for their individual qualities and not by their ethnic or religious personae. Unless Jews abandon the global sectors of the economy for a more precarious source of livelihood—a most unlikely choice indeed—the Jewish people will remain vulnerable to intermarriage and the weakened Jewish identity intermarriage spins off. If a unique Jewish identity is to be sustained under these circumstances, some sense of Jewish authenticity is a requisite. Although this authenticity may not be easy to come by, the dynamics of Jewish history explicit in the Unity Principle allow for options, even mutational ones, should the need arise. History also demonstrates the Jewish will to constantly retain a Jewish identity. The Aaronides chose a mutational option, as did the Scribes-Pharisees, and the founders of Reform and liberal Judaism. Even Jewish secularists and nationalists turned toward this mutational option when neither simple replication nor radical variation offered a viable identity. This *traditional* Jewish option is by no means foreclosed now, for Jewish identity lies deep within the globalization process itself. The Jews, after all, have always been a global people by virtue of their global God, of the universalist visions of Amos and Isaiah, and of their long and widespread Diaspora, which exposed the Jews to the full gamut of the rise and triumph of western civilization and the globalization process it has now unleashed. By virtue of its history the Jewish people already have included the rest of the world within their peoplehood, and Judaism already is a religion fit for the spiritual needs of those who would be citizens of the globe.

The continuation of American Jewry—and British Jews display a similar profile—thus ultimately depends on the successful outcome of the process of globalization, a process that carries with it both economic security and the religious risk of intermarriage. *At the same time, the Jewish people and Judaism offer to non-Jews on the frontier a meaningful historical global identity that has God-seeking (and thus knowledge) as its essential dynamic, thereby becoming both a model and a choice.*

2
American Jewry
and Israeli Jewry

෫෧ There is another crisis of Jewish identity inherent in the role Jews are playing on the global frontier in the United States and Great Britain, a crisis that is compounded by the intermittent peace process in the Middle East. If successful, the peace process will radically transform Israel and Israel's relationship to western Jewries. Throughout the decades that followed the birth of the State of Israel, and especially in the decades following the Six Day War, world Jewry's concern over Israel's security forged a unity transcending whatever differences divided Jews along denominational, communal, and regional lines. For many Jews, Israel became the touchstone of their Jewish identity and the motivation for an active role in Jewish life. American Jews pressured the President and Congress to regard Israel as America's prime asset in the Middle East, if not the world at large. They spent and lent vast sums of money on the building of an infrastructure in Israel that would enable Israel to become the only fully developed westernized nation in the Middle East—a nation with a profile in many ways comparable to that of the United States and Great Britain. A secure Israel, an Israel that was strong enough to hold its own against hostile Arab nations and gain the recognition of legitimacy she so desperately needed, was deemed imperative. Hence, sovereignty and security were seen as two sides of the same coin. The possibility that Israel's real security might ultimately come to lie in becoming the equivalent of the Hong Kong of the Middle East—and beyond—was given little or no thought. It was simply assumed that whatever peace might be made with Israel's Arab neighbors would be a peace dependent on Israel's armed might, and not on the sharing of common regional and global interests with former enemies. That Yasir Arafat could someday call for the nullification of the Palestine Liberation Organization's covenant demanding the destruction of Israel was unthinkable. Security undergirded by armed sovereignty was taken for granted. It was this imperative need for security that spurred American Jewry to lobby with might and main for all the arms Israel might require.

All this potentially changed with the handshake that shook the world. The Oslo Accords (1992), which officially opened negotiations between the State of Israel and the PLO, pointed to a new kind of security, a security to be assured not by arms but by the potential for a Middle East community. Israel's then Prime Minister Shimon Peres broached such an idea as far back as 1986 when, after meetings with Mrs. Margaret Thatcher and Sir Geoffrey Howe, he called for a Marshall Plan for the Middle East—*a plan to be funded by Europe and Japan irrespective of whether or not the United States decided to participate.* Subsequently, it was spelled out in detail by Peres in his book *The New Middle East,* published shortly after the peace process was launched. If such a process were successful, Israel's security would no longer be dependent as in the past on its arsenal of weapons, but on the role that Israel alone can play in triggering economic development for the entire Middle East. As the only fully westernized economy and polity in the region; as a nation with close ties to both the European Union and the United States, whose products, skills, and knowhow are in worldwide demand; and as a nation that could easily and rapidly become the key financial center of the Middle East, Israel is already positioned to become, as it were, the Hong Kong of the Middle East. Its security would be assured by the services rendered to its Arab neighbors and the wealth of nations worldwide, not by the weapons it could flaunt. (Even Mao Zedong at the height of his power never touched Hong Kong, and even its return of sovereignty to China is not likely to alter its unique role, given that China is bound by international treaty to guarantee Hong Kong's special capitalist way of life for fifty years. Indeed, the Golden Age of Hong Kong may just be aborning.)

Just as the Jews of the United States owe their security and well-being to the services they uniquely render on the frontiers of America's knowledge-based economy, so the Jews of Israel may in the not too distant future find their security guaranteed by the services Israel uniquely renders as the most precociously developed society of the Middle East. Over time it may turn out that, far from needing economic or military aid from the United States and American Jewry, Israel might very well find itself a significant creditor nation with heavy investments in the United States and large holdings of United States bonds and equities. American Jewry, never having anticipated such a turn of the tables, may thus become exposed to an identity crisis for which it is not prepared. American Jews whose Jewish identity was tied up with Israel's insecurity may ask themselves what meaningful Jewish identity is open to them should the peace process prevail and Israel's security be assured.

Israeli Jewry faces its own identity crisis. It is not so severe as that faced by American Jewry, since the very existence of a Jewish state guarantees the continued existence of the Jewish people. Nevertheless, the Israeli identity crisis is palpable. An Israel less isolated and less threatened will no longer need huge sums to provide for its security. These sums may be released instead for economic growth and development.

To the degree, then, that Israel becomes more and more the epicenter of a Middle East community, to that degree will Israeli national interests become more and more entwined with the globalization of the world economy. This will be especially so if Israel also becomes one of the great financial centers of the world. Should this occur, Israeli and American Jews would find themselves occupying the same frontiers and having an equivalent stake in a global economy and the knowledge sectors of that economy. An optimal Israeli Jewish identity would thus become more globalist and less nationalist. The Jews of Israel may come to view Jewish peoplehood as an anomalous but not abnormal peoplehood, the remarkable survival of which was possible only because sovereignty and territoriality had actually proved nonessential. Ironically, it may well turn out that the State of Israel, a state whose establishment was to restore the "normality" that the *Galut*, the "Exile," had for so long denied — a normality based on being a nation like all other nations, a nation whose sovereignty seemed essential for its security (an assumption which, by the way, has little historical justification, given that historically the greater the power Israel has had at its disposal, the more uncertain was its ultimate destiny) — may find itself so secure that sovereignty becomes in a sense nominal.

Should this prove to be the case then the "abnormality" of the Diaspora experience shaped an East European Jewry so imbued with the secular nationalism of western nations that they built an anomalous nation-state in the Middle East. Israel arose as a modern westernized nation thoroughly out of joint with the Middle East profile, a nation-state that in a few brief years began to play a critical role in the building of a global economy — a role so invaluable that it was essential for all the nations of the world (including Arab states) to protect Israel's security. Ironically, it turns out that the Jewish people in the Diaspora and the Jewish people in Israel seem to have shared the same destiny: to serve other peoples so that their security might be assured, even when having a sovereign nation-state of their own. If the peace process moves, however slowly and jaggedly, in the direction of achieving its ends of a confederated union of sovereign nation-states committed to the free flow of capital, goods, services, and people within the Middle East community—as is the case today within the European Union, made up as it is of nations that had waged devastating wars against one another for centuries—then a time could come when Israel's security and that of Palestine, Egypt, Jordan, Lebanon, Syria, and Saudi Arabia, *et al.*, will be one and the same.

Should this eventuate, our traditional concept of "normality" will have to undergo a radical change in meaning. *The so-called "normal" nation-states throughout history will come to be viewed as having been, as it were, "abnormal," while the people and State of Israel will come to be viewed as "normal."* Concentration by nations on sovereignty and territory in the past justified the most destructive of wars, the unleashing of the Holocaust and genocidal impulses, the erecting of barriers to the free flow of capital, goods, and people throughout the world, and the wasting of the wealth of nations in weapons of destruction. It is in this sense that being a "normal" nation will be seen in retrospect to have been "abnormal." It always carried with it a high cost in human life, a dedication to the destruction of the wealth of hostile nations, and a subsequent loss of spiritual values within the nation itself. Through globalization, nation-states will find absolute sovereignty an impediment to their prosperity and grandeur rather than, as in the past, a prerequisite.

3
The Place of
the Holocaust

ۏ Just as the globalization process has generated a crisis in American Jewish identity and the peace process in Israel is radically altering the status of Israel, so the turbulence following the end of the Cold War has cast the Holocaust in a new light. The Holocaust could be and was indeed looked upon as a *tremendum of tremendums* beyond rational explanation because genocide on so gruesome a scale simply could not otherwise be fathomed. Only against Jews could a hatred so diabolical and so murderous be possible. There could be no counterpart. The bombing of Dresden, of Hamburg, of Hiroshima and Nagasaki, however grievous, cruel, and aimed at civilian populations, were after all looked upon as an instrument of waging war, whether for good or for ill.

The systematic extermination of the Jewish people, however, a people who waged no war, had no arms with which to defend themselves against those who would destroy them, and no means for retaliation in kind, was *sui generis.* The Holocaust therefore belonged to the Jews; it was not for sharing. It was something very special, fraught with meaning, and ineffable. The Jews had to be on guard, like no other people, lest this *tremendum of tremendums* recur. Its ghastly memory became critical to one's Jewish identity. Every effort was made to call attention to the horrors of the Holocaust by building museums for all to see the gruesome reality, producing films of dramatic and emotional impact, and gaining the support of politicians and mind-shapers for weaving the memory of the Holocaust into the warp and woof of American and western consciousness.

Efforts such as these were successful, but, it seems, not successful enough. Not successful enough, because what had not been sufficiently appreciated was that anti-Semitism is too precious a tool for scapegoating to be given up, however false its claims may be and however exhaustively they have been refuted. In the 1980's the defamatory pamphlet, *The Protocols of the Elders of Zion,* was sold by the hundreds of thousands in Japan, a country where virtually no Jews live. Even though the *Protocols* has been exposed as falsehood for nigh on a hundred years, it still sells well, even in the West where large numbers of Jews live. The reason for this is that anti-Semitism's stock and trade is the systemic breakdown of a society, or sectors thereof, and the alleged responsibility of the Jews for this breakdown. The *Protocols* singles out the Jews as the critical cause of the breakdown of a system, a breakdown that Jews could not possibly have had the power to bring about. When a systemic breakdown occurs and generates anxieties from the loss of livelihood and self-esteem, what becomes relevant for the victims are the pain and injustice, not the fact that a systemic breakdown is not some casual happening that can be triggered by a Jewish conspiracy. From these feelings of pain, holocaustal impulses are stirred by demagogues who are interested in power, not facts, and who themselves cannot effect about a constructive systemic rectification. Those who listen to them have only one interest: to wipe out the enemy who has inflicted so much pain upon them. Anti-Semites are not interested in facts because they know the "real" facts, and those "facts" are that the Jews have done them in. Thus, all the strenuous efforts to document the horrors of the Holocaust failed to alleviate anti-Semitism. Revisionist historians simply asserted that the Holocaust did not occur, and the Farrakhans and Buchanans had all the grist they needed for their mill. The Holocaust, they alleged, far from being evil incarnate, either did not occur, or if it did occur the Jews brought it upon themselves by subjugating the rest of humankind. Hence they deserved what they got.

Once respectability is given to the claim of self-proclaimed academics that there was no Holocaust, a Buchanan could exploit this claim to justify his conservative anti-Semitism and a Farrakhan could add it to his already bursting files as a falsehood to appeal to an emerging black permanent underclass, as well as disgruntled black intellectuals and college youth. Thus the Holocaust, far from becoming a deterrent, became a model for Farrakhan when, in a speech to a 25,000-plus crowd in Madison Square Garden in 1984, he urged that the Jews be burned in holy ovens!

In addition, the Holocaust began to look less exceptional as genocidal horrors became epidemic in troubled parts of the world—Cambodia, East Timor, India, Africa, and Bosnia. Holocaustal impulses, far from being limited to the Germans against the Jews, seemed to be the handmaiden of national, ethnic, racial, cultural, and religious rivalries and hatreds. Human beings of whatever stripe, when desperate enough, showed themselves quite capable of inflicting every kind of shocking violence on defenseless innocents. No line of demarcation seems to bar holocaustal impulses from full expression when rage, anger, and fear reach an apogee of intensity. Given this human propensity for extinguishing one's own rage by exterminating those held accountable for arousing it, the Holocaust has taken on a universal dimension that is only now beginning to be appreciated.

Jews, it is now clear, are not the only people who need fear extermination. There are others, many others. As we know from Stalinism, holocaustal impulses were no monopoly of the Germans, even while Hitler was exterminating the Jews. These impulses live deep within the hearts of us all. Whenever and wherever human beings experience fear and terror, they can experience the impulse to eradicate these painful emotions by eradicating their perceived cause. Ethnic, national, religious, and cultural rivalries seed the grapes of wrath when scarcity precludes just and equitable means for righting traditional wrongs. So long as human triage is virtually mandated by the unresolved problem of nation-state rivalries and superpower drives for hegemony, holocaustal impulses will seethe and on occasion explode. Since, at its roots, the Holocaust itself was an effort by Hitler to solve the seemingly insoluble problem of surplus populations — triage *über alles* — by exterminating first six million Jews and then 33 million Slavs — these roots are to be found wherever starvation, homelessness, and helplessness are endemic and ethnic and religious hatreds abound. The Holocaust thus casts its shadow on the frightening dilemma that humankind has been wrestling with throughout the post-World War II era: who will live and who will die when there are more lives than the existing structure of the world economy can sustain, constricted as it is by the existing nation-state system and its rivalries.

Once the Holocaust is recognized for what it truly is — an indictment of humankind's failure to solve the problems of scarcity, surplus populations, nation-state rivalry, and bids for global and regional hegemony — its role in informing a Jewish identity ceases to be its uniqueness as an exclusively Jewish experience, but rather an experience that like no other, no matter how genocidal, calls attention to the as yet unresolved problems human beings face, problems that instigate genocidal impulses and bring them to the boiling point.

The Holocaust thus may be viewed, as Christian theologians have often viewed it, as a Jewish "sacrifice" for humanity as a whole — a warning of what could be the fate of any nation people or race so long as the United States and European Union, the superpowers of the world, fail to abandon their own hegemonic rivalries. Such rivalries militate against building a single global economy capable of creating wealth on a scale so vast as to enable all nations, races, and peoples to sustain themselves without the need for waging war to hold what they have, or to gain what they want and need at the expense of other nations; or to fight civil wars to rectify injustices stemming from the failure of nations to create sufficient wealth to satisfy the minimum needs of their peoples. The Holocaust is, as it were, the handwriting on the wall for all peoples, nations, races, classes, and individuals, and not just for one people alone, even though it was unique, a *tremendum of tremendums*. This could hardly be otherwise, given that the Jews are an anomalous people with no state or territory, no cities or towns in which civilian populations could be freely bombed with saturation bombings or nuclear blasts, and their destruction could not be justified as a legitimate act of nation-state warfare.

The fact, then, that the very existence of the Holocaust could be brought into question—not only by those who, like Hitler, lust for the power that lies in wretchedness, helplessness, and despair, but by those who would gain notoriety for themselves as dedicated academics laying claim to facts that do not exist, evidence that is not to be found, and testimony that cannot be true—demonstrates that facts themselves not only do not deter but can even serve as inspiration. *Anti-Semitism is a function of anxiety, not truth.*

If, after years of studying and teaching the Holocaust in the United States and decades of building museums to display its terrors vividly, a Farrakhan can still urge the masses to perpetuate another Holocaust and revisionists can blithely bring into question the Holocaust's historicity, it becomes self-evident that anti-Semitism is a function of anxiety and not ignorance. A systemic breakdown of an economy or a society of necessity stirs up anxiety to the panic point, and demands an easy target on which to wreak vengeance and a quick fix to set everything right instantaneously.

The Jews may be an easy target, but getting rid of them does not provide a quick fix. The Jews can be identified and isolated as an independent entity from all others who enjoy wealth, power, and influence, and can be held exclusively responsible for a systemic breakdown no individual or group could possibly have brought about. Nevertheless, America's huge trade deficits, its multi-trillion-dollar national debt, its status as a debtor nation, its permanent underclass, its tarnished image as a world power — all are the outcome of a long and complex process which cannot be attributed to any particular group or cause. *All* groupings and interests were party to creating the anxieties that make the American people less than happy. Jews as such were part of this process but were not its cause. The fact that Jews were not hurt by structural breakdowns to the same degree as blacks or others was a derivative of Jewish history, a history that had thrust Jews out onto the frontiers of a knowledge-based economy and thus spared them the breakdown that hit more traditional sectors of the economy. *But all those on these frontiers — Jews, Gentiles, or what have you — were either unaffected or were beneficiaries of globalization.* Computers, high technologies, and information highways enriched those who were caught up in their networks, irrespective of their ethnic origins, race, gender, or cultural and religious particularities. There was no Jewish conspiracy to be on that frontier, no plot to use Jewish advantages to trigger a systemic dislocation of the economy. Quite the reverse: it was always clear that systemic well-being would be a boost, not a loss. The same unique history of the Jews that exposed them to the Holocaust exposed them to the frontiers of a knowledge-based economy and its handsome rewards. This is simply a matter of fact, not a plot or a conspiracy. It would be ridiculous to argue that the Jews plotted the Holocaust or conspired to have it come about in order to reach their present position. Likewise, the fact that a very different history precluded blacks, Hispanics, or Native Americans, along with a large number of whites, from pioneering these frontiers and enjoying the rewards they bring is simply a matter of fact and not a deliberate effort on the part of the Jews to read them out of the equation. The Holocaust almost wiped out the Jews of Europe because of their unique history. The frontiers of a knowledge-based economy, for its part, have spared most Jews, also because of their unique history, from the pain of unemployment, homelessness, loss of self-esteem, and the dismal fate of a permanent underclass doomed to a carcinoma of the mind, body, and spirit.

Though the Jews are not the cause of systemic breakdown, their long history of being the victims of such breakdowns with their anti-Semitic reverberations affords no end of a lesson: unless the systemic breakdown is repaired, objective anxieties will grow apace, discontents will multiply, demagogues will abound, and ugly and fearful feelings will proliferate. Contrariwise, systemic wholeness drains anxieties, releases the wellsprings of hope, loosens the grip of fear, and gives space for harmony and good feelings to flourish. This has happened of its own accord in the past. It could happen in the future, too, as the process of repair mends its way to prosperity and well-being, even as the contrary happened of its own accord as the process of breakdown sapped the wealth and power of the host peoples among whom Jews lived.

There was not a single society in the past that did not of its own accord grant Jews safe haven and broad opportunity, despite glaring religious and ideological differences—so long, that is, as that society was enjoying economic well-being and social stability. So, too, there was not a single society weakened by systemic breakdown that did not turn on the Jews and hold them to account for the breakdown, despite long years of cordial, even privileged, and indulgent treatment.

Once this causal connection is fully appreciated, Jews and all other classes, ethnic groupings, and genders in American society can come to realize that systemic repair, not scapegoating, is the necessity of the day. There is no other long-term solution. But—and here is the rub—there can be no quick fix of systemic flaws, especially when, as in the case of the United States today, there are grave problems that must be solved in America's relationship to the European Union, Russia, Japan, and China before the American economy and American society can be permanently secure. In the interim, American Jews may enjoy relative security insofar as their overall well-being is concerned, so long as the knowledge-based sectors of the economy thrive, but at the same time may find themselves insecure and vulnerable to scapegoating from a relatively permanent and wretched underclass of the unemployable and the rejects of society, with all their potential for violence, as well as from "downsized" members of the middle class, should the economy suffer a severe recession or a real depression.

4
The Lure of Fundamentalism

❧ In an age of global turbulence such as we are now experiencing, when anxiety and bewilderment grip society as a whole, the appeal of an inward-focusing religion becomes well nigh irresistible. In just such an age, at the time of the Hasmonean Revolt, the Scribes-Pharisees sealed off the blows and the sound and fury of a hostile and threatening external world by proclaiming to those who internalized and obeyed the twofold Law that one's soul was immortal and one's body bound for resurrection. So, in similar fashion, do highly westernized American Jews turn back to those modes of life and symbols that time and practice have hallowed as authentic — a 25-hour a day religion, not some watered-down version of the Sabbath and festivals, with Rosh Hashanah and Yom Kippur being for some the only occasions for public worship.

This tug of anxiety for inner security in an external world seemingly betrayed by science, technology, and rationalism has encouraged the rebirth of an ultra-halakhic orthodoxy and a militant Hasidism that could be seen in no crystal ball when *The Shaping of Jewish History* was published in 1971. Nor was there more than a glimpse back then of a Reform Judaism moving as far in the direction of a traditional and halakhic revivalism as it has, however much this revivalism may have been tempered by the rapid growth of intermarriages and the championing of patrilinear descent to help smooth the way for the progeny of the intermarried to hold onto a Jewish identity. The lines between right-wing Reform and left-wing conservatism became more and more blurred as Reform theology and ideology lost their sting. Living an "authentic" Jewish life became as important if not more so than being a light unto the nations and a beacon to the peoples.

From the perspective of the Unity Principle and its threefold dynamic — replication, variation, mutation — what is at stake here is not whether this flight from anxiety to traditionalism is good or bad. It is not a matter of sitting in judgment of the militant Habad movement or the anticipation of the imminent coming of the Messiah. Nor is it a matter of praising or indicting the rightward shift of Reform. What is at stake is something far more important; namely, the very essence of Jewish peoplehood and of Judaism. That essence is not in the halakhah or its denial, nor in the renaissance of militant orthodoxy, nor in Reform Judaism's traditional revivalism. Rather, it is to be found in the flexible responsiveness of the Jewish people to the spirit of the age, its resistance to mere replication of a Jewish shape or form, and its open-endedness to becoming other than it had been — its mosaic of authentic options.

The debate, then, over what Judaism ought to be is not a debate that can be settled by marshaling texts, piling up rational proofs, or pointing to logical necessity. *Judaism in the present as in the past is the outcome of the vicissitudes of historical process, and not the outcome of some dogmatic or doctrinal claim.* In the fullness of time, the turbulence of our age may in all likelihood be looked upon as just another turbulence affecting the shaping and reshaping of the Jewish people, a shaping and reshaping that has been in process for millennia. What it is likely to show is the degree to which the Jewish people were replicating, the degree to which it was variegating, the degree to which it was mutating. *To be aware of this essence is to allow for a transcendence without precluding a choice.* The transcendence is in seeing the threefold dynamic as the *traditional* way in which the Jewish people and Judaism have responded to the winds of change and the shifting spirit of each age throughout the ages. The choice is the personal response to *this* time, *this* place, *this* crisis, and the spirit of *this* age as a legitimate mode of response but not one divinely mandated for all time.

What is historically mandated is the search for the answer to the questions: Whence the cause of the winds of change? Whence the cause of the shifting spirit of the age? What do these changes mean for the Jewish people, Judaism, and humankind as a whole? What do they mean for the possibility of the realization of the teaching of the first chapter of Genesis that a single individual, both male and female, was created in God's image; or of the visions of Isaiah that nations will not lift up swords against nations or know war anymore; or that objective anxieties will fade away; or that, at the end of days, Egypt, Assyria, and Israel will each be God's people?

And should it turn out that the answers to these questions are not hopeful, then a search is in order to see if there are forces at work that may have gone unnoted, forces that may in time succeed in bringing these ideals and visions to pass.

What, then, is the critical cause for the renaissance of ultra-orthodoxy, the phenomenon of militant Hasidism, the rightward drift of Reform Judaism? We can suggest that all of these have been a response to the radical shift in the spirit of the age that followed in the wake of the rise of militant Islamic fundamentalism and Ayatollah Khomeini's successful revolution in 1979 against the Shah and westernizing Iran. For what Khomeini demonstrated was that militant fundamentalism could be used effectively to bring modernization and westernization to a halt, even though the Shah had the full support of the United States. Khomeini could do this because fundamentalist Muslims do not look to this world for their reward or punishment, but, like orthodox Jews, look to the world to come. Rationalism, modernization, westernization, even nationalism proved no match for such an intrepid belief. Millions of Muslims who had benefited little, if at all, from modernization, westernization, and nationalism in this world had little motivation for giving up their one hope for a glorious eternal life; Khomeini's *Weltanschauung,* lifted out of the Middle Ages, thus had great appeal. This revolution (or, perhaps more accurately, counter-revolution) gave a boost to all fundamentalists worldwide as America's loss of Iran set in motion a process that eroded America's global power, influence, and leadership — a process, as we have seen, that is by no means at an end.

All this discomfiture was grist to anxiety's mill and fundamentalist mind-sets. Rationalism, science, and technology were made to appear the source of the distemper of our time, not its solution. Old-time religion, the spirit within, the security of shared beliefs, seductive symbols, and the patina of yesteryear—all these made sense in a world that made no sense, a world that was drifting into a future leading nowhere and was rent by violence, conflict, and genocide as human life became trivialized in Bosnia, Rwanda, Afghanistan, Palestine, and elsewhere. Little wonder, then, that even those Jews who were on the cutting edge of globalism could find little hope or comfort in the turbulence that preceded the end of the Cold War, or in the turbulence that followed on its passing. Indeed, globalism could even be seen as an agent provocateur. People needed a God and a religion they could call upon—a religion they did not have. They needed a God and religious options that were congruent with a world gone astray; a world falling apart; a world whose destiny was not some glorious end of days but a hodgepodge makeshift, a random collage, some witches' brew concocted from bits and pieces of good and evil served up without spoon, fork, or knife to sort them out. If God there is, she or he seemed to give sanction to turbulence and not serenity; to disorder, not order; to violence, not peace; to holocaustal, not loving, impulses; to terrorism, not conciliation. Insofar as the external world was concerned, God could not be relied upon to be redemptive. If God there is, she or he must be sought not somewhere outside but within the heart, soul, and spirit of each individual. When found, such a God can become that wellspring of love, caring, kindness, compassion, and creativity that lifts us out of time and into eternity. For Judaism to be relevant in a world bludgeoned by chance and seemingly unredeemed by God, it had to tack with the times, go with the tide, and fill its sails with the spirit of the age. And this it did, as ultra-orthodoxy burst into new life, militant Hasidism fought for lost souls, and Reform Judaism reached out for time-tested symbols and traditional halakhah-based lifestyles and prayers hallowed by the ages.

Throughout this burgeoning of spiritual concerns, little thought was given to the causal matrix. Remove the Khomeini Revolution, remove the sagging of American global power and leadership; remove, in a word, the drastic changes in the world's direction that occurred externally, and no such drastic changes in the spiritual and religious worlds would have followed. The corollary of this is clear enough. If the external world were once again to change drastically; if instead of growing disorder there would be growing order; if instead of turbulence there would be intimations of serenity; if instead of a future without hope there would be glimpses of a future with hope abounding; if instead of irrational happenstance there would emerge some rational design; if instead of science and technology serving as the handmaiden of violence, pollution, and unemployment, it would become the handmaiden of sustainable and non-lethal economic growth, peace, and collaboration among nations; and if science and technology would serve to heighten the quality of life for all — then we could expect the spirit of the age to change and the role of God and religion to be reexamined. The external world and the internal world would then cease to be worlds in collision.

But are there signs that change so drastic may be in the offing? Are there winds of change blowing that are no less powerful than the winds of change that brought on the sound and fury of Islamic fundamentalism and the present age of turbulence? There are, I would suggest, such winds rustling, and this rustling is pregnant with hope. There are designs on tap that are both visionary and hardheaded, designs inspired by forces so powerful that they border on the inexorable. But — and this is the sticking point — they will take time. It may take another generation or more before they become self-evident. In the meanwhile, as time slowly ticks, there will be suffering, there will be obstacles, there will be acts of terror and violence. Living through this period of transition with hope unfrayed will be daunting and demanding. A generation in God's sight may be no time at all, but for human beings it can seem an eternity. Nonetheless there are potent forces at work that in a generation or so might usher in a golden age.

What are these powerful forces? They are the economic forces now constructing a single global economic system, in the face of the high barriers and obstructive deterrents erected by sovereign nation-states. Ironically, the very states that at present block a smooth transition — the United States and Brito-Europe — are also the most responsible for the inexorability of the globalist process. Economic globalization desperately needs a state system that strengthens and supports the economic process, not one that sets up barriers, limitations, and constraints. As pressure for harmonization increases, more and more states are likely to realize that their national interests are best served by a global economy in which capital, trade, labor, and (most urgently) knowledge move freely; and national interests are hampered if this freedom of movement is constrained in any way or allowed to proceed in haphazard and irresponsible fashion because of economic and historic hegemonic rivalries. An awareness is growing that the wealth of all nations is augmented by a single global economic system within a secure confederated framework of nation-state collaboration. Nation-states may come to realize that a single global economic system need not in and of itself threaten existing political entities with any loss of sovereignty in those spheres that do not impact on the optimal functioning of a single global economic system. They may come to realize that the negative consequences of globalization can be largely offset by a high degree of joint design and planning, which will protect the environment and spare scarce natural resources and indigenous cultures from the ravages of unrestricted plundering without necessarily stripping nations of their individuality or their sovereignty.

For more than two hundred years, the United States has functioned as a federal union with a shared sovereignty that has proved most advantageous for its individual states. More recently, the European Union has been in the process of seeking the same goals through a confederated union rather than a federal union, with results that are most impressive. This is a remarkable achievement, given that its members have had long histories of proud nation-state sovereignty, different languages, cultures, and religious preferences. Most remarkable, indeed, is that its members carry hallowed memories of bitter wars fought against one another. Adhering to the principle of sovereignty, these states retain all sovereign rights that do not impinge on the optimal functioning of a single market. By demonstrating that the economic realm is a universal realm that enhances the wealth, well-being, and security of each nation, the European Union offers a paradigm for what may be possible to accomplish not only on a continental scale but on a global scale as well—a commonwealth, as it were, of the sovereign nation-states of the world, states that have agreed to forego their sovereignty in the economic sphere insofar as it affects the optimal functioning of a global market economy, even as they continue to exercise their sovereignty in all other realms.

Another paradigm, though lacking as yet the single market component, is that of the sovereign nation-states associating themselves voluntarily to enhance their mutual interests as members of the new post-imperial Commonwealth with the Queen of the United Kingdom as its head. Biannually, the heads of fifty-four states gather together for informal discussions and non-binding resolutions, resolutions that have had far more impact on the course of events than is generally realized or acknowledged — for example, in bringing about the end of apartheid in South Africa without a bloody civil war.

The point is that there is a process at work in Europe that is bent on drawing into the European Union not only nations that formerly were members of the Soviet bloc but also Russia, the Ukraine, and other members of the new post-Soviet commonwealth as well. There is also in the former British Commonwealth a process at work facilitating a relationship between its members that seeks to ward off resort to violent solutions in clashes of national interest among its members, thereby enhancing wealth creation. The fact that the United Kingdom, the hated former imperial power is the acknowledged first among equals and that the Queen who sits on Queen Victoria's throne is the head of this Commonwealth of more than fifty-former colonial subject states speaks volumes for future possibilities of world peace and harmony.

Recognizing the dramatic global implications of the enlargement of the European Union in the 1980's by the inclusion of Greece, Spain, Portugal, and Greater Germany and the establishment of a single market comprising fifteen sovereign nation-states, and recognizing the end of the Cold War as an opportunity for a new world order, Mrs. Thatcher, in August, 1990, unveiled a blueprint for just such a new world order. This blueprint envisioned a free-market global economy — a global economy free of regional trading blocs and other barriers to the free flow of capital, goods, services, and labor worldwide. Mrs. Thatcher urged that there should be no West European bloc, no North American bloc, no Asian bloc. Wealth creation could thereby be enhanced worldwide — with all that could mean for peace, security, and prosperity within a single global economic system. This could be done, she averred, without foregoing state sovereignty or distinctive modes of national life or culture. Having exercised its sovereign right to keep its hands off the free movement of capital, goods, and services, each nation could then hold fast to its sovereignty in all other areas.

Although this blueprint made little headway, it was an indication. Even a hardheaded government official like Mrs. Thatcher was able to phrase serious political thought in visionary terms. Indeed, her successors have set 2020 as the target date for a single world market. Such a prognosis is predicated on the assumption that the tempo of the globalization of the world economy will continue to speed up, be it by regionalization or other means, to the point where the joint interest of the United States, Brito-Europe, Japan, and other capitalistic powers will virtually compel a global equivalent of the European Union.

There are powerful forces, however fractious, at work pressing for a global commonwealth of nations, modeled on the European Union and committed to a single world market, on the one hand, and to national sovereign rights in all other areas, on the other. Once harmony of national interests transcends existing rivalries, it is likely that wars between the nations of the world will be ruled out as surely as wars between Germany and France and other members of the European Union are now ruled out. And with the fading away of the need to wage war in the national interest, the trillions of dollars hitherto needed for armaments to defend or augment the national interest can be siphoned off for augmenting the good and welfare of the peoples of the world and for the dissolution of objective anxieties—hunger, homelessness, plague, pestilence, and premature death.

5
Judaism as a
Religion of Process

ૐ   The turbulence we are now experiencing is near at hand, while what we can hope for is at best a long way off. In the meantime, the Jewish people is confronted by the need to find a *raison d'être* in the present if there is to be a Jewish people in the future to witness any possible fulfillment of Isaiah's vision. Fortunately, Judaism through the ages has been a Judaism for all times and all seasons, a Judaism equipped to deal as effectively with turbulence as with tranquility.

In essence, adaptability and absorption have always been the genius of Jewish peoplehood. Judaism has ever sought to adapt itself and its God to the vicissitudes of time, tide, and circumstance. Adaptability permitted ideas, hopes, values and visions to blossom forth. Adaptability allowed Judaism to envision a God who not only makes elevated human aspirations ultimately possible but also, by imposing free will on creation, enables human beings to choose, however flawed these choices at times may have been. God did not endow human beings at their inception with the knowledge of how the universe came to be, how it works, how objective anxieties can be alleviated, how wars can be ended, what the purpose of the universe is, and what it is that God requires of the individual.

The experience of the Jewish people, like the experience of no other people, has been an experience with history, with what God is or might be—an experience that goes beyond doctrine, dogma, and belief. Experience compels and has always compelled Jews in their struggle for creative survival to envision a God for all seasons, for all vicissitudes, for all occasions. God is not a Rock, but an outcome. In wrestling with the concept of God, the Jewish people reaped a harvest of knowledge as to the way the world works and conceived and reconceived the ways in which God relates to the children of God. What is required in this process is the knowledge of how the highest of human aspirations can be fulfilled.

At this moment in their history, then, Jews need to seek out the causes of the turbulence of our time. Jews need to find and assess the means for subduing the turbulence. And Jews need to identify the long-range forces now at work that could make for the shaping of an harmonious world order. In the interim, "Jewish" values that have proved to be universal and timeless — love, justice, compassion, faith, and hope — provide an invaluable beachhead, irrespective of the spirit of the age or the harshness of external realities. These values Jews preserve and celebrate through helpful and appropriate signs, symbols, and prayers. Above all, Jews must cleave to the essence of Judaism as process, lest the emergence of new shapes and forms be proscribed and the long sought-for God remain unfound.

Fortunately, in this period, when hope is at a premium and bleakness prevails, there are lights to be glimpsed beyond the shadows. Among these lights are those that reveal that even the most tenacious hatred between people, cultures, and religions are not so tenacious as to be immune to the forces that dictate harmony. This has been made clear beyond all peradventure by the aggregate experience of the Jewish people throughout its history. However deep the differences between the belief and loyalties of the Jews and their host peoples — whether in antiquity, the Middle Ages, or the modern period — they never precluded renewing cooperation as soon as conditions became favorable to harmonious rather than discordant relationships. In recent times, this was evident when Menachem Begin and Anwar al-Sadat embraced each other, Nelson Mandela and his lifelong adversary F. W. de Klerk brought an end to apartheid, Yitzhak Rabin and Yasir Arafat shook hands, and King Hussein of Jordan and Prime Minister Rabin declared themselves to be brothers. Even more notable was the way in which the Catholic Church, in Vatican II (1962-65), tossed aside vintage dogmas to bring the Church in line with the spirit of the age. Among these vintage dogmas were those that condemned Judaism as a superceded religion and the Jews as Christ-killers. In their stead, the Church has given due legitimacy to Judaism and has given due recognition to the Jewish people as a people of God. It has abjured anti-Semitism by calling for continuous and respectful dialogue and in doing so has underwritten a leitmotif of *The Unity Principle*; namely, that even the most hostile of ideologies, ideologies believed to be immutable, lose their force and power when objective anxieties lessen for those who adhere to them. This held true for Islam and Christianity in the past; it could hold true for Islam and Christianity in the future. Vatican II makes this only too clear to those who would learn from history and not be blinded by it.

6
The Destiny of the Jewish People

ટ‌ો If we were to draw up a balance sheet today as to where the Jewish people stand in relation to where they have been and where they might be going, and what their destiny may hold in store, it would reveal a profile of exquisite complexity and plasticity. Because of their anomalous history, the Jewish people find themselves to be a people the majority of whom not only live in a widespread "Diaspora" but thrive there more affluently and securely than those Jews who live in Israel. Indeed, the Jewish profile in the west — the United States, Canada, Great Britain, Australia and New Zealand — is the profile that the State of Israel aspires to. At the same time, Israel herself is a sovereign nation-state that is compelled to face a whole array of problems that the Jews of the Diaspora do not have to face directly, but only as concerned fellow Jews. Among these problems two stand out: 1) The ultimate outcome of the peace process and its consequences. In a word, will Israel become, as it were, the Hong Kong of a Middle East community of sovereign nation-states on the model of the European union, a confederation whose security would be assured by the community as a whole and the world at large that benefits from the services Israel renders to the increasing of the wealth of nations, or will it continue to be plagued by unresolved conflict with its neighbors? 2) The ultimate outcome of the *Kulterkampf* that threatens to stifle the emergence of a society in Israel where freedom of religion becomes an unalienable right and the politicization of religion becomes a relic of the past. One of the unintended gifts the Diaspora bestowed upon the Jewish people was that when the emancipation process began the Jews had no land and enjoyed no sovereignty. They were liberated from discrimination and their reduced status and given the right to be co-citizens, but they were given neither a land nor sovereign rights. The Diaspora profile was therefore undergirded by the right of the individual Jew to determine his or her Jewish identity; ultra-Orthodox Jews could not use the machinery of the state to compel non-Orthodox Jews to abide by the halakhah, and so it has remained. By contrast to the western profile, the Israeli profile carries with it the imposition of as much of the halakhah as the political representatives of the Orthodox can carry through the Knesset. Particularly sensitive, since they have a direct impact not only on non-halakhic Israelis but on the Jews of the Diaspora as well, are such critical issues as "Who is a Jew," the barring of non-halakhic conversions, and the non-recognition of forms of Judaism that do not bind themselves by the halakhah as taught and interpreted by the Orthodox.

Given this complexity and plasticity of present being, what meaning, if any, can be elicited from the history of the Jewish people? The meaning I suggest is to be seen in the very complexity and plasticity of the profiles that we now see, profiles that are the outcome of that history. The complexity and plasticity comes from the fact that the history of the Jewish people itself has been highly complex and plastic. The Unity Principle, which has generated this history, is a principle that generates not only replication, but variation and mutation as well. It has been a history of changing shapes and forms, a history in which the image of God has assumed many faces. Little wonder, then, that when we take an accounting of the Jewish people today we should find such complexity, especially now that certain cohering and unifying factors are no longer as binding as they once were.

What final assessment can we make at this moment as to the significance and destiny of the Jewish people? First, its significance lies in the anomalous nature of its history. The Jewish people is the only community in the history of western civilization that had its beginning in a semi-nomadic people at the dawn of western civilization in the Ancient Near East and remains very much alive both in a widespread Diaspora and the State of Israel.

Second, with regard to the future of the Jewish people, the balance sheet is inconclusive. It must be inconclusive because at this moment it is far from clear whether the globalization process will bring hegemonic rivalry to an end or intensify it. If the latter pertains, then our present age of turbulence will long be with us. If the former is the case, an age of tranquility may very well be the outcome in the form of a global commonwealth of nations modeled on the European Union. If, however, the age of turbulence persists and globalization nonetheless proceeds apace but within a framework of nation-state rivalries and conflicts over hegemonies, then ongoing turbulence will continue to be the order of the day, especially if terrorism, more and more the preferred instrument for waging war, becomes more rife than it already is.

As for the Jews, whereas a world commonwealth of nations would assure them of the well-being and security that they have been seeking throughout the millennia in the Diaspora and Israel, national and hegemonic rivalries will continue to generate anxieties and insecurities that affect all people, irrespective of their wealth, station in life, or political clout. As long as Jews can be of service on the frontiers of globalization, they are likely to fare better than other groupings whose services, being unneeded or difficult to utilize, are condemned to an apartheid-like existence. As rejects of society, the disinherited may become highly combustible and easily inflamed by power-hungry demagogues who urge them to hold the more fortunate Jews responsible. All that having been said, the fate and destiny of the Jews seem to be inextricably bound up with the fate and destiny of the globalization process—a fate and destiny that can by no means be spelled out with certainty.

7
The Unity Principle

ﷺ   Although the destiny of Jewish history cannot as yet be
conclusively predicted, the metaphysical import of Judaism
can be discerned. This metaphysical import may perhaps best
be seen if we set it alongside the myth of Sisyphus. The metaphysical import of the myth of Sisyphus is that the gods mock
human aspirations. By contrast, the metaphysical import of
Jewish history is that God teaches. The myth of Sisyphus
makes it clear that the ultimate outcome of even the most
strenuous of human efforts to achieve human ends is doomed
to tragic failure, so there is no point in sacrificing the present
for the future. Gods are determined that human beings will
not become gods. This is the lesson of life. It is the lesson of
history. Thus, from the Sisyphus perspective, the process of
globalization is nothing more than another attempt to roll the
stone to the top of the mountain. It will not, for it cannot, bring
about the end of objective anxieties. The age of turbulence will
not give birth to an age of permanent tranquility, no matter
how many tranquil oases may crop up from time to time. One
has only to recollect the hopes and dreams of a new world order that were stirred up by the end of the Cold War to have
evidence on that score. The dreams were quickly dashed by a
turbulence that gives few signs of abating. That the gods
mock is a truth which is ever-present, persuasive, and powerful—and nowhere more so in fact than in the history of the
Jewish people, a people who again and again were lifted up to
high expectations by host societies that had treated them well
and endowed them with privileges, only to have these expectations shattered by the same host societies with humiliations,
pogroms, impoverishment, and exile. Even now in the United
States, where in the post-World War II period American Jews

were fully liberated from their minority status and given free reign to make their mark, virulent anti-Semitism rears its head whenever anxiety grips one segment of the American people or another. However much this anti-Semitism is still contained and relatively nonviolent, it is there nonetheless. It has not totally withered away. It is just an additional insecurity that Jews must face, along with the insecurities that even the highest and mightiest have to face in turbulent times. This is the Jewish metaphysic, as it might be described from the perspective of Sisyphus.

The metaphysic of Judaism, however, occupies the polar opposite. God does not mock, but teaches. This is a metaphysic that stems from the historical experience of the Jewish people and the meaning put on that experience by the author of the first chapter of Genesis and by the prophecies of Amos, Hosea, Micah, Isaiah, Jeremiah, and those throughout the centuries who persisted in holding fast to this metaphysic in face of the facts and in spite of the facts. It is most clearly espoused in the visions of the Prophet Isaiah, visions that focus on an end of days when swords will be beaten into plowshares and war will be no more; when the wolf will lie down with the lamb; when children will play in the basilisk's den; when fear will terrorize no more; when Egypt, Israel, and Assyria will be equally peoples of God. Isaiah was certain that day would come because God could not be a mocking God. God does not raise expectations and then shatter them. Expectations are not only capable of being fulfilled at some future time, but they will be fulfilled — provided, of course, that human beings come to understand God's way with humankind as illuminated by the experience of the Jewish people. God does not mock, but neither does God give solutions to humankind on a silver platter. It is up to human beings to discover the preconditions for achieving ideal ends such as peace, tranquility, righteousness, justice, love, and compassion. As is made clear in the first chapter of Genesis, the world God created is a world of goodly—and Godly—possibilities, but this goodness is dependent on the free choices made by human beings, not by God.

The implications are manifest. God is powerless to prevent a Holocaust. Only human beings can bring on a Holocaust. Contrariwise, only human beings can make holocausts impossible. And they can be made impossible only if the preconditions for a holocaust are thoroughly understood and steps are taken to see to it that these preconditions do not recur. In the case of the Holocaust, the preconditions were the breakdown of nation-state capitalism and the harsh and provocative terms of the Treaty of Versailles. Assure a sustained economic growth worldwide and nations the opportunity to create wealth without a penalty, and holocausts are ruled out, because when there is more than enough wealth generated by a global economic system—a system in which capital, good, services, and labor move freely—objective anxieties are diminished and holocaustal impulses are stilled.

It must be remembered that at the time Isaiah had his vision there was no empirical basis whatsoever for his certainty that there would be a golden end of days. There was nothing going for this as a future possibility; nothing, that is, other than Isaiah's faith in his beliefs that God is omnipotent and that God intends that humankind be ultimately capable of fulfilling the highest of aspirations. For such assumptions, Isaiah had no empirical grounds. Quite the contrary. God's claims to omnipotence had been delivered a mortal blow. When the chips were down, God proved incapable of protecting the Kingdom of Israel—its people and its land—from the onslaught of the Assyrians, though Jerusalem and the Kingdom of Judah were spared for the nonce. Far from Assyria being the rod of God's anger, Assyria was the mighty sword of its god, Assur.

Isaiah's vision of an end of days may have been a vision to be sure, but it is the stuff that dreams are made of, not the facts that make up the real world. Isaiah's vision was thus contra-empirical. Isaiah's concept of the omnipotence of God was actually grounded in God's impotence. Powerless to defend the people and the land, Isaiah was forced to the conclusion that the all-powerful God had used Assyria to chastise the people. The more thorough the chastising, the more omnipotent God appeared to be. Omnipotent by definition, God may be shielded from the bludgeoning of the empirical. Whatever occurs, be it good or evil, may be taken as a sign of God's omnipotence. When faced with the choice of the empirical evidence of God's impotence and Isaiah's stubborn faith that God was omnipotent the people sided with Isaiah, and in doing so assured the survival of the Jewish people by sealing off their God from, so to speak, the facts of life. The people held fast to Isaiah's vision of a glorious end of days, however rough the going. Faith in the impossible proved to be of higher survival value than faith in the empirical.

The god Assur's potency proved to be short-lived, as did the potency of the gods of the Medes and the Persians, the Greeks and the Romans, and the Sassanians. Isaiah's omnipotent God continued to prevail. Thus, belief in a God whose omnipotence could not be subverted by the facts became itself a fact to be reckoned with. The idea of such a God is always tantamount to God being what the idea attests to through Israel's creative survival in the real, empirical world— without a land, without sovereignty, and without sword, shield, or buckler. And when we look closer at this idea and trace its historical vicissitudes, we see that this idea was above all else a principle—the Unity Principle—a principle that had the generative power at one and the same time to continuously image new concepts of God and elicit new shapes and forms for the Jewish people.

The God pictured by Isaiah may have altered radically over the ages, but the Unity Principle that drew the face of Isaiah's God is the same Unity Principle that drew all those many faces of God that were needed to cope with and adapt to the vicissitudes of Israel's history. It is this principle, as it unfolded in the history of the Jewish people, that can lay claim to be none other than *the God as revealed by history*. As we analyze the threefold dynamics of the historical process operating through the history of the only people that believed, from the outset, that they had covenanted with a God that would have the power to sustain them through thick and thin, we can affirm that God is a revealing, not a revealed, God; that God is a search, not a finding; that God is not bound to any transient assumption of what God is. Herein we may glimpse the dual meaning of the name God revealed to Moses at the burning bush—a name sometimes translated as "I am that I am" and sometimes as "I will be what I will be." So, too, a people of God is likewise a people that cannot be bound by transient shapes and forms, however immutable they may seem to be at one moment or another.

In a word, the essence of the Jewish experience has been God-seeking, and God-seeking has meant coming to a more profound knowledge of the way God works in the world, in human nature, and in the process of human interaction with nature. Through such a growing understanding and historical process, not only the Jewish people but humankind itself may be able to achieve the glorious end of days envisaged by Isaiah. The belief that God teaches can be juxtaposed against the myth of Sisyphus that portrays the gods as mocking, and not found wanting.

As we enter the millennium, neither of the two metaphysics has won out. The view of Isaiah that God teaches is evident in the creation of the European community, the end of apartheid without bloody civil war in South Africa, and the peace process both in Israel and Northern Ireland, however uncertain their outcomes. The view of the Sisyphus myth that the gods mock is evident in the straits of turbulence we are traversing as we face terrorism, genocidal conflicts, recurrent anti-Semitism and xenophobia, and all the uncertainties affecting the outcome of the globalization process.

Until such time as one or the other of these two metaphysics triumphs, the experience of the Jewish people reveals a faith in a God that teaches and will not block the way to a glorious end of days when war will be no more, hunger will be no more, poverty will be no more, premature death will be no more, hopelessness will be no more—should that way be found. God will not block the audacious belief that such an age must necessarily come—a contra-empirical belief to be sure, but a belief that sustained the people of Israel through their trials and tribulations with their God. And in the hope that Isaiah's vision may yet will out, Jews find themselves pioneering on the frontiers of the globalization process as an anomalous people whose power lay not in land or sovereignty but in service to the peoples of the world and to every individual among those peoples, individuals who, as on the day of creation of the individual, are minted in Gods image and after God's likeness—male and female, a people who covenanted through Abraham to be a blessing to all the peoples of the earth.

Preface to the First Edition

[Editor's note: The Shaping of Jewish History was first published in 1971. Its message and teachings remain fresh and lucid, giving impetus to this much-revised edition with its entirely new Postlude. The original Preface continues to be important, but in light of the many years since it was penned, it made sense to place it here, at the end of the book, to make it clear that the present work is in no wise merely a reprint of the earlier edition. - SR]

❧ The impulse to write this book was sparked by an invitation to give a series of lectures on Jewish history in September 1967, on the occasion of the establishment of the Joseph Rosenblatt Lectureship in Judaica at the University of Utah. The warm reception given my theme by scholars and laymen, along with the strong urging of Mr. Rosenblatt that these ideas not be limited to the community of scholars, encouraged me to transform the lectures into a book. In the process the lectures dissolved into a far more ambitious undertaking than originally anticipated, for though the leitmotif — the Unity Principle as the dynamic element within Jewish history — remains unaltered, its development is worked through in a more elaborate and, it is hoped, more enriching and enlightening way. I am grateful to the History Department of the University of Utah for the opportunity afforded me to share my ideas and benefit from critical reactions. Likewise I am grateful to Mr. Joseph Rosenblatt, who made the lectureship possible and responded to the lectures with such genuine and keen appreciation that I was convinced that I ought to work through the theme in book form. I should also like to express my appreciation to my good friend, Professor Louis Zucker of the University of Utah, for his suggestion that I give the Rosenblatt Lectures, for his critical appreciation of what I was trying to do, and for the many stimulating discussions we had during my visit.

Writing a book such as this could not but heighten my awareness of how deeply I was influenced by my home, my teachers, my students, my colleagues, my friends, and my family. I am convinced that without my upbringing in a home of totally committed orthodoxy, where there were no boundaries between the Law and life, where God was both a loving *and* demanding Father, where the world to come and resurrection were no less real than the earth and sky, and where *mitzvah* and *averah* — saving commandment and provocative sin — vied for preference, I could never have appreciated the elemental power of Pharisaism to preserve a people, and drive a Paul to frenzied despair. Nor would I have been exposed from a tender age to the Pentateuch, the prophets, Rashi, the Mishnah, and Gemara — in the original, and glowing with divine consolation, and salvation.

Three of my teachers opened up for me other paths. Dr. Louis L. Kaplan, formerly dean of the Baltimore Hebrew College, was the first to bring to me awareness of a world of Jewish creativity beyond the halakhah. Through him I was exposed not only to the full range of Judaica, but also to the desperate need for lifting Jewish history out of its parochial setting and integrating it with world history. Indeed, it was his wise counsel that I prepare myself first as a general historian and only then specialize in Jewish history. Rarely has advice proved so perceptive, and friendship so rewarding.

Dr. Harry M. Orlinsky, now Professor of Bible at the Hebrew Union College-Jewish Institute of Religion, New York, but then a teacher of Jewish History at the Baltimore Hebrew College, was the individual most responsible for bringing about that radical reorientation that turned me from the well-marked paths of tradition to the rugged trails leading to unforeseeable destinations. He did this not by proselytizing—no one could have been so respectful of another's autonomy—but simply by teaching Jewish history in such a way that the dynamics of the historical process were revealed as operative in Jewish history, no less than in general history. He was especially appreciative of economic factors as powerful determinants and was keenly alert to the blinding effects of ideology. Indeed, it was his critical exposure of Stalinism that not only spared me the disillusionments of Popular Frontism, but liberated me from the authoritarian enchantments of either Right or Left. Since those formative years he has continued to be both my wise teacher and my intimate friend.

Professor Frederic C. Lane, Professor Emeritus at Johns Hopkins University, extended my range of historical vision and shared with me the analytical tools that he had shaped and sharpened. It was Professor Lane's probing analysis of the forces responsible for the development of Western civilization from earliest times that sparked my interest in Jewish history as the medium by which this process might be clarified and its essential dynamics revealed. It was also Lane's stress on the crucial role of economic factors that disciplined me to look for the interconnection between economic forces and ideational systems, and to assign causal weights only after judicious deliberation. Like Lane, I have sought to *appreciate* the power of economic determinants without *depreciating* the creative role of ideas and symbols. My deep interest in capitalistic development that looms so large in the latter chapters of this book is largely to be attributed to my years of study under Professor Lane, whose contributions to this field have gained for him worldwide recognition. This book is permeated with Lane's influence, however far it may have fallen short of doing justice to his teaching. I should like to add that, like Orlinsky, Lane has not only been my teacher these past thirty years or so, but has been a grand and noble friend.

There is one scholar who has had a profound influence on my thinking, not directly as a teacher, but through writings. He is Professor Solomon Zeitlin of Dropsie University. Since my undergraduate days I have been impressed by the creative quality of his scholarship. My deep interest in Pharisaism as a revolutionary breakthrough in Jewish and world history was sparked by Zeitlin's highly creative approach to the problem of Pharisaic identity. Although I have gone my own way on the Pharisaic problem, I am the first to recognize that if it proves right, it was Professor Zeitlin who pointed it out—even if he does not follow along with me. Zeitlin's influence is by no means limited to his writings on Pharisaism. His insights have proven fruitful to me in virtually every area of Jewish history. I cannot recall anything of his that I have read—whether I agreed or disagreed—that did not set me thinking. His phenomenal knowledge of sources, his independence of thought, his intuitive understanding of historical processes, his iconoclasm—all have had deep effect upon me. I am certain that there is more in this book that reveals my indebtedness to Zeitlin than even I am able to discern. I would wish the reader to be aware that there may be much that is insightful whose origins may be snuggled away in some sentence or paragraph written by Professor Zeitlin a half century ago or only recently.

I had every reason to believe that when this book appeared the late Dr. Nelson Glueck, for so many years the gifted President of the Hebrew Union College, would be alive to read of my deep esteem and appreciation. When he appointed me to the faculty in 1949, he reassured me that, for him, Judaism and the pursuit of truth could not be in conflict. And so it proved to be. I was given absolute freedom to explore all the crevices of Jewish and world history; to experiment with daring re-conceptualizations; to teach as freely as the mind and spirit moved; to publish my findings without doctrinal or creedal concern. Like other members of our faculty, I benefited from his own intense commitment to scientific scholarship, and from his warm encouragement to publish the fruits of research and thinking. The impress of his devotion to intellectual and spiritual freedom will, I am certain, always mark off the Hebrew Union College for distinction.

To Dr. Jacob R. Marcus, my cherished colleague and dear friend, I owe so much that I find it difficult to convey it in a few sentences. He was responsible for seeking me out for the Hebrew Union College faculty. It was he who assured me that my academic freedom would never be infringed, and that I would be perfectly free to teach Jewish history as I saw fit. He has been my wise counselor, helpful colleague, and steadfast friend. This friendship has deepened and matured through the years as he encouraged me in the development of the ideas that permeate this book. He has always been sympathetic to my gropings, understanding of my uncertainties, reassuring of the value of my researches.

For affording me the opportunity to explore the role of the Jews in the development of modern capitalism, I am most grateful to the Simon Guggenheim Foundation and the American Philosophic Society. A Guggenheim Fellowship for 1962-63 enabled me to work in the notarial archives in Amsterdam and to think through without pressures the problems of Marrano entrepreneurship. An American Philosophic Society grant for the summer of 1965 permitted me to extend my researches to Vienna and Dubrovnik. The chapter on the Marranos and capitalism in this book is the fruit of these researches; it was originally presented as a paper at the Third International Congress on Economic History in 1965.

My former student and my very good friend, Rabbi Jack Bemporad, has been most helpful, encouraging, and constructively critical. His disciplined philosophic mind was always placed freely at my disposal. He read through several versions of the manuscript, made many worthwhile suggestions, and alerted me to the many pitfalls that a theme such as this is bound to encounter. Rabbi Mayer Selekman, likewise a former student, has been my very close friend these past three years. He likewise read through the manuscript again and again with patient care and friendly concern, shared with me both his appreciation and criticism with heartening candor, and was a refreshing source of intellectual stimulation and encouragement. I have had the benefit, through the years, of the critically discriminating mind of my brother-in-law, Dr. Herbert C. Zafren, Director of Libraries, Hebrew Union College-Jewish Institute of Religion. He has made me acutely aware, on more than one occasion, of the ease with which fuzziness can pass for clear thinking, and he has always been at hand for consultation and discussion. My colleagues Professors Michael Meyer and Lewis Barth were kind enough to read through the manuscript at one stage or another and to offer well-taken criticisms. Professor Joseph Gutmann, of Wayne State University and formerly of the Hebrew Union College, read the manuscript carefully and made some excellent suggestions, as did Professor Gerson Shaked of the Hebrew University. I also benefited greatly from the critical reactions and stylistic suggestions of Professor Herbert Leibowitz, now at Washington University in St. Louis. Rabbi Herbert Opalek of Dropsie University and Rabbi Barton Lee were also most helpful.

To my students, over the years, I am indebted for their provocative, challenging, and stimulating inspiration to transform knowledge into wisdom. There are so many students, friends, and colleagues that had some part in the making of this book that I fear I am bound to overlook some quite unintentionally. I trust that such individuals will be understanding and weigh the balance in my favor.

Mrs. Rissa Alex, Executive Secretary of the Hebrew Union College, deserves special mention for her splendid cooperation in arranging for the transcribing of the tapes of the original lectures and for seeing to it that the final manuscript was ready in time. This she managed despite formidable obstacles. Her efforts were another instance of the collaboration that has marked our relationship through the years. To Mrs. Helen Lederer I owe a special kind of thanks. She has worked for me for well over fifteen years, typing my manuscripts, translating sources from the German for my students, making extremely valuable suggestions. She has been both a creative collaborator and a devoted friend. I consider myself most fortunate to have had such a talented associate for my scholarly work.

I have been most fortunate in having Norman Kotker as my editor. He has demonstrated that rare gift of being able to prune without damage and re-phrase without alteration. He has done an impressive job of smoothing the jagged, extracting the superfluous, and seasoning the bland. It has been a real privilege for me to work with him and to learn from him. To Carol Hallman, Michael Dine, and Mrs. Leslie Freund I am grateful for helping out in the typing of the manuscript. My good friend Dan Ransohoff took the photo for the book jacket.

I am indebted to my daughter, Roslyn Weinberger, for her reading of the manuscript and for the many shrewd criticisms and stylistic suggestions that could not but improve the book. To my daughter Sharon, I am grateful for her reactions, since they gave me some glimmer of hope that the Unity Principle might be able to bridge the generation gap. The sort of gratefulness that I feel towards my wife, Zelda, is really not expressible. My dedication of this book to her seeks, however inadequately, to convey my appreciation and my love.

Index